TOLSTOY AND THE CRITICS:
LITERATURE AND AESTHETICS

Holley Gene Duffield
Wayne State University

Manuel Bilsky
Eastern Michigan University

SCOTT, FORESMAN AND COMPANY
Chicago   Atlanta   Dallas   Palo Alto   Fair Lawn, N.J.

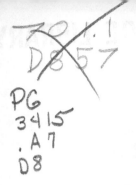

To Donna and Mark
and
to the memory of
Thomas Edward Duffield

Librairie Félix Alcan: For excerpt from "Beauty Is Not All: An Appeal for Esthetic Pluralism" from *The Way of Things: A Philosophy of Knowledge, Nature and Value* by William Pepperell Montague. As adapted from *Deuxième congrés international d'esthetique et de science de l'art* (Paris: Librairie Félix Alcan, 1937), Vol. I, pp. 142–145.

The Ann Arbor News: For "Khrushchev Hits 'Donkey' Art."

The Aristotelian Society: For excerpt from "The Concept of Artistic Expression" by John Hospers. Reprinted from *Proceedings of the Aristotelian Society* (1954–1955) by courtesy of the Editor of The Aristotelian Society.

Ernest Benn, Limited: For "Tolstoi on Art" from *Gospels of Anarchy* by Vernon Lee. Reprinted by permission of Ernest Benn, Limited, successor to T. Fisher Unwin.

British Journal of Psychology: For "Communication Versus Expression in Art" by Lascelles Abercrombie and for excerpt from "Psychical Distance as a Factor in Art and an Aesthetic Principle" by Edward Bullough.

Mrs. Pamela Diamond and *The Hogarth Press:* For excerpt from *The Artist and Psycho-Analysis* by Roger Fry. No. 2 of The Hogarth Essays pamphlets. Reprinted by permission of Mrs. Diamond and The Hogarth Press.

Dodd, Mead & Company: For excerpt from "Tolstoi's Theory of Art" from *Life and Literature* by Lafcadio Hearn. Reprinted by permission of Dodd, Mead & Company.

Eastern Michigan University: For "Confronting the Work of Art" by Manuel Bilsky. Reprinted from the *University College Quarterly.*

International Publishers Co., Inc.: For "Art Is Communication" from *Art and Society* by Sidney Finklestein. Reprinted by permission of International Publishers Co., Inc.

Journal of Aesthetics and Art Criticism: For "The Role of Theory in Aesthetics" by Morris Weitz.

Journal of Philosophy: For "What Has Beauty To Do with Art?" by C. J. Ducasse and for "Tolstoi's Esthetic Definition of Art" by Israel Knox.

The Kenyon Review: For excerpt from "The Formalist Critics" by Cleanth Brooks.

Macmillan & Co., Ltd.: For "Tolstoi's Moral Theory of Art" by John Albert Macy. Reprinted from *Century Magazine* by permission of Macmillan & Co., Ltd., London.

David McKay Company, Inc.: For "Tolstoy" from *Artists and Thinkers* by William L. Flaccus. Reprinted by permission of David McKay Company, Inc., successors to Longmans, Green.

Oxford University Press: For "God Sees the Truth, But Waits" and "A Prisoner in the Caucasus" from *Twenty-Three Tales* by Leo Tolstoy, tr. by Louise and Aylmer Maude, reprinted by permission of Oxford University Press; for excerpts from *The Mirror and the Lamp* by M. H. Abrams, copyright 1953 by Oxford University Press, Inc., reprinted by permission; and for excerpts from *What is Art?* by Leo Tolstoy, tr. by Aylmer Maude.

Princeton University Press: For excerpts from *The Dehumanization of Art, and Notes on the Novel* by José Ortega y Gasset, tr. by Helen Weyl. Reprinted by permission of Princeton University Press.

The University of Chicago Press: For "Notes on the Moralistic Theory of Art: Plato and Tolstoy" by Israel Knox. Reprinted from the *International Journal of Ethics,* 41, 1930, by permission of The University of Chicago Press.

Frederick Warne & Co., Ltd.: For excerpts from "Art Criticism" from *Leo Tolstoy: A Biographical and Critical Study* by T. S. Knowlson. Reprinted by permission of Frederick Warne & Co., Ltd.

The cover is a composite of Russian embroidery, reproduced from plates in *Peasant Art in Russia* (1912), edited by Charles Holme.

Library of Congress Catalog Card #65-11912
Copyright © 1965 by Scott, Foresman and Company
Printed in the United States of America

✳

PREFACE

Here are some typical assertions about literature and art: *X is a tragedy; X is not a tragedy; X is a good tragedy; X is a bad tragedy; art is imitation; art is expression; art is beauty created by humans; art is the perfect conjunction of form and content; art is disguised wish fulfillment; art teaches; art delights; art teaches and delights; art is a special kind of medicine; art is for art's sake; art is useless; X is a work of art; X is not a work of art; X is a good work of art; X is a bad work of art;* and so on. The main purpose of this book is to present many of the criteria and methods people use to define and to evaluate literature and art.[1]

The book is centered upon Leo Tolstoy's theory and practice of art. Part One introduces and exemplifies, to some extent, M. H. Abrams' idea that theories of literature and art are orientated toward one of the four elements—the universe, the audience, the artist, and the work of art—which exist in what he calls the "total situation of a work of art."[2] Selections from the works of Aristotle, Sir Philip Sidney, Eugene Véron, and Cleanth Brooks exemplify Abrams' idea. In effect, Part One gives the reader material he can use to understand and to discuss Tolstoy's theory of literature and art.

Part Two contains extensive excerpts from *What Is Art?* (published in 1898) and the complete texts of "God Sees the Truth, But Waits" and "A Prisoner in the Caucasus." In the selections from *What Is Art?* Tolstoy discusses, for example, definitions of art as beauty, the value of the art critic, what art really is (or ought to be), what bad art is, what good art is, and the types of good art. Needless to say, when Tolstoy applies his standards for good art to such a work as Beethoven's *Ninth Symphony* and concludes that it is bad art, he causes many people to be rather irritated with him and his ideas.[3] Only "God Sees the Truth, But Waits" and "A Prisoner in the Caucasus" survive his severe criticism of his own work written before 1898. To him, both stories are good art—the former good religious art and the latter good universal art. Both stories give the reader ample opportunity to apply not only Tolstoy's tests for good art but also the tests of other literary and art theorists.

Part Three is a series of essays whose material is directly and indirectly related to Tolstoy's theory of literature and art.[4] These essays are in two groups. The essays in the first group directly defend, attack, and explain various aspects

[1] The editors would like to note here that the range of material and aims of this book make it practical for several kinds of college courses. It can be used, for example, in introductory composition and literature courses, in other literature courses, in literary criticism courses, in aesthetics courses, in humanities courses, and, quite possibly, in many fine arts courses. Some of these courses are beyond the scope of most source books.

[2] M. H. Abrams, *The Mirror and the Lamp* (New York: Oxford University Press, 1953), p. 6.

[3] By the fact of their irritation, such people are expressing their own opinions of the *Ninth Symphony* and of art. For example, those who claim that the *Ninth Symphony* is a good work of art must have some conception of what art is and some conception of what good art is.

[4] The reader should carefully note that the writers of these essays are also advocating criteria and methods for defining and evaluating literature and art.

of his theory.[5] For example, Lafcadio Hearn and John Albert Macy differ on Tolstoy's idea that the peasant is a qualified art critic. The essays in the second group indirectly defend, attack, and explain Tolstoy's ideas. For example, when Oscar Wilde says in his Preface to *The Picture of Dorian Gray* that "all art is quite useless," he is obviously opposing Tolstoy's contention that good art has social value. Finally, some of the material in Part Three directly compliments the material in Part One. The essay by Manuel Bilsky, for example, is an application of the formalist critic's position advocated by Cleanth Brooks.

The final section of the book contains Edgar Allan Poe's "The Cask of Amontillado" for the reader's use in conjunction with the various theories he has studied, some detailed study questions on the material in all three parts of the book, some topics for essays, and a selected bibliography.

Note on the text: All material is reprinted, completely or in part, in its original form. Numbers between slash bars (/22/) are the page numbers of the original text. Editorial apparatus and comments appear in brackets, except in three places: the brackets and comments on page 304 of Macy's essay, on page 93 of Bullough's essay, and in Bilsky's essay were in the original sources.

July 1964

H. G. D.
M. B.

---

[5] The editors have allowed much of the exposition of Tolstoy's theory to remain in these essays for three reasons: it is sometimes necessary to the logic of the construction of the essays; it is interesting because it is sometimes quite diverse; and it sometimes includes material not reprinted in the excerpt of *What Is Art?* in this book.

CONTENTS

APPENDICES

PART I

Preliminaries

✳ SOME CO-ORDINATES OF ART CRITICISM

M. H. Abrams

Four elements in the total situation of a work of art are discriminated and made salient, by one or another synonym, in almost all theories which aim to be comprehensive. First, there is the *work,* the artistic product itself. And since this is a human product, an artifact, the second common element is the artificer, the *artist.* Third, the work is taken to have a subject which, directly or deviously, is derived from existing things — to be about, or signify, or reflect something which either is, or bears some relation to, an objective state of affairs. This third element, whether held to consist of people and actions, ideas and feelings, material things and events, or super-sensible essences, has frequently been denoted by that word-of-all-work, 'nature'; but let us use the more neutral and comprehensive term, *universe,* instead. For the final element we have the *audience:* the listeners, spectators, or readers to whom the work is addressed, or to whose attention, at any rate, it becomes available.

. . . let us arrange the four co-ordinates in a convenient pattern. A triangle will do, with the work of art, the thing to be explained, in the center.

UNIVERSE
↑
WORK
↙   ↘
ARTIST   AUDIENCE

Although any reasonably adequate theory takes some account of all four elements, almost all theories, as we shall see, exhibit a discernible orientation toward one only. That is, a critic tends to derive from one of these terms his principal categories for defining, classifying, and analyzing a work of art, as well as the major criteria by which he judges its value. Application of this analytic scheme, therefore, will sort attempts to explain the nature /6/ and worth of a work of art into four broad classes. Three will explain the work of art prin-

From "Orientation of Critical Theories," in *The Mirror and the Lamp* (New York: Oxford University Press, 1953), pp. 3–29.

cipally by relating it to another thing: the universe, the audience, or the artist. The fourth will explain the work by considering it in isolation, as an autonomous whole, whose significance and value are determined without any reference beyond itself.

To find the major orientation of a critical theory, however, is only the beginning of an adequate analysis. For one thing, these four co-ordinates are not constants, but variables; they differ in significance according to the theory in which they occur. Take what I have called the *universe* as an example. In any one theory, the aspects of nature which an artist is said to imitate, or is exhorted to imitate, may be either particulars or types, and they may be only the beautiful or the moral aspects of the world, or else any aspect without discrimination. It may be maintained that the artist's world is that of imaginative intuition, or of common sense, or of natural science; and this world may be held to include, or not to include, gods, witches, chimeras, and Platonic Ideas. Consequently, theories which agree in assigning to the represented universe the primary control over a legitimate work of art may vary from recommending the most uncompromising realism to the most remote idealism. Each of our other terms . . . also varies, both in meaning and functioning, according to the critical theory in which it occurs, the method of reasoning which the theorist characteristically uses, and the explicit or implicit 'world-view' of which these theories are an integral part. /7/

⌘ DEFINITION OF TRAGEDY. SIX ELEMENTS OF TRAGEDY.

Aristotle

Tragedy, then, is an imitation of an action that is serious, complete, and of a certain magnitude; in language embellished with each kind of artistic ornament, the several kinds being found in separate parts of the play; in the form of action, not of narrative; through pity and fear effecting the proper purgation of these emotions. By 'language embellished,' I mean language into which rhythm, 'harmony,' and song enter. By 'the several kinds in separate parts,' I mean, that some parts are rendered through the medium of verse alone, others again with the aid of song.

Now as tragic imitation implies persons acting, it necessarily follows, in the first place, that Spectacular equipment will be a part of Tragedy. Next, Song and Diction, for these are the medium of imitation. By 'Diction' /23/ I mean the mere metrical arrangement of the words: as for 'Song,' it is a term whose sense every one understands.

Again, Tragedy is the imitation of an action; and an action implies personal agents, who necessarily possess certain distinctive qualities both of character and thought; for it is by these that we qualify actions themselves, and these—thought and character—are the two natural causes from which actions spring, and on actions again all success or failure depends. Hence, the Plot is the imitation of the action:—for by plot I here mean the arrangement of the incidents. By Character I mean that in virtue of which we ascribe certain qualities to the

From *The Poetics of Aristotle,* trans. S. H. Butcher (London: The Macmillan Co., Ltd., 1907). The English translation appears on alternate pages with the Greek text.

agents. Thought is required wherever a statement is proved, or, it may be, a general truth enunciated. Every Tragedy, therefore, must have six parts, which parts determine its quality—namely, Plot, Character, Diction, Thought, Spectacle, Song. Two of the parts constitute the medium of imitation, one the manner, and three the objects of imitation. And these complete the list. These elements have been employed, we may say, by the poets to a man; in fact, every play contains Spectacular elements as well as Character, Plot, Diction, Song, and Thought.

But most important of all is the structure of the /25/ incidents. For Tragedy is an imitation, not of men, but of an action and of life, and life consists in action, and its end is a mode of action, not a quality. Now character determines men's qualities, but it is by their actions that they are happy or the reverse. Dramatic action, therefore, is not with a view to the representation of character: character comes in as subsidiary to the actions. Hence the incidents and the plot are the end of a tragedy; and the end is the chief thing of all. Again, without action there cannot be a tragedy; there may be without character. The tragedies of most of our modern poets fail in the rendering of character; and of poets in general this is often true. It is the same in painting; and here lies the difference between Zeuxis and Polygnotus. Polygnotus delineates character well: the style of Zeuxis is devoid of ethical quality. Again, if you string together a set of speeches expressive of character, and well finished in point of diction and thought, you will not produce the essential tragic effect nearly so well as with a play which, however deficient in these respects, yet has a plot and artistically constructed incidents. Besides which, the most powerful elements of emotional interest in Tragedy—Peripeteia or Reversal of the Situation, and Recognition scenes—are parts of the plot. A further proof is, that novices in the art attain to finish of diction and precision of portraiture before they can construct the plot. It is the same with almost all the early poets.

The Plot, then, is the first principle, and, as it were, /27/ the soul of a tragedy: Character holds the second place. A similar fact is seen in painting. The most beautiful colours, laid on confusedly, will not give as much pleasure as the chalk outline of a portrait. Thus Tragedy is the imitation of an action, and of the agents mainly with a view to the action.

Third in order is Thought,—that is, the faculty of saying what is possible and pertinent in given circumstances. In the case of oratory, this is the function of the political art and of the art of rhetoric: and so indeed the older poets make their characters speak the language of civic life; the poets of our time, the language of the rhetoricians. Character is that which reveals moral purpose, showing what kind of things a man chooses or avoids. Speeches, therefore, which do not make this manifest, or in which the speaker does not choose or avoid anything whatever, are not expressive of character. Thought, on the other hand, is found where something is proved to be or not to be, or a general maxim is enunciated.

Fourth among the elements enumerated comes Diction; by which I mean, as has been already said, the expression of the meaning in words; and its essence is the same both in verse and prose.

Of the remaining elements Song holds the chief place among the embellishments.

The Spectacle has, indeed, an emotional attraction of its own, but, of all the parts, it is the least artistic, and connected least with the art of poetry. For the power of Tragedy, we may be sure, is felt even apart from representation and actors. Besides, the production of /29/ spectacular effects depends more on the art of the stage machinist than on that of the poet. /31/

✖ DEFINITION, KINDS, AND VALUE OF POETRY

Sir Philip Sidney

Poesy, therefore, is an art of imitation, for so Aristotle termeth it in his word *mimesis,* that is to say, a representing, counterfeiting, or figuring forth; to speak metaphorically, a speaking picture, with this end, — to teach and delight.

Of this have been three general kinds. The chief, both in antiquity and excellency, were they that did imitate the inconceivable excellencies of God. Such were David in his Psalms; Solomon in his Song of Songs, in his Ecclesiastes and Proverbs; Moses and Deborah in their Hymns; and the writer of Job; which, beside other, the learned Emanuel Tremellius and Franciscus Junius do entitle the poetical part of the Scripture. Against these none will speak that hath the Holy Ghost in due holy reverence. In this kind, though in a full wrong divinity, were Orpheus, Amphion, Homer in his Hymns, and many other, both Greeks and Romans. And this poesy must be used by whosoever will follow St. James' counsel in singing psalms when they are merry; and I know is used with the fruit of comfort by some, when, in sorrowful pangs of their death-bringing sins, they find the consolation of the never-leaving goodness.

The second kind is of them that deal with matters philosophical: either moral, as Tyrtaeus, Phocylides, and /9/ Cato; or natural, as Lucretius and Virgil's *Georgics;* or astronomical, as Manilius and Pontanus; or historical, as Lucan; which who mislike, the fault is in their judgment quite out of taste, and not in the sweet food of sweetly uttered knowledge.

But because this second sort is wrapped within the fold of the proposed subject, and takes not the free course of his own invention, whether they properly be poets or no let grammarians dispute, and go to the third, indeed right poets, of whom chiefly this question ariseth. Betwixt whom and these second is such a kind of difference as betwixt the meaner sort of painters, who counterfeit only such faces as are set before them, and the more excellent, who having no law but wit, bestow that in colors upon you which is fittest for the eye to see, — as the constant though lamenting look of Lucretia, when she punished in herself another's fault; wherein he painteth not Lucretia, whom he never saw, but painteth the outward beauty of such a virtue. For these third be they which most properly do imitate to teach and delight; and to imitate borrow nothing of what is, hath been, or shall be; but range, only reined with learned discretion, into the divine consideration of what may be and should be. These be they that, as the first and most noble sort, may justly be termed *vates;* so these are waited on in the excellentest languages and best understandings with the foredescribed name of poets. For these, indeed, do merely make to imitate, and imitate both to delight and teach, and delight to move men to take that goodness in hand, which without delight they would fly as from a stranger; and teach to make them know that goodness whereunto they are moved: — which being the noblest scope to which ever any learning was directed, yet want there not idle tongues to bark at them. /10/

These be subdivided into sundry more special denominations. The most notable be the heroic, lyric, tragic, comic, satiric, iambic, elegiac, pastoral, and certain others, some of these being termed according to the matter they deal with, some by the sort of verse they liked best to write in, — for indeed the greatest part of poets have apparelled their poetical inventions in that numberous kind of writing which is called verse. Indeed but apparelled, verse being but an ornament and no cause to poetry, since there have been many most excel-

From *The Defense of Poesy,* ed. Albert S. Cook (Boston: Ginn and Company, 1890).

lent poets that never versified, and now swarm many versifiers that need never answer to the name of poets. For Xenophon, who did imitate so excellently as to give us *effigiem justi imperii*—the portraiture of a just empire under the name of Cyrus (as Cicero saith of him)—made therein an absolute heroical poem; so did Heliodorus in his sugared invention of that picture of love in Theagenes and Chariclea; and yet both these wrote in prose. Which I speak to show that it is not riming and versing that maketh a poet—no more than a long gown maketh an advocate, who, though he pleaded in armor, should be an advocate and no soldier—but it is that feigning notable images of virtues, vices, or what else, with that delightful teaching, which must be the right describing note to know a poet by. Although indeed the senate of poets hath chosen verse as their fittest raiment, meaning, as in matter they passed all in all, so in manner to go beyond them; not speaking, table-talk fashion, or like men in a dream, words as they chanceably fall from the mouth, but peizing each syllable of each word by just proportion, according to the dignity of the subject.

Now therefore it shall not be amiss, first to weigh this latter sort of poetry by his works, and then by his parts; and if in neither of these anatomies he be condemnable, I hope we shall obtain a more favorable sentence. /11/ This purifying of wit, this enriching of memory, enabling of judgment, and enlarging of conceit, which commonly we call learning, under what name soever it come forth or to what immediate end soever it be directed, the final end is to lead and draw us to as high a perfection as our degenerate souls, made worse by their clay lodgings, can be capable of. This, according to the inclination of man, bred many formed impressions. For some that thought this felicity principally to be gotten by knowledge, and no knowledge to be so high or heavenly as acquaintance with the stars, gave themselves to astronomy; others, persuading themselves to be demi-gods if they knew the causes of things, became natural and supernatural philosophers. Some an admirable delight drew to music, and some the certainty of demonstration to the mathematics; but all, one and other, having this scope:—to know, and by knowledge to lift up the mind from the dungeon of the body to the enjoying his own divine essence. But when by the balance of experience it was found that the astronomer, looking to the stars, might fall into a ditch, that the inquiring philosopher might be blind in himself, and the mathematician might draw forth a straight line with a crooked heart; then lo! did proof, the overruler of opinions, make manifest, that all these are but serving sciences, which, as they have each a private end in themselves, so yet are they all directed to the highest end of the mistress-knowledge . . . even as the saddler's next end is to make a good saddle, but his further end to serve a nobler faculty, which is horsemanship; so the horseman's to soldiery; and the soldier not only to have the skill, but to perform the /12/ practice of a soldier. So that the ending end of all earthly learning being virtuous action, those skills that most serve to bring forth that have a most just title to be princes over all the rest; wherein . . . the poet is worthy to have it before any other competitors. /13/

❧ ART AS EXPRESSION OF EMOTION

Eugene Véron

GENERAL DEFINITION OF ART

We have seen that art, far from being the blossom and fruit of civilization, is rather, its germ. It began to give evidence of its existence so soon as man became self-conscious, and is to be found clearly defined in his very earliest works.

By its psychologic origin it is bound up with the constituent principles of humanity. The salient and essential characteristic of man is his incessant cerebral activity which is propagated and developed by countless acts and works of varied kind. The aim and rule of this activity is the search after *the best;* that is to say, the more and more complete satisfaction of physical and moral wants. This instinct, common to all animals, is seconded in man by an exceptionally well-developed faculty to adapt the means to the end.

The effort to satisfy physical wants has given birth to all the industries that defend, preserve, and smooth the path of life; the effort to satisfy the moral wants — of which one of the most important is the gratification of our cerebral activity itself — has created the arts, long before it could give them power sufficient for the conscious elaboration of ideas. The life of sentiment preceded the manifestations of intellectual life by many centuries.

The gratification, *in esse* or *in posse,* of either real or imaginary wants, is the cause of happiness, joy, pleasure, and of all the feelings connected with them; the contrary is marked by grief, sadness, fear etc.: but in both cases there is emotion, whether grave or gay, and it is the nature of such emotion to give more or less /88/ lively evidence of its existence by means of exterior signs. When expressed by gesture and rhythmic movement, such motion produces the dance; when by rhythmic notes, music; when by rhythmic words, poetry.

As in another aspect man is essentially sympathetic and his joy or pain is often caused as much by the good or evil fortunes of others as by his own; as, besides, he possesses in a very high degree the faculty of combining series of fictitious facts, and of representing them in colours even more lively than those of reality: it results that the domain of art is of infinite extent for him. For the causes of emotion are multiplied for every man — not only by the number of similar beings who live around him and are attached to him by the more or less closely knit bonds of affection, alliance, similitude of situation or community of ideas and interests; but, also, by the never-ending multitude of beings and events that are able to originate or direct the imaginings of poets.

To these elements of emotion and moral enjoyment, must be added the combinations of lines, of forms and of colours, the dispositions and opposition of light and shade, etc. The instinctive search after this kind of emotion or pleasure, the special organ of which is the eye, has given birth to what are called the arts of design — sculpture, painting and architecture.

We may say then, by way of general definition, that art is the manifestation of emotion, obtaining external interpretation, now by expressive arrangements of line, form or colour, now by a series of gestures, sounds, or words governed by particular rhythmical cadence. /89/

If our definition is exact, we must conclude, from it, that the merit of a work of art, whatever it may be, can be finally measured by the power with which it manifests or interprets the emotion that was its determining cause, and

From *Aesthetics,* trans. W. H. Armstrong (London: Chapman and Hall, 1879).

that, for a like reason, must constitute its innermost and supreme unity. . . . /90/

Imitation is no more the aim of art, than a mere collection of letters and syllables is the aim of a writer who wishes to express his thoughts and feelings by the aid of the words which they form. The poet arranging his verses, the musician composing his airs and harmonies, are well aware that their real object lies beyond words and notes. This distinction, as we have here explained it, is perhaps less clear in matters of painting and sculpture. Some artists, and these not the least capable, are quite convinced that when they have a model before them, their one duty is to imitate it. And indeed they do nothing else; and, by virtue of such imitation they succeed in producing works of incontestable artistic value.

Here we have simply a misunderstanding. If an artist were really able to reduce himself to the condition of a copying machine; if he could so far efface and suppress himself as to confine his work to the servile reproduction of all the features and details of an object or event passing before his eyes: the only value his work would possess, would be that of a more or less exact *procès verbal*, and it would perforce remain inferior to reality. Where is the artist who would attempt to depict sunlight without taking refuge in some legerdemain, calling to his aim devices which the true sun would despise? But enough of this. Just because he is endowed with sensibility and imaginative power, the artist, in presence of the facts of nature or the events of history, finds himself, whether he will or not, in a peculiar situation. However /105/ thorough a realist he may think himself, he does not leave himself to chance. Now, choice of subject alone is enough to prove that, from the very beginning, some preference has existed, the result of a more or less predeterminate impression, and of a more or less unconscious agreement between the character of the object and that of the artist. This impression and agreement he sets to work to embody in outward form; it is the real aim of his work, and its possession gives him his claim to the name of artist. Without wishing or even knowing it, he moulds the features of nature to his dominant impression and to the idea that caused him to take pencil in hand. His work has an accidental stamp, in addition to that of the permanent genius which constitutes his individuality. Poet, musician, sculptor and architect, all pay more or less strict obedience to the same law. To it, point all those rules of artistic composition which pedantic academicism has subtly multiplied until they contradict each other.

The more of this personal character that a work possesses; the more harmonious its details and their combined expression; the more clearly each part communicates the impression of the artist, whether of grandeur, of melancholy or of joy; in fine, the more that expression of human sensation and will predominates over mere imitation: the better will be its chance of obtaining sooner or later the admiration of the world — always supposing that the sentiment expressed be a generous one, and that the execution be not of such a kind as to repel or baffle connoisseurs. It is not of course impossible, that an artist endowed with an ill-regulated or morbid imagination may place himself outside all normal conditions and condemn himself to the eternal misapprehension of the public. Impressions that are too particular, eccentric feelings, fantastic execution or processes, which do nothing to raise the intrinsic value or power of inspiration of a work, may give it so strange and ultra-individual a character, that it may become impossible for us to arrive at its real merit. The best qualities, when exaggerated, become faults; and that very personality or individuality which, when added to imitative power, results in a /106/ work of art, produces when pushed to extravagance nothing but an enigma.

We see, then, if we have succeeded in making ourselves understood, that the beautiful in art springs mainly from the intervention of the genius of man when more or less excited by special emotion.

A work is beautiful when it bears strong marks of the individuality of its author, of the permanent personality of the artist, and of the more or less accidental impression produced upon him by the sight of the object or event rendered.

In a word, it is from the worth of the artist that that of his work is derived. It is the manifestation of the faculties and qualities he possesses which attracts and fascinates us. The more sympathetic power and individuality that these faculties and qualities display, the easier is it for them to obtain our love and admiration. On the other hand, we, for a similar reason, reject and contemn bold and vulgar works that by their shortcomings demonstrate the moral and intellectual mediocrity of their authors, and prove the latter to have mistaken their vocation.

Consequently, then, beauty in art is a purely human creation. Imitation may be its means, as in sculpture and painting; or, on the other hand, it may have nothing to do with it, as in poetry and music. This beauty is of so peculiar a nature that it may exist even in ugliness itself; inasmuch as the exact reproduction of an ugly model may be a beautiful work of art, by the ensemble of qualities which the composition of it may prove are possessed by its author.

The very theory of imitation is but the incomplete and superficial statement of the ideas which we are here advocating. What is it that we admire in imitation? The resemblance? We have that much better in the object itself. But how is it that the similitude of an ugly object can be beautiful? It is obvious that between the object and its counterfeit some new element intervenes. This element is the personality, or, at least, the skill of the artist. This latter, indeed, is what they admire who will have /107/ it that beauty consists in imitation. What these applaud, in fact, is the talent of the artist. If we look below the surface and analyse their admiration we shall find that it is so; whether they mean it or not, what they praise in a work is the worker.

This was the opinion of Bürger, who, in his *Salon of* 1863, says: "In works which interest us the authors in a way substitute themselves for nature. However common or vulgar the latter may be, they have some rare and peculiar way of looking at it. It is Chardin himself whom we admire in his representation of a glass of water. We admire the genius of Rembrandt in the profound and individual character which he imparted to every head that posed before him. Thus did they seem to him, and this explains everything simple or fantastic in his expression and execution."

After all this, we need not stop to refute the theory which would found artistic beauty upon the imitation of "beautiful nature." In spite of the brilliant reputation that its triumph in three academies has given to M. Ch. Sevêyne's book upon the science of beauty, it does not seem to us to be founded upon arguments worthy of respect; it has not shown us where "beautiful nature" *(la belle nature)* is to be found in *Le Pouilleux,* in the *Raft of the Medusa,* in the *Battlefield of Eylau,* in the character of *Tartuffe,* or of *La Marneffe.*

The only beauty in a work of art is that placed there by the artist. It is both the result of his efforts and the foundation of his success. As often as he is struck by any vivid impression—whether moral, intellectual, or physical—and expresses that impression by some outward process—by poetry, music, sculpture, painting or architecture—in such a way as to cause its communication with the soul of spectator or auditor; so often does he produce a work of art the beauty of which will be in exact proportion to the intelligence and depth of the sentiment displayed, and the power shown in giving it outward form.

The union of all these conditions constitutes artistic beauty in its most complete expression.

With a few reservations, then, we may preserve the definition of /108/ æsthetics which usage' has sanctified — *The Science of Beauty.* For the sake of clearness, however, and to prevent confusion, we prefer to call it the *Science of Beauty in Art.* Had not the tyranny of formulæ by custom become too strong, we would willingly refrain from using the word "beauty" at all, for it has the drawback of being too exclusively connected with the sense of seeing, and of calling up too much the idea of visible form. The employment of this word became general when *the* art *par excellence* was sculpture. To make it apply to the other arts, it was necessary to foist upon it a series of extensions which deprived it of all accuracy. Language possesses no word more vague or less precise. This absence of precision has perhaps contributed more than might at first be supposed to that confusion of ideas which can alone explain the multiplicity and absurdity of current æsthetic theories.

All these inconveniences and obscurities may be avoided by simply putting it thus: —

Æsthetics is the science whose object is the study and elucidation of the manifestations of artistic genius. . . . /109/

RESUMÉ

To sum up — there are two distinct kinds of art. The one, decorative art, we understand to be that whose main object is the gratification of the eye and ear, and whose chief means to perfection of form are harmony and grace of contour, diction or sound. Such art rests upon the desire for beauty, and has nothing in view beyond the peculiar delight caused by the sight of beautiful objects. It has produced admirable works in the past, and may produce them again now or in the future, on condition that its inspiration be sought in actual and existing life, and not in the imitation of works sanctified by time. We must recognize, however, that modern art has no tendency in this latter direction. Beauty no longer suffices for us. Indeed, for the last two thousand years something more has been required; for even among the chefs d'œuvre of the Greeks not a few owe their creation to a different sentiment. Some of the great artists of antiquity were certainly occupied with the interpretation of the moral life; and had not time destroyed their painted works, we should, at the present moment, probably be able to show absolute proofs of this tendency. But we may readily dispense with the confirmation which they would have afforded to our arguments; for we find more than sufficient evidence in the avowed character of the music of the Greeks, in many of the most important works of their sculptors, and in most of their great poems.

The chief characteristic of modern art — of art, that is, left to follow its own inspiration free from academic patronage — is power of expression. Through form this, the second kind of art, traces the moral life, and endeavours to occupy man, body and soul, but with no thought of sacrificing the one to the other. It is ever becoming more imbued with the quite modern idea that the whole being is *one*, metaphysicians notwithstanding, and that its aim can only be complete by refusing to separate the organ from its function. The moral life is but the general result of the conditions of the physical. The one is bound to the other by necessary /126/ connections which cannot be broken without destroying both. The first care of the artist should be to seek out and grasp the methods of manifestation so as to comprehend and master their unity.

Art, thus understood, demands from its votary an ensemble of intellectual faculties higher and more robust than if founded solely upon an ideal of beauty. Art founded upon the latter notion would be sufficiently served by one possessing an acute sense of the beautiful — the degree of his sensibility being indicated by the plastic perfection of his work. But expressive art demands a capability of being moved by many varying sentiments, demands the power to penetrate beneath outward appearances and to seize a hidden thought, the power to grasp either the permanent characteristic or the particular and momentary emotion; in a word, it demands that complete eloquence of representation which art might have dispensed with while it confined itself to the investigation or delineation of a single expression, but which became absolutely indispensable from the moment that the interpretation of the entire man became its avowed object.

We may say, too, that modern art is doubly expressive; because, while the artist is indicating by form and sound the sentiments and ideas of the personages whom he introduces, he is also by the power and manner of such manifestation giving an unerring measure of his own sensibility, imagination, and intelligence.

Expressive art is in no way hostile to beauty; it makes use of it as one element in the subjects which require it, but its domain is not enclosed within the narrow bounds of such a conception. It is by no means indifferent to the pleasures of sight and hearing, but it sees something beyond them. Its worth must not be measured only by perfection of form, but also and chiefly, by the double power of expression which we have pointed out, and, as we must not omit to add, by the value of the sentiments and ideas expressed. This latter point is too often and wrongly ignored by artists.

Between two works which give evidence of equal talent — that is to say, of equal facility to grasp the true accents and charac- /127/ teristics of nature, and equal power to bring out both the inner meaning of things and the personality of the artist — we, for our part, would not hesitate to accord the preference to that of which the *Conception* showed the more vigorous intelligence and elevated feeling. The art critics seem to have made it one of their principles to take no account of choice of subject, but only to look at the technical result. Such a principle is plausible rather than true. The individuality of the author can never be excluded from a work, and choice of subject is frequently one of the points by which this individuality is most clearly indicated.

It is true, of course, that elevation of sentiment can never take the place of art talent. On this point we cannot too strongly comdemn the practice of academic juries who, on the one hand, reward mere mechanical labour simply because it has been exercised upon what are called classic subjects; and, on the other, persecute more independent artists to punish their obstinacy in deserting the beaten track. Nothing, then, can be further from our thoughts than to require critics to substitute, in every case, consideration of the subject for that of the work itself; or to condemn *à priori* all artists who remain faithful to the traditions, ideas, and sentiments of the past. In these, indeed, some find their only inspiration. We only wish to affirm our conviction that choice of subject is not so indifferent a matter as some say it is, and that it must be taken into account as of considerable weight in determining an opinion of a work of art.

The necessity for this is one consequence of the distinction which we have established between decorative and expressive art. The former, solely devoted to the gratification of eye and ear, affords no measure of its success beyond the pleasure which it gives. The latter, whose chief object is to express the feelings and ideas, and, through them, to manifest the power of conception and expansion possessed by the artist, must obviously be estimated, partly at least, by the moral or other value of the ideas and sentiments in question. And, as the value of a work depends directly upon the capability of its author, and as many artists /128/ have been about equal in their technical ability, we must be ready to acknowledge that moral and intellectual superiority is a real superiority, and is naturally marked by the possession of an instinctive and spontaneous power of sympathy. . . . /129/

STYLE

Style is the man, says Buffon; and he is right. Get some one who *can* read, to read a page of Demosthenes *and* of Cicero, of Bossuet and of Massillon, of Corneille and of Racine, of Lamartine and of Victor Hugo. However slight may be your literary perceptions, you will at once notice that no two of them sound the same. Apart altogether from the subjects or ideas, which may be identical, each one has an air, an accent, which can never either be confounded or replaced. In some of them we find elegance, finesse, grace, the most seductive and soothing harmony; in others, a force and *élan* like the sound of a trumpet, enough to awaken the Seven Sleepers.

Style only exists by virtue of what Bürger calls *the law of separation.* "A being only exists in consequence of his separation from other beings. . . . . [*sic*] This law of successive detachment — which alone renders progress possible — may be proved to influence the course of religion, of politics, of literature and of art. What was the renaissance but a break in the continuity of the middle ages?" It is by style, by the manner of comprehension, of feeling and interpretation, that epochs, races, schools and individuals are separated and distinguished one from the other. In all the arts, analogous differences are to be found; plainly marked, in proportion as a more or less extensive field is offered for the development of artistic personality. Michael /130/ Angelo and Raphael, Leonardo and Veronese, Titian and Correggio, Rubens and Rembrandt, resembled each other no more and no less than Beethoven resembled Rossini; Weber, Mozart; or Wagner resembles Verdi. Each has his own style, his peculiar mode of thinking and feeling, and of expressing those feelings and thoughts.

Why have mediocre artists no style? For the same reasons that they are mediocrities. The particular characteristic of mediocrity is commonness or vulgarity of thought and feeling. At each moment in the evolution of a social system, there is a general level which marks, for that moment, the average value of the human soul and intellect. Such works as rise above this general level, imply an amount of talent or genius in exact proportion to the amount of superior elevation and spontaneity which they display. Mediocrity comes up to the general level, but does not pass it; thus the mediocre artist thinks and feels like the ordinary run of mankind, and has nothing to "separate" him from the crowd. He may have a manner, an ensemble of habits of working peculiar to himself; but he can have no style in the accurate sense of the word. Facility is not style; for the latter is really a product, a reverberation, if we may use the word, from the soul itself, and can no more be artificially acquired than can the sonorousness of bronze or silver be acquired by lead. . . . /131/

. . . Style, which is a simple reflection of the artist's personality, is naturally found in the work of every artist who possesses any personality. The indescribable quality, the "je ne sais quoi" of which Fromentin speaks, is precisely the assemblage of qualities, the condition of being and temperament which caused Rubens to see things differently to Rembrandt. The two extracted from one and the same object or subject, emotions widely different though congenial to their respective natures; just as a tightened string in a concert room will vibrate in response to the note which it would itself produce if struck. The one thing needful is the power to vibrate, which is too often wanting.

The question of style has considerable importance. We might even say that it includes the whole of æsthetics, which is in fact the question of personality in art. . . . /139/

Truth and personality: these are the alpha and omega of art formulas; *truth* as to facts, and the *personality* of the artist. But, if we look more closely, we shall see that these two terms are in reality but one. Truth as to fact, so far as art is concerned, is above all the truth of our own sensations, of our own sentiments. It is truth as we see it, as it appears modified by our own temperaments, preferences, and physical organs. It is, in fact, our personality itself. Reality, as given by the photographer, reality taken from a point of view without connection with us or our impressions, is the very negation of art. When this kind of truth predominates in a work of art, we cry, "There is realism for you!" Now, realism partakes of the nature of art, only because the most downright of realists must, whether he will or not, put something of his own individuality into his work. When, on the other hand, the dominant quality is what we call human or personal truth, then we at once exclaim, "Here is an artist!"

And the latter is the right meaning of the word. Art consists essentially in the predominance of subjectivity over objectivity; it is the chief distinction between it and science. The man intended for science, is he whose imagination has no modifying influence over the results of his direct observation. The artist, on the other hand, is one whose imagination, impressionability—in a word, whose personality, is so lively and excitable, that it spontaneously transforms everything, dyeing them in its own colours, and unconsciously exaggerating them in accordance with its own preferences.

We think ourselves justified, then, in calling art the direct and spontaneous manifestation of human personality. But we must not omit also to remember the fact that such personality—individual and particular as it is from some points of view—is nevertheless exposed to many successive and temporary modifications caused by the various kinds of civilisation through which it has had to pass. . . . /389/

✳ THE FORMALIST CRITICS

Cleanth Brooks

Here are some articles of faith I could subscribe to:

That literary criticism is a description and an evaluation of its object.

That the primary concern of criticism is with the problem of unity—the kind of whole which the literary work forms or fails to form and the relation of the various parts to each other in building up this whole.

That the formal relations in a work of literature may include, but certainly exceed, those of logic.

That in a successful work, form and content cannot be separated.

That form is meaning.

That literature is ultimately metaphorical and symbolic.

From "The Formalist Critics," *The Kenyon Review*, 13 (1951), 72–81.

That the general and the universal are not seized upon by abstraction, but got at through the concrete and the particular.

That literature is not a surrogate for religion.

That, as Allen Tate says, "specific moral problems" are the subject matter of literature but that the purpose of literature is not to point a moral.

That the principles of criticism define the area relevant to literary criticism; they do not constitute a method for carrying out the criticism. /72/

Such statements as these would not, however, even though greatly elaborated, serve any useful purpose here. The interested reader already knows the general nature of the critical position adumbrated – or, if he does not, he can find it set forth in writings of mine or of other critics of like sympathy. Moreover, a condensed restatement of the position here would probably beget as many misunderstandings as have past attempts to set it forth. It seems much more profitable to use the present occasion for dealing with some persistent misunderstandings and objections.

In the first place, to make the poem or the novel the central concern of criticism has appeared to mean cutting it loose from its author and from his life as a man, with his own particular hopes, fears, interests, conflicts, etc. A criticism so limited may seem bloodless and hollow. It will seem so to the typical professor of literature in the graduate school, where the study of literature is still primarily a study of the ideas and personality of the author as revealed in his letters, his diaries, and the recorded conversations of his friends. It will certainly seem so to literary gossip columnists who purvey literary chitchat. It may also seem so to the young poet or novelist, beset with his own problems of composition and with his struggles to find a subject and a style and to get a hearing for himself.

In the second place, to emphasize the work seems to involve severing it from those who actually read it, and this severance may seem drastic and therefore disastrous. After all, literature is written to be read. Wordsworth's poet was a man speaking to men. In each Sunday *Times,* Mr. J. Donald Adams points out that the hungry sheep look up and are not fed; and less strenuous moralists than Mr. Adams are bound to feel a proper revulsion against "mere aestheticism." Moreover, if we neglect the audience which reads the work, including that for which it was presumably written, the literary historian is prompt to point out that the kind of audience that Pope had did condition the kind of poetry /73/ that he wrote. The poem has its roots in history, past or present. Its place in the historical context simply cannot be ignored.

I have stated these objections as sharply as I can because I am sympathetic with the state of mind which is prone to voice them. Man's experience is indeed a seamless garment, no part of which can be separated from the rest. Yet if we urge this fact of inseparability against the drawing of distinctions, then there is no point in talking about criticism at all. I am assuming that distinctions are necessary and useful and indeed inevitable.

The formalist critic knows as well as anyone that poems and plays and novels are written by men – that they do not somehow happen – and that they are written as expressions of particular personalities and are written from all sorts of motives – for money, from a desire to express oneself, for the sake of a cause, etc. Moreover, the formalist critic knows as well as anyone that literary works are merely potential until they are read – that is, that they are re-created in the minds of actual readers, who vary enormously in their capabilities, their interests, their prejudices, their ideas. But the formalist critic is concerned primarily with the work itself. Speculation on the mental processes of the author takes the critic away from the work into biography and psychology. There is no reason, of course, why he should not turn away into biography and psychology. Such explorations are very much worth making. But they should not be confused with an account of the work. Such studies describe the process of composition, not the structure of the thing composed, and they may be performed quite as validly for the poor work as for the good one. They may be validly performed for any kind of expression — non-literary as well as literary.

On the other hand, exploration of the various readings which the work has received also takes the critic away from the work into psychology and the history of taste. The /74/ various imports of a given work may well be worth studying. I. A. Richards has put us all in his debt by demonstrating what different experiences may be derived from the same poem by an apparently homogeneous group of readers; and the scholars have pointed out, all along, how different Shakespeare appeared to an 18th Century as compared with a 19th Century audience; or how sharply divergent are the estimates of John Donne's lyrics from historical period to historical period. But such work, valuable and necessary as it may be, is to be distinguished from a criticism of the work itself. The formalist critic, because he wants to criticize the work itself, makes two assumptions: (1) he assumes that the relevant part of the author's intention is what he got actually into his work; that is, he assumes that the author's intention *as realized* is the "intention" that counts, not necessarily what he was conscious of trying to do, or what he now remembers he was then trying to do. And (2) the formalist critic assumes an ideal reader: that is, instead of focusing on the varying spectrum of possible readings, he attempts to find a central point of reference from which he can focus upon the structure of the poem or novel.

But there *is* no ideal reader, someone is prompt to point out, and he will probably add that it is sheer arrogance that allows the critic, with his own blindsides and prejudices, to put himself in the position of that ideal reader. There is no ideal reader, of course, and I suppose that the practising critic can never be too often reminded of the gap between his reading and the "true" reading of the poem. But for the purpose of focusing upon the poem rather than upon his own reactions, it is a defensible strategy. Finally, of course, it is the strategy that all critics of whatever persuasion are forced to adopt. (The alternatives are desperate: either we say that one person's reading is as good as another's and equate those readings on a basis of absolute equality and thus deny the possibility of any standard reading. Or else we take a lowest common denominator of the various readings that /75/ have been made; that is, we frankly move from literary criticism into socio-psychology. To propose taking a consensus of the opinions of "qualified" readers is simply to split the ideal reader into a group of ideal readers.) As consequences of the distinction just referred to, the formalist critic rejects two popular tests for literary value. The first proves the value of the work from the author's "sincerity" (or the intensity of the author's feelings as he composed it). If we heard that Mr. Guest testified that he put his heart and soul into his poems, we would not be very much impressed, though I should see no reason to doubt such a statement from Mr. Guest. It would simply be critically irrelevant. Ernest Hemingway's statement in a recent issue of *Time* magazine that he counts his last novel his best is of interest for Hemingway's biography, but most readers of *Across the River and Into the Trees* would agree that it proves nothing at all about the value of the novel — that in this case the judgment is simply pathetically inept. We discount also such tests for poetry as that proposed by A. E. Housman — the bristling of his beard at the reading of a good poem. The intensity of his reaction has critical significance only in proportion as we have already learned to trust him as a reader. Even so, what it tells us is something about Housman – nothing decisive about the poem.

It is unfortunate if this playing down of such responses seems to deny humanity to either writer or reader. The critic may enjoy certain works very much and may be indeed intensely moved by them. I am, and I have no embarrassment in admitting the fact; but a detailed description of my emotional state on reading certain works has little to do with indicating to an interested reader what the work is and how the parts of it are related.

Should all criticism, then, be self-effacing and analytic? I hope that the answer is implicit in what I have already written, but I shall go on to spell it out. Of course not. That will depend upon the occasion and the audience. In /76/ practice, the critic's job is rarely a purely critical one. He is much more likely to be involved in dozens of more or less related tasks, some of them trivial, some of them important. He may be trying to get a hearing for a new author, or to get the attention of the freshman sitting in the back row. He may be comparing two authors, or editing a text; writing a brief newspaper review or reading a paper before the Modern Language Association. He may even be simply talking with a friend, talking about literature for the hell of it. Parable, anecdote, epigram, metaphor – these and a hundred other devices may be thoroughly legitimate for his varying purposes. He is certainly not to be asked to suppress his personal enthusiasms or his interest in social history or in politics. Least of all is he being asked to *present* his criticisms as the close reading of a text. Tact, common sense, and uncommon sense if he has it, are all requisite if the practising critic is to do his various jobs well.

But it will do the critic no harm to have a clear idea of what his specific job as a critic is. I can sympathize with writers who are tired of reading rather drab "critical analyses," and who recommend brighter, more amateur, and more "human" criticism. As ideals, these are excellent; as recipes for improving criticism, I have my doubts. Appropriate vulgarizations of these ideals are already flourishing, and have long flourished – in the class room presided over by the college lecturer of infectious enthusiasm, in the gossipy Book-of-the-Month Club bulletins, and in the columns of the *Saturday Review of Literature*.

I have assigned the critic a modest, though I think an important, role. With reference to the help which the critic can give to the practising artist, the role is even more modest. As critic, he can give only negative help. Literature is not written by formula: he can have no formula to offer. Perhaps he can do little more than indicate whether in his opinion the work has succeeded or failed. Healthy criticism and healthy creation do tend to go hand in hand. Every- /77/ thing else being equal, the creative artist is better off for being in touch with a vigorous criticism. But the other considerations are never equal, the case is always special, and in a given case the proper advice *could* be: quit reading criticism altogether, or read political science or history or philosophy – or join the army, or join the church.

There is certainly no doubt that the kind of specific and positive help that someone like Ezra Pound was able to give to several writers of our time is in one sense the most important kind of criticism that there can be. I think that it is not unrelated to the kind of criticism that I have described: there is the same intense concern with the text which is being built up, the same concern with "technical problems." But many other things are involved – matters which lie outside the specific ambit of criticism altogether, among them a knowledge of the personality of the particular writer, the ability to stimulate, to make positive suggestions.

A literary work is a document and as a document can be analysed in terms of the forces that have produced it, or it may be manipulated as a force in its own right. It mirrors the past, it may influence the future. These facts it would be futile to deny, and I know of no critic who does deny them. But the reduction of a work of literature to its causes does not constitute literary criticism; nor does an estimate of its effects. Good literature is more than effective rhetoric applied to true ideas—even if we could agree upon a philosophical yardstick for measuring the truth of ideas and even if we could find some way that transcended nose-counting for determining the effectiveness of the rhetoric. . . . /78/

PART II

Leo Tolstoy

Leo Tolstoy

CHAPTER IV

. . . Not reckoning the thoroughly inaccurate definitions of beauty which fail to cover the conception of art, and which suppose beauty to consist either in utility, or in adjustment to a purpose, or in symmetry, or in order, or in proportion, or in smoothness, or in harmony of the parts, or in unity amid variety, or in various combinations of these,—not reckoning these unsatisfactory attempts at objective definition, all the æsthetic definitions of beauty lead to two fundamental conceptions. The first is that beauty is something having an independent existence (existing in itself), that it is one of the manifestations of the absolutely Perfect, of the Idea, of the Spirit, of Will, or of God; the other is that beauty is a kind of pleasure received by us, not having personal advantage for its object.

The first of these definitions was accepted by Fichte, Schelling, Hegel, Schopenhauer, and the philosophising Frenchmen, Cousin, Jouffroy, Ravaisson, and others, not to enumerate the second-rate æsthetic philosophers. And this same objective-mystical definition of beauty is held by a majority of the educated people of our day. It is a conception very widely spread, especially among the elder generation.

The second view, that beauty is a certain kind of pleasure received by us, not having personal advantage for its aim, finds favour chiefly among the English æsthetic writers, and is shared by the other part of our society, principally by the younger generation. /38/

So there are (and it could not be otherwise) only two definitions of beauty: the one objective, mystical, merging this conception into that of the highest perfection, God—a fantastic definition, founded on nothing; the other, on the contrary, a very simple and intelligible subjective one, which considers beauty to be that which pleases (I do not add to the word "pleases" the words "without the aim of advantage," because "pleases" naturally presupposes the absence of the idea of profit).

On the one hand, beauty is viewed as something mystical and very elevated, but unfortunately at the same time very indefinite, and consequently embracing philosophy, religion, and life itself (as in the theories of Schelling and Hegel, and their German and French followers); or, on the other hand (as necessarily

From *What Is Art?* trans. Aylmer Maude (London: Walter Scott, Ltd., 1899).

follows from the definition of Kant and his adherents), beauty is simply a certain
kind of disinterested pleasure received by us. And this conception of beauty,
although it seems very clear, is, unfortunately, again inexact; for it widens out on
the other side, *i.e.* it includes the pleasure derived from drink, from food, from
touching a delicate skin, etc., as is acknowledged by Guyau, Kralik, and others.

It is true that, following the development of the æsthetic doctrines on
beauty, we may notice that, though at first (in the times when the foundations
of the science of æsthetics were being laid) the metaphysical definition of beauty
prevailed, yet the nearer we get to our own times the more does an experimental
definition (recently assuming a physiological form) come to the front, so that at
last we even meet with such æstheticians as Véron and Sully, who try to escape
entirely from the conception of beauty. But such æstheticians have very little
success, and with the majority of the public, as well as of artists and the learned,
a conception of beauty is firmly held which agrees with the definitions contained
in most of the æsthetic treatises, *i.e.* which regards /39/ beauty either as something mystical or metaphysical, or as a special kind of enjoyment.

What then is this conception of beauty, so stubbornly held to by people of
our circle and day as furnishing a definition of art?

In the subjective aspect, we call beauty that which supplies us with a particular kind of pleasure.

In the objective aspect, we call beauty something absolutely perfect, and we
acknowledge it to be so only because we receive, from the manifestation of this
absolute perfection, a certain kind of pleasure; so that this objective definition
is nothing but the subjective conception differently expressed. In reality both
conceptions of beauty amount to one and the same thing, namely, the reception
by us of a certain kind of pleasure, *i.e.* we call "beauty" that which pleases us
without evoking in us desire.

Such being the position of affairs, it would seem only natural that the science
of art should decline to content itself with a definition of art based on beauty
(*i.e.* on that which pleases), and seek a general definition, which should apply to
all artistic productions, and by reference to which we might decide whether a
certain article belonged to the realm of art or not. But no such definition is
supplied, as the reader may see from those summaries of the æsthetic theories
which I have given, and as he may discover even more clearly from the original
æsthetic works, if he will be at the pains to read them. All attempts to define
absolute beauty in itself—whether as an imitation of nature, or as suitability to
its object, or as a correspondence of parts, or as symmetry, or as harmony, or as
unity in variety, etc.—either define nothing at all, or define only some traits of
some artistic productions, and are far from including all that everybody has
always held, and still holds, to be art.

There is no objective definition of beauty. The existing definitions, (both
the metaphysical and the experimental), /40/ amount only to one and the same
subjective definition which (strange as it seems to say so) is, that art is that which
makes beauty manifest, and beauty is that which pleases (without exciting desire). Many æstheticians have felt the insufficiency and instability of such a
definition, and, in order to give it a firm basis, have asked themselves why a
thing pleases. And they have converted the discussion on beauty into a question
concerning taste, as did Hutcheson, Voltaire, Diderot, and others. But all
attempts to define what taste is must lead to nothing, as the reader may see both
from the history of æsthetics and experimentally. There is and can be no explanation of why one thing pleases one man and displeases another, or *vice
versâ*. So that the whole existing science of æsthetics fails to do what we might
expect from it, being a mental activity calling itself a science, namely, it does

not define the qualities and laws of art, or of the beautiful (if that be the content of art), or the nature of taste (if taste decides the question of art and its merit), and then, on the basis of such definitions, acknowledge as art those productions which correspond to these laws, and reject those which do not come under them. But this science of æsthetics consists in first acknowledging a certain set of productions to be art (because they please us), and then framing such a theory of art that all those productions which please a certain circle of people should fit into it. There exists an art canon, according to which certain productions favoured by our circle are acknowledged as being art, — Phidias, Sophocles, Homer, Titian, Raphael, Bach, Beethoven, Dante, Shakespear, Goethe, and others, — and the æsthetic laws must be such as to embrace all these productions. In æsthetic literature you will incessantly meet with opinions on the merit and importance of art, founded not on any certain laws by which this or that is held to be good or bad, but merely on the consideration whether this art tallies with the art canon we have drawn up. . . . /41/

So that the theory of art, founded on beauty, expounded by æsthetics, and, in dim outline, professed by the public, is nothing but the setting up as good, of that which has pleased and pleases us, *i.e.* pleases a certain class of people.

In order to define any human activity, it is necessary to understand its sense and importance. And, in order to do that, it is primarily necessary to examine that activity in itself, in its dependence on its causes, and in connection with its effects, and not merely in relation to the pleasure we can get from it.

If we say that the aim of any activity is merely our pleasure, and define it solely by that pleasure, our definition will evidently be a false one. But this is precisely what has occurred in the efforts to define art. Now, if we consider the food question, it will not occur to anyone to affirm that the importance of food consists in the pleasure we receive when eating it. Everyone understands that the satisfaction of our taste cannot serve as a basis for our definition of the merits of food, and that we have therefore no right to presuppose that the dinners with cayenne pepper, Limburg cheese, alcohol, etc., to which we are accustomed and which please us, form the very best human food.

And in the same way, beauty, or that which pleases us, can in no sense serve as the basis for the definition of art; nor can a series of objects which afford us pleasure serve as the model of what art should be.

To see the aim and purpose of art in the pleasure we get from it, is like assuming (as is done by people of the lowest moral development, *e.g.* by savages) that the purpose and aim of food is the pleasure derived when consuming it.

Just as people who conceive the aim and purpose of food to be pleasure cannot recognise the real meaning of eating, /43/ so people who consider the aim of art to be pleasure cannot realise its true meaning and purpose, because they attribute to an activity, the meaning of which lies in its connection with other phenomena of life, the false and exceptional aim of pleasure. People come to understand that the meaning of eating lies in the nourishment of the body only when they cease to consider that the object of that activity is pleasure. And it is the same with regard to art. People will come to understand the meaning of art only when they cease to consider that the aim of that activity is beauty, *i.e.* pleasure. The acknowledgment of beauty (*i.e.* of a certain kind of pleasure received from art) as being the aim of art, not only fails to assist us in finding a definition of what art is, but, on the contrary, by transferring the question into a region quite foreign to art (into metaphysical, psychological, physiological, and even historical discussions as to why such a production pleases one person, and such another displeases or pleases someone else), it renders such definition impossible. And since discussions as to why one man likes pears and another prefers meat do not help towards finding a definition of what is essential in nourishment, so the solution of questions of taste in art (to which the discussions on art involuntarily come) not only does not help to make clear what this particular human activity which we call art really consists in, but renders such elucidation quite impossible, until we rid ourselves of a conception which justifies every kind of art, at the cost of confusing the whole matter.

To the question, What is this art, to which is offered up the labour of millions, the very lives of men, and even morality itself? we have extracted replies from the existing æsthetics, which all amount to this: that the aim of art is beauty, that beauty is recognised by the enjoyment it gives, and that artistic enjoyment is a good and important thing, because it *is* enjoyment. In a word, that enjoyment is good /44/ because it is enjoyment. Thus, what is considered the definition of art is no definition at all, but only a shuffle to justify existing art. Therefore, however strange it may seem to say so, in spite of the mountains of books written about art, no exact definition of art has been constructed. And the reason of this is that the conception of art has been based on the conception of beauty. /45/

CHAPTER V

What is art, if we put aside the conception of beauty, which confuses the whole matter? The latest and most comprehensible definitions of art, apart from the conception of beauty, are the following: — (1 *a*) Art is an activity arising even in the animal kingdom, and springing from sexual desire and the propensity to play (Schiller, Darwin, Spencer), and (1 *b*) accompanied by a pleasurable excitement of the nervous system (Grant Allen). This is the physiological-evolutionary definition. (2) Art is the external manifestation, by means of lines, colours, movements, sounds, or words, of emotions felt by man (Véron). This is the experimental definition. According to the very latest definition (Sully), (3) Art is "the production of some permanent object, or passing action, which is fitted not only to supply an active enjoyment to the producer, but to convey a pleasurable impression to a number of spectators or listeners, quite apart from any personal advantage to be derived from it."

Notwithstanding the superiority of these definitions to the metaphysical definitions which depended on the conception of beauty, they are yet far from exact. (1 *a*) The first, the physiological-evolutionary definition, is inexact, because, instead of speaking about the artistic activity itself, which is the real matter in hand, it treats of the derivation of art. The modification of it (1 *b*), based on the physiological effects on the human organism, is inexact, because within the limits of such definition many other human activities can be included, as has occurred in the neo-æsthetic theories, which /46/ reckon as art the preparation of handsome clothes, pleasant scents, and even of victuals.

The experimental definition (2), which makes art consist in the expression of emotions, is inexact, because a man may express his emotions by means of lines, colours, sounds, or words, and yet may not act on others by such expression; and then the manifestation of his emotions is not art.

The third definition (that of Sully) is inexact, because in the production of objects or actions affording pleasure to the producer and a pleasant emotion to the spectators or hearers apart from personal advantage, may be included the showing of conjuring tricks or gymnastic exercises, and other activities which are not art. And, further, many things, the production of which does not afford pleasure to the producer, and the sensation received from which is unpleasant, such as gloomy, heart-rending scenes in a poetic description or a play, may nevertheless be undoubted works of art.

The inaccuracy of all these definitions arises from the fact that in them all (as also in the metaphysical definitions) the object considered is the pleasure art may give, and not the purpose it may serve in the life of man and of humanity.

In order correctly to define art, it is necessary, first of all, to cease to consider it as a means to pleasure, and to consider it as one of the conditions of human life. Viewing it in this way, we cannot fail to observe that art is one of the means of intercourse between man and man.

Every work of art causes the receiver to enter into a certain kind of relationship both with him who produced, or is producing, the art, and with all those who, simultaneously, previously or subsequently, receive the same artistic impression.

Speech, transmitting the thoughts and experiences of men, serves as a means of union among them, and art acts in a similar manner. The peculiarity of this latter means /47/ of intercourse, distinguishing it from intercourse by means of words, consists in this, that whereas by words a man transmits his thoughts to another, by means of art he transmits his feelings.

The activity of art is based on the fact that a man, receiving through his sense of hearing or sight another man's expression of feeling, is capable of experiencing the emotion which moved the man who expressed it. To take the simplest example: one man laughs, and another, who hears, becomes merry; or a man weeps, and another, who hears, feels sorrow. A man is excited or irritated, and another man, seeing him, comes to a similar state of mind. By his movements, or by the sounds of his voice, a man expresses courage and determination, or sadness and calmness, and this state of mind passes on to others. A man suffers, expressing his sufferings by groans and spasms, and this suffering transmits itself to other people; a man expresses his feeling of admiration, devotion, fear, respect, or love to certain objects, persons, or phenomena, and others are infected by the same feelings of admiration, devotion, fear, respect, or love to the same objects, persons, and phenomena.

And it is on this capacity of man to receive another man's expression of feeling, and experience those feelings himself, that the activity of art is based.

If a man infects another or others, directly, immediately, by his appearance, or by the sounds he gives vent to at the very time he experiences the feeling; if he causes another man to yawn when he himself cannot help yawning, or to laugh or cry when he himself is obliged to laugh or cry, or to suffer when he himself is suffering—that does not amount to art.

Art begins when one person, with the object of joining another or others to himself in one and the same feeling, expresses that feeling by certain external indications. To take the simplest example: a boy, having experienced, let us /48/ say, fear on encountering a wolf, relates that encounter; and, in order to evoke in others the feeling he has experienced, describes himself, his condition before the encounter, the surroundings, the wood, his own lightheartedness, and then the wolf's appearance, its movements, the distance between himself and the wolf, etc. All this, if only the boy when telling the story, again experiences the feelings he had lived through and infects the hearers and compels them to feel what the narrator had experienced, is art. If even the boy had not seen a wolf but had frequently been afraid of one, and if, wishing to evoke in others the fear he had felt, he invented an encounter with a wolf, and recounted it so as to make his hearers share the feelings he experienced when he feared the wolf, that also would be art. And just in the same way it is art if a man, having experienced either the fear of suffering or the attraction of enjoyment (whether in reality or in imagination), expresses these feelings on canvas or in marble so that others are infected by them. And it is also art if a man feels or imagines to himself feelings of delight, gladness, sorrow, despair, courage, or despondency, and the transition from one to another of these feelings, and expresses these feelings by sounds, so that the hearers are infected by them, and experience them as they were experienced by the composer.

The feelings with which the artist infects others may be most various — very strong or very weak, very important or very insignificant, very bad or very good: feelings of love for native land, self-devotion and submission to fate or to God expressed in a drama, raptures of lovers described in a novel, feelings of voluptuousness expressed in a picture, courage expressed in a triumphal march, merriment evoked by a dance, humour evoked by a funny story, the feeling of quietness transmitted by an evening landscape or by a lullaby, or the feeling of admiration evoked by a beautiful arabesque — it is all art. /49/

If only the spectators or auditors are infected by the feelings which the author has felt, it is art.

To evoke in oneself a feeling one has once experienced, and having evoked it in oneself, then, by means of movements, lines, colours, sounds, or forms expressed in words, so to transmit that feeling that others may experience the same feeling — this is the activity of art.

Art is a human activity, consisting in this, that one man consciously, by means of certain external signs, hands on to others feelings he has lived through, and that other people are infected by these feelings, and also experience them.

Art is not, as the metaphysicians say, the manifestation of some mysterious Idea of beauty, or God; it is not, as the æsthetical physiologists say, a game in which man lets off his excess of stored-up energy; it is not the expression of man's emotions by external signs; it is not the production of pleasing objects; and, above all, it is not pleasure; but it is a means of union among men, joining them together in the same feelings, and indispensable for the life and progress towards well-being of individuals and of humanity.

As, thanks to man's capacity to express thoughts by words, every man may know all that has been done for him in the realms of thought by all humanity before his day, and can, in the present, thanks to this capacity to understand the thoughts of others, become a sharer in their activity, and can himself hand on to his contemporaries and descendants the thoughts he has assimilated from others, as well as those which have arisen within himself; so, thanks to man's capacity to be infected with the feelings of others by means of art, all that is being lived through by his contemporaries is accessible to him, as well as the feelings experienced by men thousands of years ago, and he has also the possibility of transmitting his own feelings to others.

If people lacked this capacity to receive the thoughts conceived by the men who preceded them, and to pass on to /50/ others their own thoughts, men would be like wild beasts, or like Kaspar Hauser.[1]

And if men lacked this other capacity of being infected by art, people might be almost more savage still, and, above all, more separated from, and more hostile to, one another.

And therefore the activity of art is a most important one, as important as the activity of speech itself, and as generally diffused.

We are accustomed to understand art to be only what we hear and see in theatres, concerts, and exhibitions; together with buildings, statues, poems,

---

[1] "The foundling of Nuremberg," found in the market-place of that town on 26th May 1828, apparently some sixteen years old. He spoke little, and was almost totally ignorant even of common objects. He subsequently explained that he had been brought up in confinement underground, and visited by only one man, whom he saw but seldom. — Trans. /51/

novels. . . . But all this is but the smallest part of the art by which we communicate with each other in life. All human life is filled with works of art of every kind—from cradle-song, jest, mimicry, the ornamentation of houses, dress and utensils, up to church services, buildings, monuments, and triumphal processions. It is all artistic activity. So that by art, in the limited sense of the word, we do not mean all human activity transmitting feelings, but only that part which we for some reason select from it and to which we attach special importance.

This special importance has always been given by all men to that part of this activity which transmits feelings flowing from their religious perception, and this small part of art they have specifically called art, attaching to it the full meaning of the word. . . . /51/

CHAPTER X

The assertion that art may be good art, and at the same time incomprehensible to a great number of people, is extremely unjust, and its consequences are ruinous to art itself; but at the same time it is so common and has so eaten into our conceptions, that it is impossible sufficiently to elucidate all the absurdity of it.

Nothing is more common than to hear it said of reputed works of art, that they are very good but very difficult to understand. We are quite used to such assertions, and yet to say that a work of art is good, but incomprehensible to the majority of men, is the same as saying of some kind of food that it is very good but that most people can't eat it. The majority of men may not like rotten cheese or putrefying grouse dishes esteemed by people with perverted tastes; but bread and fruit are only good when they please the majority of men. And it is the same with art. Perverted art may not please the majority of men, but good art always pleases everyone.

It is said that the very best works of art are such that /100/ they cannot be understood by the mass, but are accessible only to the elect who are prepared to understand these great works. But if the majority of men do not understand, the knowledge necessary to enable them to understand should be taught and explained to them. But it turns out that there is no such knowledge, that the works cannot be explained, and that those who say the majority do not understand good works of art, still do not explain those works, but only tell us that, in order to understand them, one must read, and see, and hear these same works over and over again. But this is not to explain, it is only to habituate! And people may habituate themselves to anything, even to the very worst things. As people may habituate themselves to bad food, to spirits, tobacco, and opium, just in the same way they may habituate themselves to bad art—and that is exactly what is being done.

Moreover, it cannot be said that the majority of people lack the taste to esteem the highest works of art. The majority always have understood, and still understand, what we also recognise as being the very best art: the epic of Genesis, the Gospel parables, folk-legends, fairy-tales, and folk-songs are understood by all. How can it be that the majority has suddenly lost its capacity to understand what is high in our art?

Of a speech it may be said that it is admirable, but incomprehensible to those who do not know the language in which it is delivered. A speech delivered in Chinese may be excellent, and may yet remain incomprehensible to me if I do not know Chinese; but what distinguishes a work of art from all other mental activity is just the fact that its language is understood by all, and that it infects all without distinction. The tears and laughter of a Chinese infect me just as the laughter and tears of a Russian; and it is the same with painting and music and poetry, when it is translated into a language I understand. The songs of a Kirghiz /101/ or of a Japanese touch me, though in a lesser degree than they touch a Kirghiz or a Japanese. I am also touched by Japanese painting, Indian architecture, and Arabian stories. If I am but little touched by a Japanese song and a Chinese novel, it is not that I do not understand these productions, but that I know and am accustomed to higher works of art. It is not because their art is above me. Great works of art are only great because they are accessible and comprehensible to everyone. The story of Joseph, translated into the Chinese language, touches a Chinese. The story of Sakya Muni touches us. And there are, and must be, buildings, pictures, statues, and music of similar power. So that, if art fails to move men, it cannot be said that this is due to the spectators' or hearers' lack of understanding; but the conclusion to be drawn may, and should be, that such art is either bad art, or is not art at all. . . . /102/

Art cannot be incomprehensible to the great masses only because it is very good, — as artists of our day are fond of telling us. Rather we are bound to conclude that this art is unintelligible to the great masses only because it is very bad art, or even is not art at all. So that the favourite argument (naïvely accepted by the cultured crowd), that in order to feel art one has first to understand it (which really only means habituate oneself to it), is the truest indication that what we are asked to understand by such a method is either very bad, exclusive art, or is not art at all. /103/

People say that works of art do not please the people because they are incapable of understanding them. But if the aim of works of art is to infect people with the emotion the artist has experienced, how can one talk about not understanding?

A man of the people reads a book, sees a picture, hears a play or a symphony, and is touched by no feeling. He is told that this is because he cannot understand. People promise to let a man see a certain show; he enters and sees nothing. He is told that this is because his sight is not prepared for this show. But the man well knows that he sees quite well, and if he does not see what people promised to show him, he only concludes (as is quite just) that those who undertook to show him the spectacle have not fulfilled their engagement. And it is perfectly just for a man who does feel the influence of some works of art to come to this conclusion concerning artists who do not, by their works, evoke feeling in him. To say that the reason a man is not touched by my art is because he is still too stupid, besides being very self-conceited and also rude, is to reverse the rôles, and for the sick to send the hale to bed. . . . /104/

CHAPTER XII

A friend of mine, speaking of the relation of critics to artists, half-jokingly defined it thus: "Critics are the stupid who discuss the wise." However partial, inexact, and rude this definition may be, it is yet partly true, and is incomparably juster than the definition which considers critics to be men who can explain works of art.

"Critics explain!" What do they explain?

The artist, if a real artist, has by his work transmitted to others the feeling he experienced. What is there, then, to explain?

If a work be good as art, then the feeling expressed by the artist — be it moral or immoral — transmits itself to other people. If transmitted to others, then they feel it, and all interpretations are superfluous. If the work does not infect people, no explanation can make it contagious. An artist's work cannot be interpreted. Had it been possible to explain in words what he wished to convey, the artist would have expressed himself in words. He expressed it by his art, only because the feeling he experienced could not be otherwise transmitted. The interpretation of works of art by words only indicates that the interpreter is himself incapable of feeling the infection of art. And this is /119/ actually the case, for, however strange it may seem to say so, critics have always been people less susceptible than other men to the contagion of art. For the most part they are able writers, educated and clever, but with their capacity of being infected by art quite perverted or atrophied. And therefore their writings have always largely contributed, and still contribute, to the perversion of the taste of that public which reads them and trusts them.

Artistic criticism did not exist—could not and cannot exist—in societies where art is undivided, and where, consequently, it is appraised by the religious understanding-of-life common to the whole people. Art criticism grew, and could grow, only on the art of the upper classes, who did not acknowledge the religious perception of their time.

Universal art has a definite and indubitable internal criterion—religious perception; upper-class art lacks this, and therefore the appreciators of that art are obliged to cling to some external criterion. And they find it·in "the judgments of the finest-nurtured," as an English æsthetician has phrased it, that is, in the authority of the people who are considered educated, nor in this alone, but also in a tradition of such authorities. This tradition is extremely misleading, both because the opinions of "the finest-nurtured" are often mistaken, and also because judgments which were valid once cease to be so with the lapse of time. But the critics, having no basis for their judgments, never cease to repeat their traditions. The classical tragedians were once considered good, and therefore criticism considers them to be so still. Dante was esteemed a great poet, Raphael a great painter, Bach a great musician—and the critics, lacking a standard by which to separate good art from bad, not only consider these artists great, but regard all their productions as admirable and worthy of imitation. Nothing has contributed, and still contributes, so much to the perversion of art as these authorities set up by criticism. A man produces a /120/ work of art, like every true artist expressing in his own peculiar manner a feeling he has experienced. Most people are infected by the artist's feeling; and his work becomes known. Then criticism, discussing the artist, says that the work is not bad, but all the same the artist is not a Dante, nor a Shakespear, nor a Goethe, nor a Raphael, nor what Beethoven was in his last period. And the young artist sets to work to copy those who are held up for his imitation, and he produces not only feeble works, but false works, counterfeits of art.

Thus, for instance, our Pushkin writes his short poems, *Evgeniy Onegin, The Gipsies,* and his stories—works all varying in quality, but all true art. But then, under the influence of false criticism extolling Shakespear, he writes *Boris Godunoff,* a cold, brain-spun work, and this production is lauded by the critics, set up as a model, and imitations of it appear: *Minin* by Ostrovsky, and *Tsar Boris* by Alexée Tolstoy, and such imitations of imitations as crowd all literatures with insignificant productions. The chief harm done by the critics is this, that themselves lacking the capacity to be infected by art (and that is the characteristic of all critics; for did they not lack this they could not attempt the impossible—the interpretation of works of art), they pay most attention to, and eulogise, brain-spun, invented works, and set these up as models worthy of imitation. That is the reason they so confidently extol, in literature, the Greek tragedians, Dante, Tasso, Milton, Shakespear, Goethe (almost all he wrote), and, among recent writers, Zola and Ibsen; in music, Beethoven's last period, and Wagner. To justify their praise of these brain-spun, invented works, they devise entire theories (of which the famous theory of beauty is one); and not only dull but also talented people compose works in strict deference to these theories; and often even real artists, doing violence to their genius, submit to them. /121/

Every false work extolled by the critics serves as a door through which the hypocrites of art at once crowd in.

It is solely due to the critics, who in our times still praise rude, savage, and, for us, often meaningless works of the ancient Greeks: Sophocles, Euripides, Æschylus, and especially Aristophanes; or, of modern writers, Dante, Tasso, Milton, Shakespear; in painting, all of Raphael, all of Michael Angelo, including his absurd "Last Judgment"; in music, the whole of Bach, and the whole of Beethoven, including his last period, — thanks only to them, have the Ibsens, Maeterlincks, Verlaines, Mallarmés, Puvis de Chavannes, Klingers, Böcklins, Stucks, Schneiders; in music, the Wagners, Liszts, Berliozes, Brahmses, and Richard Strausses, etc., and all that immense mass of good-for-nothing imitators of these imitators, become possible in our day.

As a good illustration of the harmful influence of criticism, take its relation to Beethoven. Among his innumerable hasty productions written to order, there are, notwithstanding their artificiality of form, works of true art. But he grows deaf, cannot hear, and begins to write invented, unfinished works, which are consequently often meaningless and musically unintelligible. I know that musicians can imagine sounds vividly enough, and can almost hear what they read, but imaginary sounds can never replace real ones, and every composer must hear his production in order to perfect it. Beethoven, however, could not hear, could not perfect his work, and consequently published productions which are artistic ravings. But criticism, having once acknowledged him to be a great composer, seizes on just these abnormal works with special gusto, and searches for extraordinary beauties in them. And, to justify its laudations (perverting the very meaning of musical art), it attributed to music the property of describing what it cannot /122/ describe. And imitators appear — an innumerable host of imitators of these abnormal attempts at artistic productions which Beethoven wrote when he was deaf.

Then Wagner appears, who at first in critical articles praises just Beethoven's last period, and connects this music with Schopenhauer's mystical theory that music is the expression of Will — not of separate manifestations of will objectivised on various planes, but of its very essence — which is in itself as absurd as this music of Beethoven. And afterwards he composes music of his own on this theory, in conjunction with another still more erroneous system of the union of all the arts. After Wagner yet new imitators appear, diverging yet further from art: Brahms, Richard Strauss, and others. . . . /123/

CHAPTER XV

Art, in our society, has been so perverted that not only has bad art come to be considered good, but even the very perception of what art really is has been lost. In order to be able to speak about the art of our society, it is, therefore, first of all necessary to distinguish art from counterfeit art.

There is one indubitable indication distinguishing real art from its counterfeit, namely, the infectiousness of art. If a man, without exercising effort and without altering his standpoint, on reading, hearing, or seeing another man's work, experiences a mental condition which unites him with that man and with other people who also partake of that work of art, then the object evoking that condition is a work of art. And however poetical, realistic, effectful, or interesting a work may be, it is not a work of art if it does not evoke that feeling (quite distinct from all other feelings) of joy, and of spiritual union with another (the author) and with others (those who are also infected by it).

It is true that this indication is an *internal* one, and that there are people who have forgotten what the action of real art is, who expect something else from art (in our society the great majority are in this state), and that therefore such people may mistake for this æsthetic feeling the feeling of divertisement and a certain excitement which they receive from counterfeits of art. But though it is impossible to undeceive these people, just as it is impossible to convince a man suffering from "Daltonism" that green is not red, yet, for all that, this indication remains perfectly definite /152/ to those whose feeling for art is neither perverted nor atrophied, and it clearly distinguishes the feeling produced by art from all other feelings.

The chief peculiarity of this feeling is that the receiver of a true artistic impression is so united to the artist that he feels as if the work were his own and not someone else's,—as if what it expresses were just what he had long been wishing to express. A real work of art destroys, in the consciousness of the receiver, the separation between himself and the artist, nor that alone, but also between himself and all whose minds receive this work of art. In this freeing of our personality from its separation and isolation, in this uniting of it with others, lies the chief characteristic and the great attractive force of art.

If a man is infected by the author's condition of soul, if he feels this emotion and this union with others, then the object which has effected this is art; but if there be no such infection, if there be not this union with the author and with others who are moved by the same work—then it is not art. And not only is infection a sure sign of art, but the degree of infectiousness is also the sole measure of excellence in art

The stronger the infection the better is the art, as art, speaking now apart from its subject-matter, *i.e.* not considering the quality of the feelings it transmits.

And the degree of the infectiousness of art depends on three conditions:—

(1) On the greater or lesser individuality of the feeling transmitted; (2) on the greater or lesser clearness with which the feeling is transmitted; (3) on the sincerity of the artist, *i.e.* on the greater or lesser force with which the artist himself feels the emotion he transmits.

The more individual the feeling transmitted the more strongly does it act on the receiver; the more individual the state of soul into which he is transferred the more /153/ pleasure does the receiver obtain, and therefore the more readily and strongly does he join in it.

The clearness of expression assists infection, because the receiver, who mingles in consciousness with the author, is the better satisfied the more clearly the feeling is transmitted, which, as it seems to him, he has long known and felt, and for which he has only now found expression.

But most of all is the degree of infectiousness of art increased by the degree of sincerity in the artist. As soon as the spectator, hearer, or reader feels that the artist is infected by his own production, and writes, sings, or plays for himself and not merely to act on others, this mental condition of the artist infects the receiver; and, contrariwise, as soon as the spectator, reader, or hearer feels that the author is not writing, singing, or playing for his own satisfaction,—does not himself feel what he wishes to express,—but is doing it for him, the receiver, a resistance immediately springs up, and the most individual and the newest feelings and the cleverest technique not only fail to produce any infection but actually repel.

I have mentioned three conditions of contagiousness in art, but they may all be summed up into one, the last, sincerity, *i.e.* that the artist should be impelled by an inner need to express his feeling. That condition includes the first; for if the artist is sincere he will express the feeling as he experienced it. And as each man is different from everyone else, his feeling will be individual for everyone else; and the more individual it is, — the more the artist has drawn it from the depths of his nature, — the more sympathetic and sincere will it be. And this same sincerity will impel the artist to find a clear expression of the feeling which he wishes to transmit.

Therefore this third condition — sincerity — is the most important of the three. It is always complied with in peasant art, and this explains why such art always acts so /154/ powerfully; but it is a condition almost entirely absent from our upper-class art, which is continually produced by artists actuated by personal aims of covetousness or vanity.

Such are the three conditions which divide art from its counterfeits, and which also decide the quality of every work of art apart from its subject-matter.

The absence of any one of these conditions excludes a work from the category of art and relegates it to that of art's counterfeits. If the work does not transmit the artist's peculiarity of feeling, and is therefore not individual, if it is unintelligibly expressed, or if it has not proceeded from the author's inner need for expression — it is not a work of art. If all these conditions are present, even in the smallest degree, then the work, even if a weak one, is yet a work of art.

The presence in various degrees of these three conditions: individuality, clearness, and sincerity, decides the merit of a work of art, as art, apart from subject-matter. All works of art take rank of merit according to the degree in which they fulfil the first, the second, and the third of these conditions. In one the individuality of the feeling transmitted may predominate; in another, clearness of expression; in a third, sincerity; while a fourth may have sincerity and individuality but be deficient in clearness; a fifth, individuality and clearness, but less sincerity; and so forth, in all possible degrees and combinations.

Thus is art divided from not art, and thus is the quality of art, as art, decided, independently of its subject-matter, *i.e.* apart from whether the feelings it transmits are good or bad.

But how are we to define good and bad art with reference to its subject-matter? /155/

CHAPTER XVI

How in art are we to decide what is good and what is bad in subject-matter?

Art, like speech, is a means of communication, and therefore of progress, *i.e.* of the movement of humanity forward towards perfection. Speech renders accessible to men of the latest generations all the knowledge discovered by the experience and reflection, both of preceding generations and of the best and foremost men of their own times; art renders accessible to men of the latest generations all the feelings experienced by their predecessors, and those also which are being felt by their best and foremost contemporaries. And as the evolution of knowledge proceeds by truer and more necessary knowledge dislodging and replacing what is mistaken and unnecessary, so the evolution of feeling proceeds through art, — feelings less kind and less needful for the well-being of mankind are replaced by others kinder and more needful for that end. That is the purpose of art. And, speaking now of its subject-matter, the more art fulfils that purpose the better the art, and the less it fulfils it the worse the art.

And the appraisement of feelings (*i.e.* the acknowledgment of these or those feelings as being more or less good, more or less necessary for the well-being of mankind) is made by the religious perception of the age.

In every period of history, and in every human society, there exists an understanding of the meaning of life which represents the highest level to which men of that society /156/ have attained, — an understanding defining the highest

good at which that society aims. And this understanding is the religious perception of the given time and society. And this religious perception is always clearly
expressed by some advanced men, and more or less vividly perceived by all the
members of the society. Such a religious perception and its corresponding expression exists always in every society. If it appears to us that in our society there
is no religious perception, this is not because there really is none, but only because we do not want to see it. And we often wish not to see it because it exposes
the fact that our life is inconsistent with that religious perception.

Religious perception in a society is like the direction of a flowing river. If
the river flows at all, it must have a direction. If a society lives, there must be a
religious perception indicating the direction in which, more or less consciously,
all its members tend.

And so there always has been, and there is, a religious perception in every
society. And it is by the standard of this religious perception that the feelings
transmitted by art have always been estimated. Only on the basis of this religious
perception of their age have men always chosen from the endlessly varied
spheres of art that art which transmitted feelings making religious perception
operative in actual life. And such art has always been highly valued and encouraged; while art transmitting feelings already outlived, flowing from the anti-
quated religious perceptions of a former age, has always been condemned and
despised. All the rest of art, transmitting those most diverse feelings by means
of which people commune together, was not condemned, and was tolerated, if
only it did not transmit feelings contrary to religious perception. Thus, for
instance, among the Greeks, art transmitting the feeling of beauty, strength,
and courage (Hesiod, Homer, Phidias) was chosen, approved, and encouraged;
while art transmitting feelings of rude sensuality, /157/ despondency, and ef-
feminacy was condemned and despised. Among the Jews, art transmitting feelings of devotion and submission to the God of the Hebrews and to His will (the
epic of Genesis, the prophets, the Psalms) was chosen and encouraged, while
art transmitting feelings of idolatry (the golden calf) was condemned and despised. All the rest of art—stories, songs, dances, ornamentation of houses, of
utensils, and of clothes—which was not contrary to religious perception, was
neither distinguished nor discussed. Thus, in regard to its subject-matter, has
art been appraised always and everywhere, and thus it should be appraised, for
this attitude towards art proceeds from the fundamental characteristics of
human nature, and those characteristics do not change.

I know that according to an opinion current in our times, religion is a super-
stition, which humanity has outgrown, and that it is therefore assumed that no
such thing exists as a religious perception common to us all by which art, in our
time, can be estimated. I know that this is the opinion current in the pseudo-
cultured circles of to-day. People who do not acknowledge Christianity in its
true meaning because it undermines all their social privileges, and who, therefore, invent all kinds of philosophic and æsthetic theories to hide from themselves the meaninglessness and wrongness of their lives, cannot think otherwise.
These people intentionally, or sometimes unintentionally, confusing the conception of a religious cult with the conception of religious perception, think that
by denying the cult they get rid of religious perception. But even the very attacks
on religion, and the attempts to establish a life-conception contrary to the religious perception of our times, most clearly demonstrate the existence of a religious perception condemning the lives that are not in harmony with it.

If humanity progresses, *i.e.* moves forward, there must inevitably be a guide
to the direction of that movement. /158/ And religions have always furnished
that guide. All history shows that the progress of humanity is accomplished not

otherwise than under the guidance of religion. But if the race cannot progress without the guidance of religion—and progress is always going on, and consequently also in our own times,—then there must be a religion of our times. So that, whether it pleases or displeases the so-called cultured people of to-day, they must admit the existence of religion—not of a religious cult, Catholic, Protestant, or another, but of religious perception—which, even in our times, is the guide always present where there is any progress. And if a religious perception exists amongst us, then our art should be appraised on the basis of that religious perception; and, as has always and everywhere been the case, art transmitting feelings flowing from the religious perception of our time should be chosen from all the indifferent art, should be acknowledged, highly esteemed, and encouraged; while art running counter to that perception should be condemned and despised, and all the remaining indifferent art should neither be distinguished nor encouraged.

The religious perception of our time, in its widest and most practical application, is the consciousness that our well-being, both material and spiritual, individual and collective, temporal and eternal, lies in the growth of brotherhood among all men—in their loving harmony with one another. This perception is not only expressed by Christ and all the best men of past ages, it is not only repeated in the most varied forms and from most diverse sides by the best men of our own times, but it already serves as a clue to all the complex labour of humanity, consisting as this labour does, on the one hand, in the destruction of physical and moral obstacles to the union of men, and, on the other hand, in establishing the principles common to all men which can and should unite them into one universal brotherhood. /159/ And it is on the basis of this perception that we should appraise all the phenomena of our life, and, among the rest, our art also; choosing from all its realms whatever transmits feelings flowing from this religious perception, highly prizing and encouraging such art, rejecting whatever is contrary to this perception, and not attributing to the rest of art an importance not properly pertaining to it.

The chief mistake made by people of the upper classes of the time of the so-called Renaissance,—a mistake which we still perpetuate,—was not that they ceased to value and to attach importance to religious art (people of that period could not attach importance to it, because, like our own upper classes, they could not believe in what the majority considered to be religion), but their mistake was that they set up in place of religious art which was lacking, an insignificant art which aimed only at giving pleasure, *i.e.* they began to choose, to value, and to encourage, in place of religious art, something which, in any case, did not deserve such esteem and encouragement.

One of the Fathers of the Church said that the great evil is not that men do not know God, but that they have set up, instead of God, that which is not God. So also with art. The great misfortune of the people of the upper classes of our time is not so much that they are without a religious art, as that, instead of a supreme religious art, chosen from all the rest as being specially important and valuable, they have chosen a most insignificant and, usually, harmful art, which aims at pleasing certain people, and which, therefore, if only by its exclusive nature, stands in contradiction to that Christian principle of universal union which forms the religious perception of our time. Instead of religious art, an empty and often vicious art is set up, and this hides from men's notice the need of that true religious art which should be present in life in order to improve it. . . . /160/

Good Christian art of our time may be unintelligible to people because of imperfections in its form, or because men are inattentive to it, but it must be such that all men can experience the feelings it transmits. It must be the art, not of some one group of people, nor of one class, nor of one nationality, nor of one religious cult; that is, it must not transmit feelings which are accessible only to a man educated in a certain way, or only to an aristocrat, or a merchant, or only to a Russian, or a native of Japan, or a Roman Catholic, or a Buddhist, etc., but it must transmit feelings accessible to everyone. Only art of this kind can be acknowledged in our time to be good art, worthy of being chosen out from all the rest of art and encouraged.

Christian art, *i.e.* the art of our time, should be catholic in the original meaning of the word, *i.e.* universal, and therefore it should unite all men. And only two kinds of feeling do unite all men: first, feelings flowing from the perception of our sonship to God and of the brotherhood of man; and next, the simple feelings of common life, accessible to everyone without exception — such as the feeling of merriment, of pity, of cheerfulness, of tranquillity, etc. Only these two kinds of feelings can now supply material for art good in its subject-matter.

And the action of these two kinds of art, apparently so dissimilar, is one and the same. The feelings flowing from perception of our sonship to God and of the brotherhood of man — such as a feeling of sureness in truth, devotion to the will of God, self-sacrifice, respect for and love of man — /164/ evoked by Christian religious perception; and the simplest feelings — such as a softened or a merry mood caused by a song or an amusing jest intelligible to everyone, or by a touching story, or a drawing, or a little doll: both alike produce one and the same effect — the loving union of man with man. Sometimes people who are together are, if not hostile to one another, at least estranged in mood and feeling, till perchance a story, a performance, a picture, or even a building, but oftenest of all music, unites them all as by an electric flash, and, in place of their former isolation or even enmity, they are all conscious of union and mutual love. Each is glad that another feels what he feels; glad of the communion established, not only between him and all present, but also with all now living who will yet share the same impression; and more than that, he feels the mysterious gladness of a communion which, reaching beyond the grave, unites us with all men of the past who have been moved by the same feelings, and with all men of the future who will yet be touched by them. And this effect is produced both by the religious art which transmits feelings of love to God and one's neighbour, and by universal art transmitting the very simplest feelings common to all men.

The art of our time should be appraised differently from former art chiefly in this, that the art of our time, *i.e.* Christian art (basing itself on a religious perception which demands the union of man), excludes from the domain of art good in subject-matter everything transmitting exclusive feelings, which do not unite but divide men. It relegates such work to the category of art bad in its subject-matter, while, on the other hand, it includes in the category of art good in subject-matter a section not formerly admitted to deserve to be chosen out and respected, namely, universal art transmitting even the most trifling and simple feelings if only they are accessible to all men without exception, /165/ and therefore unite them. Such art cannot, in our time, but be esteemed good, for it attains the end which the religious perception of our time, *i.e.* Christianity, sets before humanity.

Christian art either evokes in men those feelings which, through love of God and of one's neighbour, draw them to greater and ever greater union, and make them ready for and capable of such union; or evokes in them those feelings which show them that they are already united in the joys and sorrows of life. And therefore the Christian art of our time can be and is of two kinds: (1) art transmitting feelings flowing from a religious perception of man's position in the world in relation to God and to his neighbour—religious art in the limited meaning of the term; and (2) art transmitting the simplest feelings of common life, but such, always, as are accessible to all men in the whole world—the art of common life—the art of a people—universal art. Only these two kinds of art can be considered good art in our time.

The first, religious art,—transmitting both positive feelings of love to God and one's neighbour, and negative feelings of indignation and horror at the violation of love,—manifests itself chiefly in the form of words, and to some extent also in painting and sculpture: the second kind (universal art) transmitting feelings accessible to all, manifests itself in words, in painting, in sculpture, in dances, in architecture, and, most of all, in music.

If I were asked to give modern examples of each of these kinds of art, then, as examples of the highest art, flowing from love of God and man (both of the higher, positive, and of the lower, negative kind), in literature I should name *The Robbers* by Schiller: Victor Hugo's *Les Pauvres Gens* and *Les Misérables:* the novels and stories of Dickens—*The Tale of Two Cities, The Christmas Carol, The Chimes,* and others: *Uncle Tom's Cabin:* Dostoievsky's works— /166/ especially his *Memoirs from the House of Death:* and *Adam Bede* by George Eliot.

In modern painting, strange to say, works of this kind, directly transmitting the Christian feeling of love of God and of one's neighbour, are hardly to be found, especially among the works of the celebrated painters. There are plenty of pictures treating of the Gospel stories; they, however, depict historical events with great wealth of detail, but do not, and cannot, transmit religious feeling not possessed by their painters. There are many pictures treating of the personal feelings of various people, but of pictures representing great deeds of self-sacrifice and of Christian love there are very few, and what there are are principally by artists who are not celebrated, and are, for the most part, not pictures but merely sketches. Such, for instance, is the drawing by Kramskoy (worth many of his finished pictures), showing a drawing-room with a balcony, past which troops are marching in triumph on their return from the war. On the balcony stands a wet-nurse holding a baby and a boy. They are admiring the procession of the troops, but the mother, covering her face with a handkerchief, has fallen back on the sofa, sobbing. Such also is the picture by Walter Langley, to which I have already referred, and such again is a picture by the French artist Morlon, depicting a lifeboat hastening, in a heavy storm, to the relief of a steamer that is being wrecked. Approaching these in kind are pictures which represent the hard-working peasant with respect and love. Such are the pictures by Millet, and, particularly, his drawing, "The Man with the Hoe," also pictures in this style by Jules Breton, L'Hermitte, Defregger, and others. As examples of pictures evoking indignation and horror at the violation of love to God and man, Gay's picture, "Judgment," may serve, and also Leizen-Mayer's, "Signing the Death Warrant." But there are also very few of this kind. Anxiety about the technique /167/ and the beauty of the picture for the most part obscures the feeling. For instance Gérôme's "Pollice Verso" expresses, not so much horror at what is being perpetrated as attraction by the beauty of the spectacle.[1]

To give examples, from the modern art of our upper classes, of art of the second kind, good universal art or even of the art of a whole people, is yet more difficult, especially in literary art and music. If there are some works which by their inner contents might be assigned to this class (such as *Don Quixote,* Molière's comedies, *David Copperfield* and *The Pickwick Papers* by Dickens, Gogol's and Pushkin's tales, and some things of Maupassant's), these works are for the most

---

[1] In this picture the spectators in the Roman Amphitheatre are turning down their thumbs to show that they wish the vanquished gladiator to be killed.—Trans. /168/

part—from the exceptional nature of the feelings they transmit, and the super-
fluity of special details of time and locality, and, above all, on account of the
poverty of their subject-matter in comparison with examples of universal ancient
art (such, for instance, as the story of Joseph)—comprehensible only to people
of their own circle. That Joseph's brethren, being jealous of his father's affection,
sell him to the merchants; that Potiphar's wife wishes to tempt the youth; that
having attained the highest station, he takes pity on his brothers, including
Benjamin the favourite,—these and all the rest are feelings accessible alike to a
Russian peasant, a Chinese, an African, a child, or an old man, educated or
uneducated; and it is all written with such restraint, is so free from any superfluous detail, that the story may be told to any circle and will be equally comprehensible and touching to everyone. But not such are the feelings of Don Quixote
or of Molière's heroes (though Molière is perhaps the most universal, and therefore the most excellent, artist of modern times), nor of Pickwick and his friends.
These feelings are not common to all /168/ men but very exceptional, and therefore, to make them infectious, the authors have surrounded them with abundant
details of time and place. And this abundance of detail makes the stories difficult
of comprehension to all people not living within reach of the conditions described by the author.

The author of the novel of Joseph did not need to describe in detail, as
would be done nowadays, the blood-stained coat of Joseph, the dwelling and
dress of Jacob, the pose and attire of Potiphar's wife, and how, adjusting the
bracelet on her left arm, she said, "Come to me," and so on, because the subject-
matter of feelings in this novel is so strong that all details, except the most
essential,—such as that Joseph went out into another room to weep,—are superfluous, and would only hinder the transmission of feelings. And therefore this
novel is accessible to all men, touches people of all nations and classes, young
and old, and has lasted to our times, and will yet last for thousands of years
to come. But strip the best novels of our times of their details, and what will
remain?

It is therefore impossible in modern literature to indicate works fully satisfying the demands of universality. Such works as exist are, to a great extent,
spoilt by what is usually called "realism," but would be better termed "provin-
cialism," in art.

In music the same occurs as in verbal art, and for similar reasons. In consequence of the poorness of the feeling they contain, the melodies of the modern
composers are amazingly empty and insignificant. And to strengthen the impression produced by these empty melodies, the new musicians pile complex
modulations on to each trivial melody, not only in their own national manner,
but also in the way characteristic of their own exclusive circle and particular
musical school. Melody—every melody—is free, and may be understood of all
men; but as soon as it is bound up /169/ with a particular harmony, it ceases to
be accessible except to people trained to such harmony, and it becomes strange,
not only to common men of another nationality, but to all who do not belong
to the circle whose members have accustomed themselves to certain forms of
harmonisation. So that music, like poetry, travels in a vicious circle. Trivial and
exclusive melodies, in order to make them attractive, are laden with harmonic,
rhythmic, and orchestral complications, and thus become yet more exclusive,
and far from being universal are not even national, *i.e.* they are not comprehensible to the whole people but only to some people.

In music, besides marches and dances by various composers, which satisfy
the demands of universal art, one can indicate very few works of this class:
Bach's famous violin *aria*, Chopin's nocturne in E flat major, and perhaps a

dozen bits (not whole pieces, but parts) selected from the works of Haydn, Mozart, Schubert, Beethoven, and Chopin.[1]

Although in painting the same thing is repeated as in poetry and in music, — namely, that in order to make them more interesting, works weak in conception are surrounded by minutely studied accessories of time and place, which give them a temporary and local interest but make them /170/ less universal, — still, in painting, more than in the other spheres of art, may be found works satisfying the demands of universal Christian art; that is to say, there are more works expressing feelings in which all men may participate.

In the arts of painting and sculpture, all pictures and statues in so-called genre style, depictions of animals, landscapes and caricatures with subjects comprehensible to everyone, and also all kinds of ornaments, are universal in subject-matter. Such productions in painting and sculpture are very numerous (*e.g.* china dolls), but for the most part such objects (for instance, ornaments of all kinds) are either not considered to be art or are considered to be art of a low quality. In reality all such objects, if only they transmit a true feeling experienced by the artist and comprehensible to everyone (however insignificant it may seem to us to be) are works of real, good, Christian art.

I fear it will here be urged against me that having denied that the conception of beauty can supply a standard for works of art, I contradict myself by acknowledging ornaments to be works of good art. The reproach is unjust, for the subject-matter of all kinds of ornamentation consists not in the beauty, but in the feeling (of admiration of, and delight in, the combination of lines and colours) which the artist has experienced and with which he infects the spectator. Art remains what it was and what it must be: nothing but the infection by one man of another, or of others, with the feelings experienced by the infector. Among those feelings is the feeling of delight at what pleases the sight. Objects pleasing the sight may be such as please a small or a large number of people, or such as please all men. And ornaments for the most part are of the latter kind. A landscape representing a very unusual view, or a genre picture of a special subject, may not please everyone, but ornaments, from Yakutsk ornaments to /171/ Greek ones, are intelligible to everyone and evoke a similar feeling of admiration in all, and therefore this despised kind of art should, in Christian society, be esteemed far above exceptional, pretentious pictures and sculptures.

So that there are only two kinds of good Christian art: all the rest of art not comprised in these two divisions should be acknowledged to be bad art, deserving not to be encouraged but to be driven out, denied and despised, as being art not uniting but dividing people. Such, in literary art, are all novels and poems which transmit Church or patriotic feelings, and also exclusive feelings pertaining only to the class of the idle rich; such as aristocratic honour, satiety, spleen, pessimism, and refined and vicious feelings flowing from sex-love — quite incomprehensible to the great majority of mankind.

In painting we must similarly place in the class of bad art all the Church, patriotic, and exclusive pictures; all the pictures representing the amusements and allurements of a rich and idle life; all the so-called symbolic pictures, in

[1] While offering as examples of art those that seem to me the best, I attach no special importance to my selection; for, besides being insufficiently informed in all branches of art, I belong to the class of people whose taste has, by false training, been perverted. And therefore my old, inured habits may cause me to err, and I may mistake for absolute merit the impression a work produced on me in my youth. My only purpose in mentioning examples of works of this or that class is to make my meaning clearer, and to show how, with my present views, I understand excellence in art in relation to its subject-matter. I must, moreover, mention that I consign my own artistic productions to the category of bad art, excepting the story *God sees the Truth*, which seeks a place in the first class, and *The Prisoner of the Caucasus*, which belongs to the second. /170/

which the very meaning of the symbol is comprehensible only to the people of a certain circle; and, above all, pictures with voluptuous subjects—all that odious female nudity which fills all the exhibitions and galleries. And to this class belongs almost all the chamber and opera music of our times,—beginning especially from Beethoven (Schumann, Berlioz, Liszt, Wagner),—by its subject-matter devoted to the expression of feelings accessible only to people who have developed in themselves an unhealthy, nervous irritation evoked by this exclusive, artificial, and complex music.

"What! the *Ninth Symphony* not a good work of art!" I hear exclaimed by indignant voices.

And I reply: Most certainly it is not. All that I have written I have written with the sole purpose of finding a clear and reasonable criterion by which to judge the /172/ merits of works of art. And this criterion, coinciding with the indications of plain and sane sense, indubitably shows me that that symphony by Beethoven is not a good work of art. Of course, to people educated in the adoration of certain productions and of their authors, to people whose taste has been perverted just by being educated in such adoration, the acknowledgment that such a celebrated work is bad is amazing and strange. But how are we to escape the indications of reason and of common sense?

Beethoven's *Ninth Symphony* is considered a great work of art. To verify its claim to be such, I must first ask myself whether this work transmits the highest religious feeling? I reply in the negative, for music in itself cannot transmit those feelings; and therefore I ask myself next, Since this work does not belong to the highest kind of religious art, has it the other characteristic of the good art of our time,—the quality of uniting all men in one common feeling: does it rank as Christian universal art? And again I have no option but to reply in the negative; for not only do I not see how the feelings transmitted by this work could unite people not specially trained to submit themselves to its complex hypnotism, but I am unable to imagine to myself a crowd of normal people who could understand anything of this long, confused, and artificial production, except short snatches which are lost in a sea of what is incomprehensible. And therefore, whether I like it or not, I am compelled to conclude that this work belongs to the rank of bad art. It is curious to note in this connection, that attached to the end of this very symphony is a poem of Schiller's which (though somewhat obscurely) expresses this very thought, namely, that feeling (Schiller speaks only of the feeling of gladness) unites people and evokes love in them. But though this poem is sung at the end of the symphony, the music does not accord with the thought expressed in the verses; for the music is exclusive and does /173/ not unite all men, but unites only a few, dividing them off from the rest of mankind.

And, just in this same way, in all branches of art, many and many works considered great by the upper classes of our society will have to be judged. By this one sure criterion we shall have to judge the celebrated *Divine Comedy* and *Jerusalem Delivered,* and a great part of Shakespeare's and Goethe's works, and in painting every representation of miracles, including Raphael's "Transfiguration," etc.

Whatever the work may be and however it may have been extolled, we have first to ask whether this work is one of real art or a counterfeit. Having acknowledged, on the basis of the indication of its infectiousness even to a small class of people, that a certain production belongs to the realm of art, it is necessary, on the basis of the indication of its accessibility, to decide the next question, Does this work belong to the category of bad, exclusive art, opposed to religious perception, or to Christian art, uniting people? And having acknowledged an article to belong to real Christian art, we must then, according to whether it transmits the feelings flowing from love to God and man, or merely the simple feelings uniting all men, assign it a place in the ranks of religious art or in those of universal art.

Only on the basis of such verification shall we find it possible to select from the whole mass of what, in our society, claims to be art, those works which form real, important, necessary spiritual food, and to separate them from all the harmful and useless art, and from the counterfeits of art which surround us. Only on the basis of such verification shall we be able to rid ourselves of the pernicious results of harmful art, and to avail ourselves of that beneficent action which is the purpose of true and good art, and which is indispensable for the spiritual life of man and of humanity. /174/

✖ GOD SEES THE TRUTH, BUT WAITS

Leo Tolstoy

In the town of Vladímir lived a young merchant named Iván Dmítrich Aksënov. He had two shops and a house of his own.

Aksënov was a handsome, fair-haired, curly-headed fellow, full of fun and very fond of singing. When quite a young man he had been given to drink and was riotous when he had had too much; but after he married he gave up drinking except now and then.

One summer Aksënov was going to the Nízhny Fair, and as he bade good-bye to his family his wife said to him, 'Iván Dmítrich, do not start to-day; I have had a bad dream about you.'

Aksënov laughed, and said, 'You are afraid that when I get to the fair I shall go on the spree.'

His wife replied: 'I do not know what I am afraid of; all I know is that I had a bad dream. I dreamt you returned from the town, and when you took off your cap I saw that your hair was quite grey.'

Aksënov laughed. 'That's a lucky sign,' said he. 'See if I don't sell out all my goods and bring you some presents from the fair.'

So he said good-bye to his family and drove away.

When he had travelled half-way, he met a merchant whom he knew, and they put up at the same inn for the night. They had some tea together, and then went to bed in adjoining rooms.

It was not Aksënov's habit to sleep late, and, wishing to travel while it was still cool, he aroused his driver before dawn and told him to put in the horses. /1/

Then he made his way across to the landlord of the inn (who lived in a cottage at the back), paid his bill, and continued his journey.

When he had gone about twenty-five miles he stopped for the horses to be fed. Aksënov rested awhile in the passage of the inn, then he stepped out into the porch and, ordering a *samovár*[1] to be heated, got out his guitar and began to play.

Suddenly a *tróyka*[2] drove up with tinkling bells, and an official alighted, fol-

"God Sees the Truth, But Waits," *Twenty-Three Tales,* trans. Louise and Aylmer Maude (London: Oxford University Press, 1906), pp. 1–10.
[1] The *samovár* ('self-boiler') is an urn in which water can be heated and kept on the boil. /2/
[2] A three-horse conveyance. /2/

lowed by two soldiers. He came to Aksënov and began to question him, asking him who he was and whence he came. Aksënov answered him fully, and said, 'Won't you have some tea with me?' But the official went on cross-questioning him and asking him, 'Where did you spend last night? Were you alone, or with a fellow-merchant? Did you see the other merchant this morning? Why did you leave the inn before dawn?'

Aksënov wondered why he was asked all these questions, but he described all that had happened, and then added, 'Why do you cross-question me as if I were a thief or a robber? I am travelling on business of my own, and there is no need to question me.'

Then the official, calling the soldiers, said, 'I am the police-officer of this district, and I question you because the merchant with whom you spent last night has been found with his throat cut. We must search your things.'

They entered the house. The soldiers and the police-officer unstrapped Aksënov's luggage and searched it. Suddenly the officer drew a knife out of a bag, crying, 'Whose knife is this?' /2/

Aksënov looked, and seeing a blood-stained knife taken from his bag, he was frightened.

'How is it there is blood on this knife?'

Aksënov tried to answer, but could hardly utter a word, and only stammered: 'I – don't know – not mine.'

Then the police-officer said, 'This morning the merchant was found in bed with his throat cut. You are the only person who could have done it. The house was locked from inside, and no one else was there. Here is this blood-stained knife in your bag, and your face and manner betray you! Tell me how you killed him and how much money you stole?'

Aksënov swore he had not done it; that he had not seen the merchant after they had had tea together; that he had no money except eight thousand rúbles[1] of his own, and that the knife was not his. But his voice was broken, his face pale, and he trembled with fear as though he were guilty.

The police-officer ordered the soldiers to bind Aksënov and to put him in the cart. As they tied his feet together and flung him into the cart, Aksënov crossed himself and wept. His money and goods were taken from him, and he was sent to the nearest town and imprisoned there. Enquiries as to his character were made in Vladímir. The merchants and other inhabitants of that town said that in former days he used to drink and waste his time, but that he was a good man. Then the trial came on: he was charged with murdering a merchant /3/ from Ryazán and robbing him of twenty thousand rúbles.

His wife was in despair, and did not know what to believe. Her children were all quite small; one was a baby at the breast. Taking them all with her, she went to the town where her husband was in gaol. At first she was not allowed to see him; but, after much begging, she obtained permission from the officials and was taken to him. When she saw her husband in prison-dress and in chains, shut up with thieves and criminals, she fell down and did not come to her senses for a long time. Then she drew her children to her, and sat down near him. She told him of things at home, and asked about what had happened to him. He told her all, and she asked, 'What can we do now?'

'We must petition the Tsar not to let an innocent man perish.'

His wife told him that she had sent a petition to the Tsar, but that it had not been accepted.

[1] The value of the rúble has varied at different times from more than three shillings to less than two shillings. For purposes of ready calculation it may be taken as two shillings. In reading these stories to children, the word 'florin' can be substituted for 'rúble' if preferred. /3/

Aksënov did not reply, but only looked downcast.

Then his wife said, 'It was not for nothing I dreamt your hair had turned grey. You remember? You should not have started that day.' And passing her fingers through his hair she said: 'Ványa dearest, tell your wife the truth; was it not you who did it?'

'So you, too, suspect me!' said Aksënov, and, hiding his face in his hands, he began to weep. Then a soldier came to say that the wife and children must go away, and Aksënov said good-bye to his family for the last time.

When they were gone, Aksënov recalled what had been said, and when he remembered that his wife also had suspected him, he said to himself, 'It seems that only God can know the truth; it is /4/ to Him alone we must appeal and from Him alone expect mercy.'

And Aksënov wrote no more petitions, gave up all hope, and only prayed to God.

Aksënov was condemned to be flogged and sent to the mines. So he was flogged with a knout, and when the wounds caused by the knout were healed, he was driven to Siberia with other convicts.

For twenty-six years Aksënov lived as a convict in Siberia. His hair turned white as snow, and his beard grew long, thin, and grey. All his mirth went; he stooped; he walked slowly, spoke little, and never laughed, but he often prayed.

In prison Aksënov learnt to make boots, and earned a little money, with which he bought *The Lives of the Saints*. He read this book when it was light enough in the prison; and on Sundays in the prison-church he read the epistle and sang in the choir, for his voice was still good.

The prison authorities liked Aksënov for his meekness, and his fellow-prisoners respected him: they called him 'Grandfather,' and 'The Saint.' When they wanted to petition the prison authorities about anything, they always made Aksënov their spokesman, and when there were quarrels among the prisoners they came to him to put things right, and to judge the matter.

No news reached Aksënov from his home, and he did not even know if his wife and children were still alive.

One day a fresh gang of convicts came to the prison. In the evening the old prisoners collected round the new ones and asked them what towns or villages they came from, and what they were sentenced for. Among the rest Aksënov sat down near the new-comers, and listened with downcast air to what was said. /5/

One of the new convicts, a tall, strong man of sixty, with a closely-cropped grey beard, was telling the others what he had been arrested for.

'Well, friends,' he said, 'I only took a horse that was tied to a sledge, and I was arrested and accused of stealing. I said I had only taken it to get home quicker, and had then let it go; besides, the driver was a personal friend of mine. So I said, "It's all right." "No," said they, "you stole it." But how or where I stole it they could not say. I once really did something wrong, and ought by rights to have come here long ago, but that time I was not found out. Now I have been sent here for nothing at all . . . Eh, but it's lies I'm telling you; I've been to Siberia before, but I did not stay long.'

'Where are you from?' asked some one.

'From Vladímir. My family are of that town. My name is Makár, and they also call me Semënich.'

Aksënov raised his head and said: 'Tell me, Semënich, do you know anything of the merchants Aksënov, of Vladímir? Are they still alive?'

'Know them? Of course I do. The Aksënovs are rich, though their father is in Siberia: a sinner like ourselves, it seems! As for you, Gran'dad, how did you come here?'

Aksënov did not like to speak of his misfortune. He only sighed, and said, 'For my sins I have been in prison these twenty-six years.'

'What sins?' asked Makár Semënich.

But Aksënov only said, 'Well, well — I must have deserved it!' He would have said no more, but his companions told the new-comer how Aksënov came to be in Siberia: how some one had killed a merchant and had put a knife among Aksënov's things, and he had been unjustly condemned.

When Makár Semënich heard this he looked at Aksënov, slapped his own knee, and exclaimed, /6/ 'Well, this is wonderful! Really wonderful! But how old you've grown, Gran'dad!'

The others asked him why he was so surprised, and where he had seen Aksënov before; but Makár Semënich did not reply. He only said: 'It's wonderful that we should meet here, lads!'

These words make Aksënov wonder whether this man knew who had killed the merchant; so he said 'Perhaps, Semënich, you have heard of that affair, or maybe you've seen me before?'

'How could I help hearing? The world's full of rumours. But it's long ago, and I've forgotten what I heard.'

'Perhaps you heard who killed the merchant?' asked Aksënov.

Makár Semënich laughed, and replied, 'It must have been him in whose bag the knife was found! If some one else hid the knife there — "He's not a thief till he's caught," as the saying is. How could any one put a knife into your bag while it was under your head? It would surely have woke you up?'

When Aksënov heard these words he felt sure this was the man who had killed the merchant. He rose and went away. All that night Aksënov lay awake. He felt terribly unhappy, and all sorts of images rose in his mind. There was the image of his wife as she was when he parted from her to go to the fair. He saw her as if she were present; her face and her eyes rose before him, he heard her speak and laugh. Then he saw his children, quite little, as they were at that time: one with a little cloak on, another at his mother's breast. And then he remembered himself as he used to be — young and merry. He remembered how he sat playing the guitar in the porch of the inn where he was arrested, and how free from care he had been. He saw in his mind the place where he was flogged, the /7/ executioner, and the people standing around; the chains, the convicts, all the twenty-six years of his prison life, and his premature old age. The thought of it all made him so wretched that he was ready to kill himself.

'And it's all that villain's doing!' thought Aksënov. And his anger was so great against Makár Semënich that he longed for vengeance, even if he himself should perish for it. He kept saying prayers all night, but could get no peace. During the day he did not go near Makár Semënich, nor even look at him.

A fortnight passed in this way. Aksënov could not sleep at nights and was so miserable that he did not know what to do.

One night as he was walking about the prison he noticed some earth that came rolling out from under one of the shelves on which the prisoners slept. He stopped to see what it was. Suddenly Makár Semënich crept out from under the shelf, and looked up at Aksënov with frightened face. Aksënov tried to pass without looking at him, but Makár seized his hand and told him that he had dug a hole under the wall, getting rid of the earth by putting it into his high boots and emptying it out every day on the road when the prisoners were driven to their work.

'Just you keep quiet, old man, and you shall get out too. If you blab they'll flog the life out of me, but I will kill you first.'

Aksënov trembled with anger as he looked at his enemy. He drew his hand away, saying, 'I have no wish to escape, and you have no need to kill me; you killed me long ago! As to telling of you—I may do so or not, as God shall direct.'

Next day, when the convicts were led out to work, the convoy soldiers noticed that one or other of the /8/ prisoners emptied some earth out of his boots. The prison was searched and the tunnel found. The Governor came and questioned all the prisoners to find out who had dug the hole. They all denied any knowledge of it. Those who knew would not betray Makár Semënich, knowing he would be flogged almost to death. At last the Governor turned to Aksënov, whom he knew to be a just man, and said:

'You are a truthful old man; tell me, before God, who dug the hole?'

Makár Semënich stood as if he were quite unconcerned, looking at the Governor and not so much as glancing at Aksënov. Aksënov's lips and hands trembled, and for a long time he could not utter a word. He thought, 'Why should I screen him who ruined my life? Let him pay for what I have suffered. But if I tell, they will probably flog the life out of him, and maybe I suspect him wrongly. And, after all, what good would it be to me?'

'Well, old man,' repeated the Governor, 'tell us the truth: who has been digging under the wall?'

Aksënov glanced at Makár Semënich and said, 'I cannot say, your honour. It is not God's will that I should tell! Do what you like with me; I am in your hands.'

However much the Governor tried, Aksënov would say no more, and so the matter had to be left.

That night, when Aksënov was lying on his bed and just beginning to doze, some one came quietly and sat down on his bed. He peered through the darkness and recognized Makár.

'What more do you want of me?' asked Aksënov. 'Why have you come here?'

Makár Semënich was silent. So Aksënov sat up and said, 'What do you want? Go away or I will call the guard!' /9/

Makár Semënich bent close over Aksënov, and whispered, 'Iván Dmítrich, forgive me!'

'What for?' asked Aksënov.

'It was I who killed the merchant and hid the knife among your things. I meant to kill you too, but I heard a noise outside; so I hid the knife in your bag and escaped through the window.'

Aksënov was silent and did not know what to say. Makár Semënich slid off the bed-shelf and knelt upon the ground. 'Iván Dmítrich,' said he, 'forgive me! For the love of God, forgive me! I will confess that it was I who killed the merchant, and you will be released and can go to your home.'

'It is easy for you to talk,' said Aksënov, 'but I have suffered for you these twenty-six years. Where could I go to now? My wife is dead, and my children have forgotten me. I have nowhere to go. . . .'

Makár Semënich did not rise, but beat his head on the floor. 'Iván Dmítrich, forgive me!' he cried. 'When they flogged me with the knout it was not so hard to bear as it is to see you now . . . yet you had pity on me and did not tell. For Christ's sake forgive me, wretch that I am!' And he began to sob.

When Aksënov heard him sobbing he, too, began to weep.

'God will forgive you!' said he. 'Maybe I am a hundred times worse than you.' And at these words his heart grew light and the longing for home left him. He no longer had any desire to leave the prison, but only hoped for his last hour to come.

In spite of what Aksënov had said, Makár Semënich confessed his guilt. But when the order for his release came, Aksënov was already dead.

(*Written in* 1872.) /10/

🎗 A PRISONER IN THE CAUCASUS

Leo Tolstoy

I

An officer named Zhílin was serving in the army in the Caucasus.

One day he received a letter from home. It was from his mother, who wrote: 'I am getting old, and should like to see my dear son once more before I die. Come and say good-bye to me and bury me, and then, if God pleases, return to service again with my blessing. But I have found a girl for you, who is sensible and good and has some property. If you can love her, you might marry her and remain at home.'

Zhílin thought it over, It was quite true, the old lady was failing fast and he might not have another chance to see her alive. He had better go, and, if the girl was nice, why not marry her?

So he went to his Colonel, obtained leave of absence, said good-bye to his comrades, stood the soldiers four pailfuls of vódka[1] as a farewell treat, and got ready to go.

It was a time of war in the Caucasus. The roads were not safe by night or day. If ever a Russian ventured to ride or walk any distance away from his fort, the Tartars killed him or carried him off to the hills. So it had been arranged that twice every week a body of soldiers should march from one fortress to the next to convoy travellers from point to point.

It was summer. At daybreak the baggage-train got ready under shelter of the fortress; the soldiers /11/ marched out; and all started along the road. Zhílin was on horseback, and a cart with his things went with the baggage-train. They had sixteen miles to go. The baggage train moved slowly; sometimes the soldiers stopped, or perhaps a wheel would come off one of the carts, or a horse refuse to go on, and then everybody had to wait.

When by the sun it was already past noon, they had not gone half the way. It was dusty and hot, the sun was scorching, and there was no shelter anywhere: a bare plain all round — not a tree, not a bush, by the road.

Zhílin rode on in front, and stopped, waiting for the baggage to overtake him. Then he heard the signal-horn sounded behind him: the company had again stopped. So he began to think: 'Hadn't I better ride on by myself? My horse is a good one: if the Tartars do attack me, I can gallop away. Perhaps, however, it would be wiser to wait.'

As he sat considering, Kostílin, an officer carrying a gun, rode up to him and said:

'Come along, Zhílin, let's go on by ourselves. It's dreadful; I am famished and the heat is terrible. My shirt is wringing wet.'

Kostílin was a stout, heavy man, and the perspiration was running down his red face. Zhílin thought awhile, and then asked: 'Is your gun loaded?'

'Yes, it is.'

'Well, then, let's go, but on condition that we keep together.'

So they rode forward along the road across the plain, talking, but keeping a look-out on both sides. They could see afar all round. But after crossing the plain the road ran through a valley between two hills, and Zhílin said: 'We had better climb that hill and have a look round, or the Tartars may be on us before we know it.' /12/

"A Prisoner in the Caucasus," *Twenty-Three Tales*, trans. Louise and Aylmer Maude (London: Oxford University Press, 1906), pp. 11–43.

[1] *Vódka* is a spirit distilled from rye. It is the commonest form of strong drink in Russia. /11/

But Kostílin answered: 'What's the use? Let us go on.'

Zhílin, however, would not agree.

'No,' he said; 'you can wait here if you like, but I'll go and look round.' And he turned his horse to the left, up the hill. Zhílin's horse was a hunter, and carried him up the hill-side as if it had wings. (He had bought it for a hundred rúbles as a colt out of a herd, and had broken it in himself.) Hardly had he reached the top of the hill, than he saw some thirty Tartars not much more than a hundred yards ahead of him. As soon as he caught sight of them he turned round, but the Tartars had also seen him, and rushed after him at full gallop, getting their guns out as they went. Down galloped Zhílin as fast as the horse's legs could go, shouting to Kostílin: 'Get your gun ready!'

And in thought he said to his horse: 'Get me well out of this, my pet; don't stumble, for if you do it's all up. Once I reach the gun, they shan't take me prisoner.'

But instead of waiting, Kostílin, as soon as he caught sight of the Tartars, turned back towards the fortress at full speed, whipping his horse now on one side now on the other, and its switching tail was all that could be seen of him in the dust.

Zhílin saw it was a bad look-out; the gun was gone, and what could he do with nothing but his sword? He turned his horse towards the escort, thinking to escape, but there were six Tartars rushing to cut him off. His horse was a good one, but theirs were still better; and besides, they were across his path. He tried to rein in his horse and to turn another way, but it was going so fast that it could not stop, and dashed on straight towards the Tartars. He saw a red-bearded Tartar on a grey horse, with his gun raised, come at him, yelling and showing his teeth. /13/

'Ah,' thought Zhílin, 'I know you, devils that you are. If you take me alive you'll put me in a pit and flog me. I will not be taken alive!'

Zhílin, though not a big fellow, was brave. He drew his sword and dashed at the red-bearded Tartar, thinking: 'Either I'll ride him down or disable him with my sword.'

He was still a horse's length away from him, when he was fired at from behind and his horse was hit. It fell to the ground with all its weight, pinning Zhílin to the earth.

He tried to rise, but two ill-savoured Tartars were already sitting on him and binding his hands behind his back. He made an effort and flung them off, but three others jumped from their horses and began beating his head with the butts of their guns. His eyes grew dim, and he fell back. The Tartars seized him, and, taking spare girths from their saddles, twisted his hands behind him and tied them with a Tartar knot. They knocked his cap off, pulled off his boots, searched him all over, tore his clothes, and took his money and his watch.

Zhílin looked round at his horse. There it lay on its side, poor thing, just as it had fallen; struggling, its legs in the air, unable to touch the ground. There was a hole in its head, and black blood was pouring out, turning the dust to mud for a couple of feet around.

One of the Tartars went up to the horse and began taking the saddle off; it still kicked, so he drew a dagger and cut its windpipe. A whistling sound came from its throat, the horse gave one plunge, and all was over.

The Tartars took the saddle and trappings. The red-bearded Tartar mounted his horse, and the others lifted Zhílin into the saddle behind him. To prevent his falling off they strapped him to the /14/ Tartar's girdle; and then they all rode away to the hills.

So there sat Zhílin, swaying from side to side, his head striking against the

Tartar's stinking back. He could see nothing but that muscular back and sinewy neck, with its closely shaven, bluish nape. Zhílin's head was wounded: the blood had dried over his eyes, and he could neither shift his position on the saddle nor wipe the blood off. His arms were bound so tightly that his collar-bones ached.

They rode up and down hills for a long way. Then they reached a river which they forded, and came to a hard road leading across a valley.

Zhílin tried to see where they were going, but his eyelids were stuck together with blood, and he could not turn.

Twilight began to fall; they crossed another river, and rode up a stony hillside. There was a smell of smoke here, and dogs were barking. They had reached an Aoul (a Tartar village). The Tartars got off their horses; Tartar children came and stood round Zhílin, shrieking with pleasure and throwing stones at him.

The Tartar drove the children away, took Zhílin off the horse, and called his man. A Nogáy[1] with high cheek-bones, and nothing on but a shirt (and that so torn that his breast was all bare), answered the call. The Tartar gave him an order. He went and fetched shackles: two blocks of oak with iron rings attached, and a clasp and lock fixed to one of the rings.

They untied Zhílin's arms, fastened the shackles on his leg, and dragged him to a barn, where they pushed him in and locked the door.

Zhílin fell on a heap of manure. He lay still awhile, then groped about to find a soft place, and settled down. /15/

II

That night Zhílin hardly slept at all. It was the time of the year when the nights are short, and daylight soon showed itself through a chink in the wall. He rose, scratched to make the chink bigger, and peeped out.

Through the hole he saw a road leading downhill; to the right was a Tartar hut with two trees near it, a black dog lay on the threshold, and a goat and kids were moving about wagging their tails. Then he saw a young Tartar woman in a long, loose, bright-coloured gown, with trousers and high boots showing from under it. She had a coat thrown over her head, on which she carried a large metal jug filled with water. She was leading by the hand a small, closely-shaven Tartar boy, who wore nothing but a shirt; and as she went along balancing herself, the muscles of her back quivered. This woman carried the water into the hut, and soon after the red-bearded Tartar of yesterday came out dressed in a silk tunic, with a silver-hilted dagger hanging by his side, shoes on his bare feet, and a tall black sheepskin cap set far back on his head. He came out, stretched himself, and stroked his red beard. He stood awhile, gave an order to his servant, and went away.

Then two lads rode past from watering their horses. The horses' noses were wet. Some other closely-shaven boys ran out, without any trousers, and wearing nothing but their shirts. They crowded together, came to the barn, picked up a twig, and began pushing it in at the chink. Zhílin gave a shout, and the boys shrieked and scampered off, their little bare knees gleaming as they ran.

Zhílin was very thirsty: his throat was parched, /16/ and he thought: 'If only they would come and so much as look at me!"

Then he heard some one unlocking the barn. The red-bearded Tartar entered, and with him was another, a smaller man, dark, with bright black eyes, red cheeks, and a short beard. He had a merry face and was always laughing. This man was even more richly dressed than the other. He wore a blue silk

---

[1] One of a certain Tartar tribe. /15/

tunic trimmed with gold, a large silver dagger in his belt, red morocco slippers worked with silver, and over these a pair of thick shoes, and he had a white sheepskin cap on his head.

The red-bearded Tartar entered, muttered something as if he were annoyed, and stood leaning against the doorpost, playing with his dagger, and glaring askance at Zhílin, like a wolf. The dark one, quick and lively, and moving as if on springs, came straight up to Zhílin, squatted down in front of him, slapped him on the shoulder, and began to talk very fast in his own language. His teeth showed, and he kept winking, clicking his tongue, and repeating, 'Good Russ, good Russ.'

Zhílin could not understand a word, but said, 'Drink! give me water to drink!'

The dark man only laughed. 'Good Russ,' he said, and went on talking in his own tongue.

Zhílin made signs with lips and hands that he wanted something to drink.

The dark man understood and laughed. Then he looked out of the door, and called to some one: 'Dína!'

A little girl came running in: she was about thirteen, slight, thin, and like the dark Tartar in face. Evidently she was his daughter. She, too, had clear black eyes, and her face was good-looking. She had on a long blue gown with wide sleeves, and no girdle. The hem of her gown, the front, and the /17/ sleeves, were trimmed with red. She wore trousers and slippers, and over the slippers stouter shoes with high heels. Round her neck she had a necklace made of Russian silver coins. She was bareheaded, and her black hair was plaited with a ribbon and ornamented with gilt braid and silver coins.

Her father gave an order, and she ran away and returned with a metal jug. She handed the water to Zhílin and sat down, crouching so that her knees were as high as her head; and there she sat with wide open eyes watching Zhílin drink, as though he were a wild animal.

When Zhílin handed the empty jug back to her, she gave such a sudden jump back, like a wild goat, that it made her father laugh. He sent her away for something else. She took the jug, ran out, and brought back some unleavened bread on a round board, and once more sat down, crouching, and looking on with staring eyes.

Then the Tartars went away and again locked the door.

After a while the Nógay came and said: '*Ayda*, the master, *Ayda!*'

He, too, knew no Russian. All Zhílin could make out was that he was told to go somewhere.

Zhílin followed the Nógay, but limped, for the shackles dragged his feet so that he could hardly step at all. On getting out of the barn he saw a Tartar village of about ten houses, and a Tartar mosque with a small tower. Three horses stood saddled before one of the houses; little boys were holding them by the reins. The dark Tartar came out of this house, beckoning with his hand for Zhílin to follow him. Then he laughed, said something in his own language, and returned into the house.

Zhílin entered. The room was a good one: the walls smoothly plastered with clay. Near the front /18/ wall lay a pile of bright-coloured feather beds; the side walls were covered with rich carpets used as hangings, and on these were fastened guns, pistols, and swords, all inlaid with silver. Close to one of the walls was a small stove on a level with the earthen floor. The floor itself was as clean as a thrashing-ground. A large space in one corner was spread over with felt, on which were rugs, and on these rugs were cushions stuffed with down. And on these five cushions sat five Tartars, the dark one, the red-haired one, and three guests. They were wearing their indoor slippers, and each had a cushion behind his back. Before them were standing millet cakes on a round board, melted butter in a bowl, and a jug of *buza*, or Tartar beer. They ate both cakes and butter with their hands.

The dark man jumped up and ordered Zhílin to be placed on one side, not on the carpet but on the bare ground, then he sat down on the carpet again, and offered millet cakes and *buza* to his guests. The servant made Zhílin sit down, after which he took off his own overshoes, put them by the door where the other shoes were standing, and sat down nearer to his masters on the felt, watching them as they ate, and licking his lips.

The Tartars ate as much as they wanted, and a woman dressed in the same way as the girl—in a long gown and trousers, with a kerchief on her head—came and took away what was left, and brought a handsome basin, and a ewer with a narrow spout. The Tartars washed their hands, folded them, went down on their knees, blew to the four quarters, and said their prayers. After they had talked for a while, one of the guests turned to Zhílin and began to speak in Russian.

'You were captured by Kazi-Mohammed,' he said, and pointed at the red-bearded Tartar. 'And /19/ Kazi-Mohammed has given you to Abdul Murad,' pointing at the dark one. 'Abdul Murad is now your master.'

Zhílin was silent. Then Abdul Murad began to talk, laughing, pointing to Zhílin, and repeating, 'Soldier Russ, good Russ.'

The interpreter said, 'He orders you to write home and tell them to send a ransom, and as soon as the money comes he will set you free.'

Zhílin thought for a moment, and said, 'How much ransom does he want?'

The Tartars talked awhile, and then the interpreter said, 'Three thousand rúbles.'

'No,' said Zhílin, 'I can't pay so much.'

Abdul jumped up and, waving his arms, talked to Zhílin, thinking, as before, that he would understand. The interpreter translated: 'How much will you give?'

Zhílin considered, and said, 'Five hundred rúbles.' At this the Tartars began speaking very quickly, all together. Abdul began to shout at the red-bearded one, and jabbered so fast that the spittle spurted out of his mouth. The red-bearded one only screwed up his eyes and clicked his tongue.

They quietened down after a while, and the interpreter said, 'Five hundred rúbles is not enough for the master. He paid two hundred for you himself. Kazi-Mohammed was in debt to him, and he took you in payment. Three thousand rúbles! Less than that won't do. If you refuse to write, you will be put into a pit and flogged with a whip!'

'Eh!' thought Zhílin, 'the more one fears them the worse it will be.'

So he sprang to his feet, and said, 'You tell that dog that if he tries to frighten me I will not write at all, and he will get nothing. I never was afraid of you dogs, and never will be!' /20/

The interpreter translated, and again they all began to talk at once.

They jabbered for a long time, and then the dark man jumped up, came to Zhílin, and said: '*Dzhigit Russ, dzhigit Russ!*' (*Dzhigit* in their language means 'brave.') And he laughed, and said something to the interpreter, who translated: 'One thousand rúbles will satisfy him.'

Zhílin stuck to it: 'I will not give more than five hundred. And if you kill me you'll get nothing at all.'

The Tartars talked awhile, then sent the servant out to fetch something, and kept looking now at Zhílin now at the door. The servant returned followed by a stout, bare-footed, tattered man, who also had his leg shackled.

Zhílin gasped with surprise: it was Kostílin. He, too, had been taken. They were put side by side, and began to tell each other what had occurred. While they talked the Tartars looked on in silence. Zhílin related what had happened to him; and Kostílin told how his horse had stopped, his gun missed fire, and this same Abdul had overtaken and captured him.

Abdul jumped up, pointed to Kostílin, and said something. The interpreter translated that they both now belonged to one master, and the one who first paid the ransom would be set free first.

'There now,' he said to Zhílin, 'you get angry, but your comrade here is gentle; he has written home, and they will send five thousand rúbles. So he will be well fed and well treated.'

Zhílin replied: 'My comrade can do as he likes; maybe he is rich, I am not. It must be as I said, Kill me, if you like — you will gain nothing by it; but I will not write for more than five hundred rúbles.'

They were silent. Suddenly up sprang Abdul, /21/ brought a little box, took out a pen, ink, and a bit of paper, gave them to Zhílin, slapped him on the shoulder, and made a sign that he should write. He had agreed to take five hundred rúbles.

'Wait a bit!' said Zhílin to the interpreter; 'tell him that he must feed us properly, give us proper clothes and boots, and let us be together. It will be more cheerful for us. And he must have these shackles taken off our feet,' and Zhílin looked at his master and laughed.

The master also laughed, heard the interpreter, and said: 'I will give them the best of clothes: a cloak and boots fit to be married in. I will feed them like princes, and if they like they can live together in the barn. But I can't take off the shackles or they will run away. They shall be taken off, however, at night.' And he jumped up and slapped Zhílin on the shoulder, exclaiming: 'You good, I good!'

Zhílin wrote the letter, but addressed it wrongly so that it should not reach its destination, thinking to himself: 'I'll run away!'

Zhílin and Kostílin were taken back to the barn and given some maize straw, a jug of water, some bread, two old cloaks, and some worn-out military boots — evidently taken from the corpses of Russian soldiers. At night their shackles were taken off their feet and they were locked up in the barn.

III

Zhílin and his friend lived in this way for a whole month. The master always laughed and said: 'You, Iván, good! I, Abdul, good!' But he fed them badly, giving them nothing but unleavened bread of millet-flour baked into flat cakes, or sometimes only unbaked dough.

Kostílin wrote home a second time and did /22/ nothing but mope and wait for the money to arrive. He would sit for days together in the barn sleeping, or counting the days till a letter could come.

Zhílin knew his letter would reach no one, and he did not write another. He thought: 'Where could my mother get enough money to ransom me? As it is she lived chiefly on what I sent her. If she had to raise five hundred rúbles, she would be quite ruined. With God's help I'll manage to escape!'

So he kept on the look-out, planning how to run away.

He would walk about the Aoul whistling; or would sit working, modelling dolls of clay, or weaving baskets out of twigs, for Zhílin was clever with his hands.

Once he modelled a doll with a nose and hands and feet and with a Tartar gown on, and put it up on the roof. When the Tartar women came out to fetch water, the master's daughter, Dína, saw the doll and called the women, who put down their jugs and stood looking and laughing. Zhílin took down the doll and held it out to them. They laughed, but dared not take it. He put down the doll and went into the barn, waiting to see what would happen.

Dína ran up to the doll, looked round, seized it, and ran away.

In the morning, at daybreak, he looked out. Dína came out of the house and sat down on the threshold with the doll, which she had dressed up in bits of red stuff, and she rocked it like a baby, singing a Tartar lullaby. An old woman came out and scolded her, and snatching the doll away broke it to bits, and sent Dína about her business.

But Zhílin made another doll, better than the first, and gave it to Dína. Once Dína brought a little jug, put it on the ground, sat down gazing at him, and laughed, pointing to the jug. /23/

'What pleases her so?' wondered Zhílin. He took the jug thinking it was water, but it turned out to be milk. He drank the milk and said: 'That's good!'

How pleased Dína was! 'Good, Iván, good!' said she, and she jumped up and clapped her hands. Then, seizing the jug, she ran away. After that, she stealthily brought him some milk every day.

The Tartars make a kind of cheese out of goat's milk which they dry on the roofs of their houses; and sometimes, on the sly, she brought him some of this cheese. And once, when Abdul had killed a sheep, she brought Zhílin a bit of mutton in her sleeve. She would just throw the things down and run away.

One day there was a heavy storm and the rain fell in torrents for a whole hour. All the streams became turbid. At the ford the water rose till it was seven feet high, and the current was so strong that it rolled the stones about. Rivulets flowed everywhere, and the rumbling in the hills never ceased. When the storm was over, the water ran in streams down the village street. Zhílin got his master to lend him a knife, and with it he shaped a small cylinder, and cutting some little boards, he made a wheel to which he fixed two dolls, one on each side. The little girls brought him some bits of stuff and he dressed the dolls, one as a peasant, the other as a peasant woman. Then he fastened them in their places and set the wheel so that the stream should work it. The wheel began to turn and the dolls danced.

The whole village collected around. Little boys and girls, Tartar men and women, all came and clicked their tongues.

'Ah, Russ! Ah, Iván!'

Abdul had a Russian clock which was broken. /24/ He called Zhílin and showed it to him, clicking his tongue.

'Give it me; I'll mend it for you,' said Zhílin.

He took it to pieces with the knife, sorted the pieces, and put them together again so that the clock went all right.

The master was delighted and made him a present of one of his old tunics which was all in holes. Zhílin had to accept it. He could at any rate use it as a coverlet at night.

After that Zhílin's fame spread; and Tartars came from distant villages, bringing him now the lock of a gun or of a pistol, now a watch, to mend. His master gave him some tools—pincers, gimlets, and a file.

One day a Tartar fell ill and they came to Zhílin, saying, 'Come and heal him!' Zhílin knew nothing about doctoring, but he went to look, and thought to himself, 'Perhaps he will get well anyway.'

He returned to the barn, mixed some water with sand, and then in the presence of the Tartars whispered some words over it and gave it to the sick man to drink. Luckily for him, the Tartar recovered.

Zhílin began to pick up their language a little, and some of the Tartars grew familiar with him. When they wanted him, they would call: 'Iván! Iván!' Others, however, still looked at him askance, as at a wild beast.

The red-bearded Tartar disliked Zhílin. Whenever he saw him he frowned and turned away or swore at him. There was also an old man there who did not live in the Aoul but used to come up from the foot of the hill. Zhílin only saw him when he passed on his way to the Mosque. He was short, and had a white cloth wound round his cap. His beard and moustaches were clipped, and white as /25/ snow, and his face was wrinkled and brick-red. His nose was hooked like a hawk's, his grey eyes looked cruel, and he had no teeth except two tusks. He would pass, with his turban on his head, leaning on his staff, and glaring round him like a wolf. If he saw Zhílin he would snort with anger and turn away.

Once Zhílin descended the hill to see where the old man lived. He went down along the pathway and came to a little garden surrounded by a stone wall, and behind the wall he saw cherry and apricot trees, and a hut with a flat roof. He came closer, and saw hives made of plaited straw, and bees flying about and humming. The old man was kneeling, busy doing something with a hive. Zhílin stretched to look and his shackles rattled. The old man turned round and, giving a yell, snatched a pistol from his belt and shot at Zhílin, who just managed to shelter himself behind the stone wall.

The old man went to Zhílin's master to complain. The master called Zhílin and said with a laugh, 'Why did you go to the old man's house?'

'I did him no harm,' replied Zhílin. 'I only wanted to see how he lived.'

The master repeated what Zhílin said.

But the old man was in a rage; he hissed and jabbered, showing his tusks and shaking his fists at Zhílin.

Zhílin could not understand all, but he gathered that the old man was telling Abdul he ought not to keep Russians in the Aoul, but ought to kill them. At last the old man went away.

Zhílin asked the master who the old man was.

'He is a great man!' said the master. 'He was the bravest of our fellows; he killed many Russians, and was at one time very rich. He had three wives and eight sons, and they all lived in one village. Then the Russians came and destroyed the village, /26/ and killed seven of his sons. Only one son was left, and he gave himself up to the Russians. The old man also went and gave himself up, and lived among the Russians for three months. At the end of that time he found his son, killed him with his own hands, and then escaped. After that he left off fighting and went to Mecca to pray to God; that is why he wears a turban. One who has been to Mecca is called "Hadji," and wears a turban. He does not like you fellows. He tells me to kill you. But I can't kill you. I have paid money for you and, besides, I have grown fond of you, Iván. Far from killing you, I would not even let you go if I had not promised.' And he laughed, saying in Russian, 'You, Iván, good; I, Abdul, good!'

IV

Zhílin lived in this way for a month. During the day he sauntered about the Aoul or busied himself with some handicraft, but at night, when all was silent in the Aoul, he dug at the floor of the barn. It was no easy task digging, because of the stones; but he worked away at them with his file, and at last had made a hole under the wall large enough to get through.

'If only I could get to know the lay of the land,' thought he, 'and which way to go! But none of the Tartars will tell me.'

So he chose a day when the master was away from home, and set off after dinner to climb the hill beyond the village and look round. But before leaving home the master always gave orders to his son to watch Zhílin and not to lose sight of him. So the lad ran after Zhílin, shouting: 'Don't go! Father does not allow it. I'll call the neighbours if you won't come back.'

Zhílin tried to persuade him, and said: 'I'm not /27/ going far;—I only wanted to climb that hill. I want to find a herb—to cure sick people with. You come with me if you like. How can I run away with these shackles on? To-morrow I'll make a bow and arrows for you.'

So he persuaded the lad and they went. To look at the hill, it did not seem far to the top, but it was hard walking with shackles on his leg. Zhílin went on and on, but it was all he could do to reach the top. There he sat down and noted how the land lay. To the south, beyond the barn, was a valley in which a herd of horses was pasturing and at the bottom of the valley one could see another Aoul. Beyond that was a steeper hill and another hill beyond that. Between the hills, in the blue distance, were forests, and still farther off were mountains, rising higher and higher. The highest of them were covered with snow, white as sugar; and one snowy peak towered above all the rest. To the east and to the west were other such hills, and here and there smoke rose from Aouls in the ravines. 'Ah,' thought he, 'all that is Tartar country.' And he turned towards the Russian side. At his feet he saw a river, and the Aoul he lived in, surrounded by little gardens. He could see women, like tiny dolls, sitting by the river rinsing clothes. Beyond the Aoul was a hill, lower than the one to the south, and beyond it two other hills well wooded; and between these, a smooth bluish plain, and far, far across the plain something that looked like a cloud of smoke. Zhílin tried to remember where the sun used to rise and set when he was living in the fort, and he saw that there was no mistake: the Russian fort must be in that plain. Between those two hills he would have to make his way when he escaped.

The sun was beginning to set. The white, snowy mountains turned red, and the dark hills turned /28/ darker; mists rose from the ravine, and the valley, where he supposed the Russian fort to be, seemed on fire with the sunset glow. Zhílin looked carefully. Something seemed to be quivering in the valley like smoke from a chimney, and he felt sure the Russian fortress was there.

It had grown late. The Mullah's cry was heard. The herds were being driven home, the cows were lowing, and the lad kept saying, 'Come home!' But Zhílin did not feel inclined to go away.

At last, however, they went back. 'Well,' thought Zhílin, 'now that I know the way, it is time to escape.' He thought of running away that night. The nights were dark—the moon had waned. But as ill-luck would have it, the Tartars returned home that evening. They generally came back driving cattle before them and in good spirits. But this time they had no cattle. All they brought home was the dead body of a Tartar—the red one's brother—who had been killed. They came back looking sullen, and they all gathered together for the burial. Zhílin also came out to see it.

They wrapped the body in a piece of linen without any coffin, and carried it out of the village, and laid it on the grass under some plane-trees. The Mullah and the old men came. They wound cloths around their caps, took off their shoes, and squatted on their heels, side by side, near the corpse.

The Mullah was in front: behind him in a row were three old men in turbans, and behind them again the other Tartars. All cast down their eyes and sat in silence. This continued a long time, until the Mullah raised his head and said: 'Allah!' (which means God). He said that one word, and they all cast down their eyes again and were again silent for a long time. They sat quite still, not moving or making any sound. /29/

Again the Mullah lifted his head and said, 'Allah!' and they all repeated: 'Allah! Allah!' and were again silent.

The dead body lay immovable on the grass and they sat as still as if they too were dead. Not one of them moved. There was no sound but that of the leaves of the plane-trees stirring in the breeze. Then the Mullah repeated a prayer, and they all rose. They lifted the body and carried it in their arms to a hole in the ground. It was not an ordinary hole, but was hollowed out under the ground like a vault. They took the body under the arms and by the legs, bent it, and let it gently down, pushing it under the earth in a sitting posture, with the hands folded in front.

The Nogáy brought some green rushes, which they stuffed into the hole, and, quickly covering it with earth, they smoothed the ground, and set an upright stone at the head of the grave. Then they trod the earth down and again sat in a row before the grave, keeping silence for a long time.

At last they rose, said 'Allah! Allah! Allah!' and sighed.

The red-bearded Tartar gave money to the old men; then he too rose, took a whip, struck himself with it three times on the forehead, and went home.

The next morning Zhílin saw the red Tartar, followed by three others, leading a mare out of the village. When they were beyond the village the red-bearded Tartar took off his tunic and turned up his sleeves, showing his stout arms. Then he drew a dagger and sharpened it on a whetstone. The other Tartars raised the mare's head and he cut her throat, threw her down, and began skinning her, loosening the hide with his big hands. Women and girls came and began to wash the entrails and the inwards. The mare was cut up, the pieces taken /30/ into the hut, and the whole village collected at the red Tartar's hut for a funeral feast.

For three days they went on eating the flesh of the mare, drinking *buza,* and praying for the dead man. All the Tartars were at home. On the fourth day at dinner-time Zhílin saw them preparing to go away. Horses were brought out, they got ready, and some ten of them (the red one among them) rode away; but Abdul stayed at home. It was new moon, and the nights were still dark.

'Ah!' thought Zhílin, 'to-night is the time to escape.' And he told Kostílin; but Kostílin's heart failed him.

'How can we escape?' he said. 'We don't even know the way.'

'I know the way,' said Zhílin.

'Even if you do,' said Kostílin, 'we can't reach the fort in one night.'

'If we can't,' said Zhílin, 'we'll sleep in the forest. See here, I have saved some cheeses. What's the good of sitting and moping here? If they send your ransom — well and good, but suppose they don't manage to collect it? The Tartars are angry now, because the Russians have killed one of their men. They are talking of killing us.'

Kostílin thought it over.

'Well, let's go,' said he.

V

Zhílin crept into the hole, widened it so that Kostílin might also get through, and then they both sat waiting till all should be quiet in the Aoul.

As soon as all was quiet, Zhílin crept under the wall, got out, and whispered to Kostílin, 'Come!' Kostílin crept out, but in so doing he caught a stone with his foot and made a noise. The master had a very vicious watch-dog, a spotted one called /31/ Ulyáshin. Zhílin had been careful to feed him for some time before. Ulyáshin heard the noise and began to bark and jump, and the other dogs did the same. Zhílin gave a slight whistle, and threw him a bit of cheese. Ulyáshin knew Zhílin, wagged his tail, and stopped barking.

But the master had heard the dog and shouted to him from his hut, 'Hayt, hayt, Ulyáshin!'

Zhílin, however, scratched Ulyáshin behind the ears, and the dog was quiet and rubbed against his legs, wagging his tail.

They sat hidden behind a corner for a while. All became silent again, only a sheep coughed inside a shed, and the water rippled over the stones in the hollow. It was dark, the stars were high overhead, and the new moon showed red as it set, horns upward, behind the hill. In the valleys the fog was white as milk.

Zhílin rose and said to his companion, 'Well, friend, come along!'

They started; but they had only gone a few steps when they heard the Mullah crying from the roof, 'Allah, Bismillah! Ilrahman!' That meant that the people would be going to the Mosque. So they sat down again, hiding behind a wall, and waited a long time till the people had passed. At last all was quiet again.

'Now then! May God be with us!' They crossed themselves and started once more. They passed through a yard and went down the hill-side to the river, crossed the river, and went along the valley.

The mist was thick but only near the ground, overhead the stars shone quite brightly. Zhílin directed their course by the stars. It was cool in the mist, and easy walking; only their boots were uncomfortable, being worn out and trodden down. Zhílin took his off, threw them away, and went /32/ barefoot, jumping from stone to stone and guiding his course by the stars. Kostílin began to lag behind.

'Walk slower,' he said, 'these confounded boots have quite blistered my feet.'

'Take them off!' said Zhílin. 'It will be easier walking without them.'

Kostílin went barefoot, but got on still worse. The stones cut his feet and he kept lagging behind. Zhílin said: 'If your feet get cut they'll heal again, but if the Tartars catch us and kill us, it will be worse!'

Kostílin did not reply, but went on, groaning all the time.

Their way lay through the valley for a long time. Then to the right they heard dogs barking. Zhílin stopped, looked about, and began climbing the hill, feeling with his hands.

'Ah!' said he, 'we have gone wrong and have come too far to the right. Here is another Aoul, one I saw from the hill. We must turn back and go up that hill to the left. There must be a wood there.'

But Kostílin said: 'Wait a minute! Let me get breath. My feet are all cut and bleeding.'

'Never mind, friend! They'll heal again. You should spring more lightly. Like this!'

And Zhílin ran back and turned to the left up the hill towards the wood.

Kostílin still lagged behind and groaned. Zhílin only said 'Hush!' and went on and on.

They went up the hill and found a wood, as Zhílin had said. They entered the wood and forced their way through the brambles, which tore their clothes. At last they came to a path and followed it.

'Stop!' They heard the tramp of hoofs on the path, and waited, listening. It sounded like the tramping of a horse's feet, but then ceased. They moved on, and again they heard the tramping. /33/ When they paused, it also stopped. Zhílin crept nearer to it and saw something standing on the path where it was not quite so dark. It looked like a horse, and yet not quite like one, and on it was something queer, not like a man. He heard it snorting. 'What can it be?' Zhílin gave a low whistle, and off it dashed from the path into the thicket, and the woods were filled with the noise of crackling, as if a hurricane were sweeping through breaking the branches.

Kostílin was so frightened that he sank to the ground. But Zhílin laughed and said: 'It's a stag. Don't you hear him breaking the branches with his antlers? We were afraid of him, and he is afraid of us.'

They went on. The Great Bear was already setting. It was near morning, and they did not know whether they were going the right way or not. Zhílin thought it was the way he had been brought by the Tartars, and that they were still some seven miles from the Russian fort; but he had nothing certain to go by, and at night one easily mistakes the way. After a time they came to a clearing. Kostílin sat down and said: 'Do as you like, I can go no farther! My feet won't carry me.'

Zhílin tried to persuade him.

'No, I shall never get there; I can't!'

Zhílin grew angry, and spoke roughly to him.

'Well, then, I shall go on alone. Good-bye!'

Kostílin jumped up and followed. They went another three miles. The mist in the wood had settled down still more densely; they could not see a yard before them and the stars had grown dim.

Suddenly they heard the sound of a horse's hoofs in front of them. They heard its shoes strike the stones. Zhílin lay down flat and listened with his ear to the ground.

'Yes, so it is! A horseman is coming towards us.' /34/

They ran off the path, crouched among the bushes, and waited. Zhílin crept to the road, looked, and saw a Tartar on horseback driving a cow and humming to himself. The Tartar rode past. Zhílin returned to Kostílin.

'God has led him past us; get up and let's go on!'

Kostílin tried to rise, but fell back again.

'I can't; on my word I can't! I have no strength left.'

He was heavy and stout and had been perspiring freely. Chilled by the mist, and with his feet all bleeding, he had grown quite limp.

Zhílin tried to lift him, when suddenly Kostílin screamed out: 'Oh, how it hurts!'

Zhílin's heart sank.

'What are you shouting for? The Tartar is still near; he'll have heard you!' And he thought to himself, 'He is really quite done up. What am I to do with him? It won't do to desert a comrade.'

'Well, then, get up and climb up on my back. I'll carry you if you really can't walk.'

He helped Kostílin up, and put his arms under his thighs. Then he went out on to the path, carrying him.

'Only, for the love of heaven,' said Zhílin, 'don't throttle me with your hands! Hold on to my shoulders.'

Zhílin found his load heavy; his feet, too, were bleeding, and he was tired out. Now and then he stooped to balance Kostílin better, jerking him up so that he should sit higher, and then went on again.

The Tartar must, however, really have heard Kostílin scream. Zhílin suddenly heard some one galloping behind and shouting in the Tartar tongue. He darted in among the bushes. The Tartar seized his gun and fired but did not hit them, shouted in his own language, and galloped off along the road. /35/

'Well, now we are lost, friend!' said Zhílin. 'That dog will gather the Tartars together to hunt us down. Unless we can get a couple of miles away from here we are lost!' And he thought to himself, 'Why the devil did I saddle myself with this block? I should have got away long ago had I been alone.'

'Go on alone,' said Kostílin. 'Why should you perish because of me?'

'No, I won't go. It won't do to desert a comrade.'

Again he took Kostílin on his shoulders and staggered on. They went on in that way for another half-mile or more. They were still in the forest and could not see the end of it. But the mist was already dispersing and clouds seemed to be gathering; the stars were no longer to be seen. Zhílin was quite done up. They came to a spring walled in with stones by the side of the path. Zhílin stopped and set Kostílin down.

'Let me have a rest and a drink,' said he, 'and let us eat some of the cheese. It can't be much farther now.'

But hardly had he lain down to get a drink, than he heard the sound of horses' feet behind him. Again they darted to the right among the bushes, and lay down under a steep slope.

They heard Tartar voices. The Tartars stopped at the very spot where they had turned off the path. The Tartars talked a bit, and then seemed to be setting a dog on the scent. There was a sound of crackling twigs and a strange dog appeared from behind the bushes. It stopped, and began to bark.

Then the Tartars, also strangers, came climbing down, seized Zhílin and Kostílin, bound them, put them on horses, and rode away with them.

When they had ridden about two miles, they met Abdul, their owner, with two other Tartars following him. After talking with the strangers, /36/ he put Zhílin and Kostílin on two of his own horses and took them back to the Aoul.

Abdul did not laugh now and did not say a word to them.

They were back at the Aoul by daybreak, and were set down in the street. The children came crowding round, throwing stones, shrieking, and beating them with whips.

The Tartars gathered together in a circle, and the old man from the foot of the hill was also there. They began discussing; and Zhílin heard them considering what should be done with him and Kostílin. Some said they ought to be sent farther into the mountains; but the old man said: 'They must be killed!'

Abdul disputed with him saying: 'I gave money for them and I must get ransom for them.' But the old man said: 'They will pay you nothing, but will only bring misfortune. It is a sin to feed Russians. Kill them, and have done with it!'

They dispersed. When they had gone the master came up to Zhílin and said: 'If the money for your ransom is not sent within a fortnight, I will flog you; and if you try to run away again, I'll kill you like a dog! Write a letter and write properly!'

Paper was brought to them, and they wrote the letters. Shackles were put on their feet, and they were taken behind the Mosque to a deep pit about twelve feet square, into which they were let down.

VI

Life was now very hard for them. Their shackles were never taken off, and they were not let out into the fresh air. Unbaked dough was thrown to them as if they were dogs, and water was let down in a can.

It was wet and close in the pit and there was a /37/ horrible stench. Kostílin grew quite ill, his body became swollen, and he ached all over and moaned or slept all the time. Zhílin, too, grew downcast; he saw it was a bad look-out and could think of no way of escape.

He tried to make a tunnel, but there was nowhere to put the earth. His master noticed it and threatened to kill him.

He was sitting on the floor of the pit one day, thinking of freedom and feeling very downhearted, when suddenly a cake fell into his lap, then another, and then a shower of cherries. He looked up and there was Dína. She looked at him, laughed, and ran away. And Zhílin thought: 'Might not Dína help me?"

He cleared out a little place in the pit, scraped up some clay, and began modelling toys. He made men, horses, and dogs, thinking, 'When Dína comes I'll throw them up to her.'

But Dína did not come next day. Zílin heard the tramp of horses; some men rode past and the Tartars gathered in council near the Mosque. They shouted and argued; the word 'Russians' was repeated several times. He could hear the voice of the old man. Though he could not distinguish what was said, he guessed that Russian troops were somewhere near, and that the Tartars, afraid they might come into the Aoul, did not know what to do with their prisoners.

After talking awhile, they went away. Suddenly he heard a rustling overhead and saw Dína crouching at the edge of the pit her knees higher than her head, and bending over so that the coins of her plait dangled above the pit. Her eyes gleamed like stars. She drew two cheeses out of her sleeve and threw them to him. Zhílin took them and said, 'Why did you not come before? I have made some /38/ toys for you. Here, catch!' And he began throwing the toys up, one by one.

But she shook her head and would not look at them.

'I don't want any,' she said. She sat silent for awhile and then went on, 'Iván, they want to kill you!' And she pointed to her own throat.

'Who wants to kill me?'

'Father; the old men say he must. But I am sorry for you!'

Zhílin answered: 'Well, if you are sorry for me, bring me a long pole.'

She shook her head, as much as to say, 'I can't!'

He clasped his hands and prayed her: 'Dína, please do! Dear Dína, I beg of you!'

'I can't!' she said, 'they would see me bringing it. They're all at home.' And she went away.

So when evening came Zhílin still sat looking up now and then, and wondering what would happen. The stars were there, but the moon had not yet risen. The Mullah's voice was heard; then all was silent. Zhílin was beginning to doze, thinking: 'The girl will be afraid to do it!'

Suddenly he felt clay falling on his head. He looked up, and saw a long pole poking into the opposite wall of the pit. It kept poking about for a time and then it came down, sliding into the pit. Zhílin was glad indeed. He took hold of it and lowered it. It was a strong pole, one that he had seen before on the roof of his master's hut.

He looked up. The stars were shining high in the sky, and just above the pit Dína's eyes gleamed in the dark like a cat's. She stooped with her face close to the edge of the pit and whispered, 'Iván! Iván!' waving her hand in front of her face to show that he should speak low.

'What?' said Zhílin.

'All but two have gone away.' /39/

Then Zhílin said, 'Well, Kostílin, come; let us have one last try; I'll help you up.'

But Kostílin would not hear of it.

'No,' said he, 'It's clear I can't get away from here. How can I go when I have hardly strength to turn round?'

'Well, good-bye, then! Don't think ill of me!' and they kissed each other. Zhílin seized the pole, told Dína to hold on, and began to climb. He slipped once or twice; the shackles hindered him. Kostílin helped him and he managed to get to the top. Dína, with her little hands, pulled with all her might at his shirt, laughing.

Zhílin drew out the pole, and said, 'Put it back in its place, Dína, or they'll notice and you will be beaten.'

She dragged the pole away, and Zhílin went down the hill. When he had gone down the steep incline, he took a sharp stone and tried to wrench the lock off the shackles. But it was a strong lock and he could not manage to break it, and besides, it was difficult to get at. Then he heard some one running down the hill, springing lightly. He thought: 'Surely, that's Dína again.'

Dína came, took a stone, and said, 'Let me try.'

She knelt down and tried to wrench the lock off, but her little hands were as slender as little twigs, and she had not the strength. She threw the stone away and began to cry. Then Zhílin set to work again at the lock, and Dína squatted beside him with her hand on his shoulder.

Zhílin looked round and saw a red light to the left behind the hill. The moon was just rising. 'Ah!' he thought, 'before the moon has risen I must have passed the valley and be in the forest.' So he rose and threw away the stone. Shackles or no, he must go on. /40/

'Good-bye, Dína dear!' he said. "I shall never forget you!'

Dína seized hold of him and felt about with her hands for a place to put some cheeses she had brought. He took them from her.

'Thank you, my little one. Who will make dolls for you when I am gone?' And he stroked her head.

Dína burst into tears, hiding her face in her hands. Then she ran up the hill like a young goat, the coins in her plait clinking against her back.

Zhílin crossed himself, took the lock of his shackles in his hand to prevent its clattering, and went along the road, dragging his shackled leg and looking towards the place where the moon was about to rise. He now knew the way. If he went straight he would have to walk nearly six miles. If only he could reach the wood before the moon had quite risen! He crossed the river; the light behind the hill was growing whiter. Still looking at it, he went along the valley. The moon was not yet visible. The light became brighter; and one side of the valley was growing lighter and lighter, and shadows were drawing in towards the foot of the hill, creeping nearer and nearer to him.

Zhílin went on, keeping in the shade. He was hurrying, but the moon was moving still faster; the tops of the hills on the right were already lit up. As he got near the wood the white moon appeared from behind the hills, and it became light as day. One could see all the leaves on the trees. It was light on the hill, but silent, as if nothing were alive; no sound could be heard but the gurgling of the river below.

Zhílin reached the wood without meeting any one, chose a dark spot, and sat down to rest.

He rested, and ate one of the cheeses. Then he /41/ found a stone and set to work again to knock off the shackles. He knocked his hands sore, but could not break the lock. He rose and went along the road. After walking the greater part of a mile he was quite done up and his feet were aching. He had to stop every ten steps. 'There is nothing else for it,' thought he. 'I must drag on as long as I have any strength left. If I sit down I shan't be able to rise again. I can't reach the fortress; but when day breaks I'll lie down in the forest, remain there all day, and go on again at night.'

He went on all night. Two Tartars on horseback passed him, but he heard them a long way off, and hid behind a tree.

The moon began to grow paler, and the dew to fall. It was getting near dawn and Zhílin had not reached the end of the forest. 'Well,' thought he, 'I'll walk another thirty steps, and then turn in among the trees and sit down.'

He walked another thirty steps and saw that he was at the end of the forest. He went to the edge; it was now quite light, and straight before him was the plain and the fortress. To the left, quite close at the foot of the slope, a fire was dying out, and the smoke from it spread around. There were men gathered about the fire.

He looked intently and saw guns glistening. They were soldiers—Cossacks!

Zhílin was filled with joy. He collected his remaining strength and set off down the hill, saying to himself: 'God forbid that any mounted Tartar should see me now, in the open field! Near as I am, I could not get there in time.'

Hardly had he said this when, a couple of hundred yards off, on a hillock to the left, he saw three Tartars.

They saw him also and made a rush. His heart /42/ sank. He waved his hands and shouted with all his might, 'Brothers, brothers! Help!'

The Cossacks heard him, and a party of them on horseback darted to cut across the Tartars' path. The Cossacks were far and the Tartars were near; but Zhílin, too, made a last effort. Lifting the shackles with his hand, he ran towards the Cossacks hardly knowing what he was doing, crossing himself and shouting, 'Brothers! Brothers! Brothers!'

There were some fifteen Cossacks. The Tartars were frightened, and stopped before reaching him. Zhílin staggered up to the Cossacks.

They surrounded him and began questioning him. 'Who are you? What are you? Where from?'

But Zhílin was quite beside himself and could only weep and repeat, 'Brothers! Brothers!'

Then the soldiers came running up and crowded round Zhílin—one giving him bread, another buckwheat, a third vódka: one wrapping a cloak round him, another breaking his shackles.

The officers recognized him, and rode with him to the fortress. The soldiers were glad to see him back, and his comrades all gathered round him.

Zhílin told them all that had happened to him.

'That's the way I went home and got married!' said he. 'No. It seems plain that fate was against it!'

So he went on serving in the Caucasus. A month passed before Kostílin was released, after paying five thousand rúbles ransom. He was nearly dead when they brought him back.

(*Written in* 1870.) /43/

PART III

The Critics

TOLSTOY'S THEORY

✻ TOLSTOI ON ART

Vernon Lee

Leo Tolstoi's recent volume on Art closes significantly the series of his ar-
raignments of what we have been pleased to call civilisation. Like all his later
works, whether treatise or play or novel or parable, this volume on art shows
Tolstoi in his character of lay prophet, with all its powers and all its weaknesses.
For it would seem—we notice it in two other great lay prophets, Carlyle and
Ruskin—that the gift of seeing through the accepted falsehoods of the present,
and foretelling the improbable realities of the future, can arise only in creatures
too far overpowered by their own magnificent nature to understand other men's
ways of being and thinking; in minds so bent upon how things should be as to
lose sight of how things are and how things came to be. While Carlyle, embodying his passionate instincts in historical narrative, was moderated at least by his
knowledge of the past and of the consequent origin and necessity of the present;
while Ruskin, accepting the whole moral and religious training of his times,
was in so far in touch with his contemporaries; Tolstoi has broken equally with
everything, if ever he had really much to break with. Destitute of all historic
sense, impervious to any form of science, and accepting /135/ the Gospel only as
the nominal text for a religion of his own making, he has become incapable of
admitting more than one side to any question, more than one solution to any
difficulty, more than one factor in any phenomenon. He is destitute of all sense
of cause and effect, all acquiescence in necessity, and all real trustfulness in the
ways of the universe. For him most things are wrong, wholly, utterly wrong;
their wrongness has never originated in any right, and never will be transformed
into right until—well, until mankind be converted to Tolstoi's theory and practice. Economic and domestic arrangements, laws, politics, religion, all wrong;
and now, art also.

Unreasonableness like this is contagious, and Tolstoi's criticisms have often
been dismissed as utterly wrong-headed. But we should not forego the benefits
which the prophetic gift can bring us, if only we know how to extract them. We
should endeavour to eliminate the hallucinations which usually accompany such
penetrating moral insight, and to apply some of this vast spiritual energy with
more discrimination than was compatible with its violent and almost tragic
production. The use of a genius like Tolstoi's is to show us in what particulars

"Tolstoi on Art," in *Gospels of Anarchy* (London: T. Fisher Unwin, 1908), pp. 135–157. This essay first
appeared in *Quarterly Review*, 191 (April 1900), 359–372.

human institutions, habits, and thoughts are morally wrong; it is for us to find out what his very prophet's onesidedness prevents his doing—the rational explanation of this wrongness.

With regard to art, Tolstoi's opinion of its moral wrongness can be analysed into two very separate and independent views. Art, as practised and conceived in our times, is immoral, according to Tolstoi, first: /136/ because it fails to accomplish its only legitimate mission of directly increasing the instincts of justice, pity, and self-renunciation; and secondly: because any mission, good or bad, which it does fulfil is limited to a very small fraction of mankind. In other words, according to Tolstoi, art is a useless, often a corrupting, luxury; and a luxury of that minority which already enjoys more luxuries than are compatible with the material welfare of the rest of the world and with its own spiritual advantage.

The two propositions must be taken separately for examination in the light of certain sciences which, alas, Tolstoi condemns outright as themselves useless, mendacious, and corrupting. Now this condemnation by Tolstoi of all science, this misconception of the very nature of science, will help us to a rapid understanding of one half of his condemnation of art—its condemnation as morally useless. There is not enough justice or sympathy, not enough purity, endurance, or self-renunciation in the world—that is the gospel Tolstoi has to preach; and, with prophetic onesidedness, he condemns everything which does not directly and obviously increase these virtues. So long as it is neither unjust nor cruel nor rapacious nor impure, it matters nothing to Tolstoi whether life be varied or monotonous, elastic and adaptive or narrow and unadaptive, lucid or dull, enterprising or stagnant, complete or mutilated, pleasant or devoid of pleasure; it never occurs to him that in the great organic give-and-take, those very qualities which he so exclusively desires depend for their existence on the fulness and energy of every side of human existence. Tolstoi wants /137/ virtue, and only virtue, dominant, exclusive; and he thinks that virtue can be got independent of everything else, perfect and instantaneous. Hence he naturally disdains mere intellectual activity, and misunderstands the object of all science.

"The important and suitable object of human science," he writes explicitly, "ought not to be the learning of those things which happen to be interesting: but the learning of the manner in which we should direct our lives: the learning of those religious, moral, and social truths without which all our so-called knowledge of nature must be either useless or fatal." Hence, practically, no science; for Tolstoi's definition of a moral or social truth is not a moral or social fact or generalisation, but simply a precept for conduct; truth, in his special vocabulary, means no longer the faithful presentation of what is, but unflinching insistence on what ought to be. As with science, so with art.

"The religious consciousness of our time consists, speaking generally, in the recognition that our happiness, material and spiritual, individual and collective, momentary and permanent, consists in the brotherhood of all men, in our union for a life in common . . . and those works of art only should be esteemed and encouraged which grow out of the religion of our day, whereas all works of art contrary to this religion should be condemned, and all the rest of art treated with indifference."

Like science, therefore, art is set by Tolstoi to enforce virtue, not, as he orders science, by precepts, but by embodying and communicating such emotion /138/ as conduces directly to greater morality; no reference being made, in this case either, to the fact that virtue cannot long exist save in a many-sided, energetic, and harmonious life, of which the impulse to art, like the impulse to science, is an essential element. On these principles, "art," continues Tolstoi, "should always be valued according to its contents," that is to say, according to the definite moral example which it exhibits, or the definite moral emotion — chiefly pity, of course — which it awakens. The practical result is the banishing, as no longer consonant with our moral purposes, of nearly all the art of former times, including Antiquity and the Middle Ages; and the absolute condemnation of more than two-thirds of all modern art, including not merely Wagner, Impressionism, Symbolism, Pre-Raphaelitism, but all Tolstoi's earlier work — "Anna Karénina" and "War and Peace" — nearly all of Goethe's, and, after minute examination, even the "Ninth Symphony." There remain, besides the Gospels, the more obviously moralising works of Victor Hugo and of Dickens, "Uncle Tom's Cabin," and whatever painting, sculpture, and music may be discovered having a moral purpose as definite and unmistakable as these.

This statement is crude, and Tolstoi's plea, judging from it, would seem to be mere fanatical dogmatism. But this is far from being the case: Tolstoi is learned and is subtle, and twists facts powerfully to suit his views. Tolstoi has read, or caused to be examined for his benefit, almost everything that ever has been written on the nature and aims of art; and, in a chapter where profound lack of sympathy is thinly /139/ disguised as intellectual impartiality, he has reviewed and dismissed every theory of art which differs from his own. The science of æsthetics, necessarily dependent as it is upon psychology, sociology, and anthropology, all as yet imperfect, is in a backward state; and an immense proportion of the "philosophy of art" is either pure metaphysics, scornful of concrete fact, or mere polemic founded on the practice of one school or period. This backward state of æsthetics has rendered it, from Plato to Spencer, and from Ruskin to Whistler, the happy hunting ground of every philosopher lacking the experience of art, and of every art connoisseur lacking the habit of philosophy; and has given Tolstoi the immense advantage of finding not merely a marvellous amount of foolish utterance to scoff at, but, what is more to his purpose, a mutual contradiction between all the main theories. All philosophers, Tolstoi is able to tell us, have insisted on the extreme nobility of art, and a great many have dogmatised about beauty being art's special object; but there is not one single intelligible account of beauty, and there are three or four conflicting main definitions of art; a proof that, as Tolstoi has so often proclaimed, all science and all philosophy are worthless, and that art can have no legitimate object save the moral one which he assigns to it. But it happens that even nowadays the psychological and historical treatment of æsthetics is beginning to put order and lucidity into the subject, and to reconcile while it explains the conflict in all previous views. It is in the light of such science, however much despised by Tolstoi, that we shall attempt to show that art, like /140/ science itself, like philosophy, like every great healthy human activity, has a right to live and a duty to fulfil, quite apart from any help it may contribute to the enforcement of a moralist's teachings.

It is necessary to premise that, like nearly every other writer on æsthetics, Tolstoi has needlessly complicated the question by considering literature as the type of all other art. Now it is clear that literature, although in one capacity an art as much as music or painting, is at the same time, and in varying degree, a mode of merely imparting opinion or stirring up emotion, the instrument, not merely of the artist, but of the thinker, the historian, the preacher, and the pleader. This being the case, it is unfair to judge the question of art by the whole practice of literature; it is necessary, on the contrary, so long as we are dealing with æsthetics, to consider only those sides of literature in which it resembles the other, more purely artistic, more typical arts. Putting literature therefore aside, on account of the multiplicity of its appeals to human interest, we shall find that, roughly speaking, while philosophers have given to art one of two large functions, imitation or expression—and practical craftsmen have inclined to judge of art as if its chief function were either invention or execution, newness of construction or dexterity of handling—the immense majority of art-loving mankind, including the philosophers and the artists in their merely human capacity, having accepted or rejected, cherished or neglected, single works of art, exactly in proportion as these works gave them the particular kind of pleasure connected with the word *beauty*. The /141/ meaning of this word *beauty* it is difficult, and, in the present backward state of æsthetic science, perhaps impossible, to define. It implies a relation between certain visible or audible phenomena (and in literature certain still more complex purely mental phenomena) and the spectator or listener; and the exact nature of these visible or audible phenomena, which we objectify in the word *form*, differs from art to art, from style to style, and from individual work to individual work, there existing practically endless numbers of ways of being *beautiful*—that is to say, of producing in the human being the very specific emotion aroused by what we call *beauty*. What may be this common character of all these different so-called beautiful visual or audible forms or patterns, is evidently a question of psychological and, in part, of physiological science; and, different as are the modes of action of different arts and different styles of art, and deficient as is at present our analysis and observation of the modes of influence of any of them, we may yet affirm with confidence that the progress of science will one day explain that particular relation between certain visible and audible forms and the human being which is brought about by what we call *beauty*, as a relation involving, whatever its particular kind, a general momentary advantage to the vital, nervous, mental, and bodily conditions, and accompanied, as all beneficent conscious phenomena are, by the condition called *pleasure*.

To recapitulate: the quality called *beauty*, recognised in the most various kinds and styles of art, marks the awakening of a specific sort of pleasure, at present /142/ neither analysable nor explicable, but which, like all the other varieties of pleasure, can be instantly identified, though not described, by any one who has experienced it. But although it is this quality of *beauty*, this specific pleasurable emotion connected with the word *beautiful*, which practically decides the eventual acceptance or rejection of a work of art, yet the theories connecting art with imitation and expression, with invention and execution, represent also a large and important side of the question. For history and anthropology point clearly to the fact that art very rarely originates from a conscious desire for beauty, but that it arises out of the practical requirements, material or spiritual—building, weaving, pottery, dress, war, and ritual—of mankind, and out of a superabundance of the great primary instincts of imitation and expression, of construction, invention, and manipulation. These instincts, which are explicable only as immediate reactions of the human organism upon its surroundings, have been carried by natural selection to an intensity so considerable as often (in the case of children, for instance) to surpass all practical requirements, so that they have to vent themselves in that gratuitous exercise which has suggested to Mr. Spencer (as it had done to Schiller) the notion that art was the result of special *play instincts*. Play instincts, as such, there are probably none; but it is certain that all art has arisen from the activity—whether utilitarian or aimless—of the tendencies to imitate, to express, to invent, to construct, to manipulate, and to perform. But what differentiates art from the mere practical or aimless exercise of these impulses /143/ is the fact that, in its case, these impulses have been controlled by that totally different and specific instinct which demands that, useful or useless, the forms presented to the mind through the eye and the ear should possess the absolutely peculiar quality of *beauty*. That which has caused the imitation of an object or the expression of an emotion to be respected after the utility thereof has vanished or the impulse to imitate or express has died out; that which has caused the shape of a building, the pattern of a stuff or a pot, the movements of a dance, the picture of an object, to be desired for their own sake, is the peculiar kind of pleasure which the quite unpractical, quite disinterested contemplation of the object or pattern or representation or game has been able to produce by virtue of its beauty. The instinct for beauty is not, in all probability, one of the creative faculties of man. It does not set people working, it does not drive them to construct, to imitate, or to express, any more than the moral instinct sets people wishing and acting, or the logical instinct sets them reasoning. It is, even more typically than the moral and logical instincts, *a categorical imperative,* which imperiously decides whether given forms are to be tolerated, cherished, or avoided.

In thus recognising that the instinct for beauty is not a creative but a regulative impulse of mankind, modern psychology, so far from diminishing its importance, increases it enormously and explains it. For the very fact that the instincts of expression and imitation, of construction, invention, manipulation, and performance, have in all their most practical applications (in building, clothing, fabrics of all sorts, /144/ and every kind of ritual) been so constantly interfered with, and in their *play capacity* (save in children) been so utterly captured, by an instinct so merely regulative as the instinct for beauty, proves, to any one accustomed to modern scientific thought, that this mysterious, unaccountable, apparently useless pleasure arising from certain form relations which we call *beautiful* must eventually be explained and accounted for by some deep-seated vital utility to the mind and the nervous system of the human race. Therefore we would answer, not to Count Tolstoi, for whom all scientific explanations are mere lumber, but to those readers of Tolstoi whom his arguments may have shaken, first: that the apparent conflict in æsthetic theory represents only the various factors of a complex problem; and secondly: that the constant return to the belief that art's eventual aim is to produce beauty, and even the very mystery which at present surrounds this indefinable and as yet inexplicable quality, go to prove that, in a world different from the monotonous ascetic, unorganic world conceived by Tolstoi, in a world of life the most complex, overflowing and organic — not merely negative moral virtue, but physical beauty, as much as intellectual lucidity, is required, and, by the nature of things, will eternally be required and produced.

But Tolstoi's plea against art is double, and we have so far disposed, even in our own eyes, of only one of its halves. Even if the theory were right, the practice would remain wrong, and could not be set right by any amount of arguing. For, however beneficial the enjoyment of beauty, the benefit must /145/ be confined to the cases where the beauty is actually enjoyed; and, however desirable a function art may fulfil in human existence, the function is limited to the lives into which art does actually enter. Now beauty, Tolstoi points out, even supposing it to exist, requires, in nine-tenths of all art, a special training before it is so much as perceived; and moreover, art of any kind, appreciated or not appreciated, does not (he says) come near the existence of the immense majority of mankind, roughly speaking, of all the classes who work with their hands. On the one hand, there are galleries, exhibitions, and concerts where works of art are displayed and performed which can give pleasure only after elaborate initiation; on the other hand, there are millions of human beings who never come near a gallery, an exhibition, or a concert room, because they have neither the money nor the leisure to enter it. This being the case — and Tolstoi seems to us irrefutably right in this matter so far at least as he is speaking of actualities, and not of what is abstractly true or possible—it is mere nonsense and cant to talk of the usefulness of art to mankind as a whole; and the only sincere statement is that of the cynical and immoral persons who calmly admit that art is one of the many luxuries of the rich and leisured minority, and is maintained for their sole enjoyment (according to Tolstoi's economics) by the labour of the poor and overworked majority.

In attempting to answer this second plea against art, we must again premise that we can do so only with the aid of those psychological and historical sciences which Tolstoi disdains like all others, and in the light more particularly of that same critical knowledge of art /146/ which he denounces as a chief source of perversion in these matters. Let us begin with the question of the necessity of training before artistic beauty can be enjoyed, and with Tolstoi's implied corollary that beauty which is not spontaneously recognised cannot really respond to any deep-seated or indeed genuine demand of human nature. One of Tolstoi's chief instances in point is that of the modern school of impressionist painters. He describes, without any exaggeration, the hopeless mental confusion of an educated person on first being introduced to a collection of impressionist pictures. We can all of us remember similar remarks on dozens of similar occasions, and, if our memory is good, and we do not happen to have been brought up in impressionist studios from our infancy, we can probably also remember having said or thought the very same things ourselves: the objects represented are in most cases not recognised, the drawing and perspective seem utterly wrong, and the effects of colour and light the result of something near akin to lunacy.

Tolstoi's description is perfectly accurate, but his deductions are unwarrantable, for what he has not seen is that impressionist painters represent the most advanced section of a school of painting which has broken with all past tradition and which is avowedly seeking to represent effects of perspective, or colour, and of light which have never been attempted before, and to do so in reference to subjects—casually chosen pieces of landscape, for instance—which have hitherto been disdained, and in disregard of all the established tenets of symmetrical composition. Now the most /147/ advanced art of any age, like the most advanced thought of any age, is really not for the period which produces it, but for the next, whether that *next* come within two years or within twenty or a hundred years; and the art of a class, like the mode of dress and speech of a class, takes time to descend to the classes below. From the nature of things no novelty can arise save in a comparatively small circle, originally in the small circle of an artistic school, or even in the mind of one individual artist. We cannot feel the beauty of an artistic form which we do not really see, any more than we can feel the cogency of an argument we do not really follow; and the act of perception is not any simpler or more rapid or spontaneous than the act of intellectual apprehension. We do not see an unfamiliar pattern, we do not hear an unusual combination of sounds, with the rapidity and completeness given by habit and by expectation. The enjoyment of the quality called *beauty* is the enjoyment of a certain set of visible or audible relations, and these relations are by no means taken in immediately. The emotion of æsthetic pleasure can take place only when any given kind of artistic form has been assimilated by the mind; and the possibility, the mode, of assimilation is handed on by imitation from the more prepared individual to the less prepared; while, on the other hand, each new form, like each new thought, is assimilated in proportion as it resembles an already familiar one. Every new work of art, nay, every form of which a whole work of art consists, is different from all its predecessors, at least in its combinations; it is a new individual, which we get to know at first by what it /148/ has in common with previous individuals of the same class. The new picture or poem or song, which we see or read or hear for the first time, represents a mental, æsthetic, emotional step made by us; it means an alteration, great or small, of attitude, like that produced by a new logical proposition, even if the new picture or poem or song be as closely connected with a previous one as a new proposition of Euclid is with earlier propositions. To expect a person totally unfamiliar with all similar art to comprehend, to *see*, let alone to enjoy, an impressionist picture, is like expecting a person, who is familiar with nothing beyond a rule-of-three sum, to follow some new problem of the higher mathematics.

Such facts and principles as these have never occurred to Tolstoi. He has never conceived the human faculties as being in a state of constant alteration and evolution; he does not recognise that what we find established and apparently spontaneous in the present has been brought about by the adjustments and the efforts of the past; and he mistakes for innate tendencies what in reality are the result of long unconscious or conscious training. "The majority of men," he says, "has always understood all that we consider as the highest art: the book of Genesis, the parables of the Gospels, and the various popular legends, stories, and songs." No doubt, the "majority of men" has understood them in those countries and times in which they happen to have been familiar. But would the opening chapters of Genesis be more comprehensible to a person brought up entirely out of touch with Christianity or Judaism than the Prologue in Heaven /149/ of "Faust"? Would the intricate forms and special allusions of the north-country ballad, of the Tuscan lyric or the Spanish song, be more intelligible to a person totally unacquainted with anything of the kind than "Sister Helen," or a "Sonnet from the Portuguese," or Verlaine's "Clair de Lune"? What Tolstoi mistakes for a naturally, inevitably intelligible and enjoyable character in art is in reality an affinity, a resemblance, with forms of art already familiar. We are now beginning to see in what way all artistic enjoyment can require a degree of previous training, and yet be, to all appearance, absolutely spontaneous. For just as a capacity to appreciate the new grows insensibly out of familiarity with the old, so also does a new form of art, under normal conditions, grow out of an old form by a series of alterations very gentle and easy to follow, although their extremes may represent styles of art as utterly unlike as the music of Wagner and the music of Mozart, or may be as far apart as the pointed architecture of the thirteenth century and the round-arched architecture of the fifth, from which it undoubtedly sprang; a process which we can realise if we remember that although Latin is no longer intelligible to an uneducated Frenchman or Italian, yet there could never have been a moment of non-comprehension during the centuries which evolved the modern languages from the ancient one.

But mere gradual evolution would not be sufficient to explain the insensible training which has made the appreciation of various artistic forms apparently spontaneous. The art, whatever it might be, was not only absolutely continuous, but widely diffused. We must /150/ here remember what we before pointed out, that the desire for beauty is a regulative function, and that it imposes its preferences upon the expressive and imitative impulses, the activities of invention, construction, and execution which mankind displays for practical purposes or as a mere pastime. Hence, in times which are normal, any artistic form is found — and all art-history is there to prove it — not merely in those very conspicuous and developed branches which we think of more particularly as *art*, but in every form of cognate craft. The language and the allusions employed by even so learned and artificial a poet as Dante were the language and allusions of the least cultivated of his contemporaries, to the extent of making his poem the favourite reading of artisans and peasants. The forms, the modelling, the

anatomy, the essential ways of being of line and surface in Greek sculpture can
be recognised, to a greater or less degree, in the commonest Greek pottery,
bronze work, cheap domestic ornaments, and so forth; the very special forms,
so difficult to imitate, and even to grasp after much study, of what we call Gothic,
appear in the very humblest building, in every chair, table, embroidery, or piece
of iron-work of the later Middle Ages; while the modulations and rhythms, and
in great part the harmonies, of every past form of music have always been common to the most humble and to the highest categories of the art: the lower, like
the more provincial branches of art, according to the law of imitation we have
before alluded to, being always just a little behind the work of the creative
masters in the highest branches and in the greatest centres. This universal
diffusion of a given fashion in art—fashion /151/ in dress is perhaps the only
modern representative of this state of things—explains how a whole population
could be, so to speak, constantly in presence of any given style of art, and able
gradually to appreciate its variations without any apparent previous training.
The mediæval artisan was as able to appreciate the most far-fetched and subtle
of all forms of art, the Gothic—and for the same reason—as the modern Japanese of the lower class is able to appreciate peculiarities of perspective, of form,
and of execution which strike even the educated European as exotic, and which
cannot be enjoyed by him without some special study.

This, as we have remarked, is the state of affairs in *normal times;* for we must
be careful to underline this qualification. Tolstoi, with his deficient historical
sense, and his tendency to believe in an unvarying typical man (more or less
represented by the Russian peasant of to-day), has not recognised the prevalence
of this normal condition throughout the past, nor, of course, the reasons
through which, as Mr. Ruskin taught some forty years ago, this normal condition
has become more and more exceptional in the present. It is, however, easy to
understand why our century, with its quite unparalleled rapidity and complexity
of change, must differ in this respect from all others. As regards the continuity
of artistic development, there have been and still are two notable causes of disturbance: the opening up of foreign civilisations and the importation of exotic
kinds of art (like that of Japan), and the archæological revival of the art of the
past, for instance, the Greek and the Gothic. From these have resulted /152/
both an impulse of imitation and an effort after novelty, the latter due both
to facility of new combinations and to resistance against foreign or historical
influence. Now an art which, like that of Burne-Jones or of Whistler, is half
archæological or half exotic, cannot possibly be appreciated without some
degree of familiarity with the Mediæval or the Japanese art from which it has
partly sprung; while, on the other hand, an art like that of Manet, Monet, and
Rodin has evidently been pushed into excessive novelty by a violent revulsion
from the officially accepted forms and methods of the painting and sculpture of
the Renaissance and of Antiquity.

There is in the art of this century a degree of individualism, an amount of
archæological and exotic research, an obvious desire for novelty at any price,
which renders it less organic, less natural, than the art of past times. The result
is that its appreciation is no longer attainable by the unconscious training which
is conferred by familiarity with previous art, and demands special initiation
through critical study. Among our contemporaries it is a matter of everyday
experience to find persons extremely appreciative of Greek or Gothic art who
yet, like Mr. Ruskin, can see absolutely nothing in the art of modern France;
while there are practical artists who can see absolutely nothing save archaic
quaintness in the art of Antiquity and of the Renaissance; to such an extent are
the perception and enjoyment of one kind of form impeded by the habit and

preoccupation of another. Such being the case with the artistic classes themselves, how much more must it be the case with the general public! And from
/153/ this general public we are obliged in our century to exclude completely
the enormous majority of mankind. Tolstoi has not exaggerated matters in
saying that barely one man in a hundred comes nowadays within reach of art,
appreciated or unappreciated. For here we find ourselves in presence of the
other and far greater difference which separates the æsthetic conditions of our
century from those of every previous one. The industrial and economic changes
accompanying the development of machinery have virtually, as Mr. Ruskin
pointed out, put an end for the moment to all that handicraft which formed
the fringe of the artistic activity of the past, and which kept the less favoured
classes in such contact with the artistic forms of their time and country that, for
instance, the pottery and brass-work of the humbler classes of Greece, and the
wood-work and textile fabrics of the poorest citizens of the Middle Ages, let
alone every kind of domestic architecture, afforded sufficient preparation for
the greatest art of temples and cathedrals: a daily, hourly preparation, embodying in many cases actual mechanical familiarity. Nowadays, on the contrary,
objects of utility, machine-made, and no longer expressive of any preferences,
are either totally without æsthetic quality, or embody, in a perfunctory and
imperfect manner, the superficial and changing æsthetic fashions of a very
small minority. Nor is this all. The extreme rapidity of scientific discovery and
mechanical invention, the growing desire for technical education and hygienic
advantage, the race for material comfort and the struggles for intellectual and
social equality—in fact, the whole immense movement of our times, both /154/
for good and for evil—have steadily tended to make art less and less a reality
even in the lives of the leisured classes, and have resulted in virtually effacing
all vestige of it from the lives of working men.

Art, therefore, we may concede to Tolstoi, is in our days largely artificial,
often unwholesome, always difficult of appreciation, and, above all, a luxury.
Violent and even fanatical as are Tolstoi's words on this subject, they hardly
exaggerate the present wrongness of things.

But we hope to have suggested in the course of these criticisms that the
present condition of art does not justify Tolstoi's proposal that in the future
art should be reduced to being a mere adjunct of ethical education, or, failing
that, should be banished from the world as futile or degrading. In pointing out,
as we have done, the imperious nature of that desire for beauty which normally
regulates all the practical constructive energies of mankind, and subdues to its
purposes all human impulses to imitation and expression, imposing a *how*
entirely separate and *sui generis;* and in clearing up that confusion among
conflicting æsthetic theories of which Tolstoi has taken such advantage, we have
brought home, we hope, to the reader the presumption that an instinct so special
and so powerful must play some very important part in the bodily and mental
harmony of man. Further, while indicating the natural mechanism by which,
under normal circumstances, the appreciation and enjoyment of artistic forms
have kept pace with their changes, and familiarity with the various kinds of
beauty in the humblest and commonest objects /155/ of utility has rendered
spontaneous the perception of the same kinds of beauty in their higher, more
complex, and less utilitarian developments, we have shown that this special and
imperious æsthetic craving has created its own natural and universal modes of
satisfaction. We have seen that art, considered as the production of beautiful
objects or arrangements, has been spontaneously produced, spontaneously enjoyed, and universally diffused, in one or other of its categories, throughout
the whole of the past; and, having taken notice of the disturbing influences

which have interrupted this normal condition of things in the present, we have shown reason to expect a return thereunto in the future. The wrong condition of things with regard to art is the result of other wrong conditions, intellectual, social, and economic, inevitable in a period of excessive, complex, and, so to speak, compound, change; and as these wrong conditions cannot fail to right themselves, the adjustment of the question of art will follow as the result of other adjustments. In what precise manner this may take place it would be presumptuous to forecast; but this much may be affirmed, that the ascetic subordination of art to ethical teaching will play no part in it. Imperfect, and even in some ways intolerable to our moral sense, as is the present condition of art, as Tolstoi has victoriously demonstrated, let those among us whom it offends reflect that even under such evident wrong conditions it is not mere selfishness to preserve the art of the past and foster the art of the present for the benefit of a more just and wholesome, a more developed and more traditionally normal, future. Moreover art, like science and like practical /156/ well-being, will in the long run take care of itself; because, despite Tolstoi's statement to the contrary, art, like morality itself, is necessary to mankind's full and harmonious life. /157/

⌘ TOLSTOI'S MORAL THEORY OF ART

John Albert Macy

Two years ago appeared a treatise on art by one of the greatest of living artists.[1] Although it attracted wide attention among the critics and was reviewed in many journals, none of the reviews, so far as I have seen them, attempted to deal fully with the stimulating questions raised in this singular volume. Yet the work is so distinctly vital and original that it demands, and will, I think, continue to demand, more extended consideration than is possible in a mere book-review. Even if Tolstoi's essay is not destined to take a permanent place in the literature of esthetics and criticism, it nevertheless discusses with great power, and in a new light, questions which will refuse to be laid aside so long as there are artists and writers on art.

Tolstoi's "What is Art?" contains a querulous exposition of existing evils, a sincere attempt to find out and formulate the causes, and some sweeping statements of dogma, based on a wide and rather ill-defined socialism, by which he hopes to see the causes removed. Like most reformers, he succeeds better in naming the disease than in prescribing the cure for it. New rules to set the world right are always inadequate and often cardinally wrong.

As a reformer, Tolstoi handles large ethical problems, and, to assess the work fairly, the critic cannot confine himself to a purely esthetic discussion. The different branches of philosophy, especially ethics and esthetics, are so interwoven that they are only abstractly capable of complete separation. This, indeed, is at the bottom of the first lesson which Tolstoi himself would teach, namely, that all art is worthless which swings away from morality. The large task he sets himself is to prevent art from wandering out of the road of good healthy life into the quagmire of moral stagnation. Thus it is in the field of ethics

"Tolstoi's Moral Theory of Art," *Century Magazine,* 62 (1901), 298–307.

[1] "What is Art?" by Count Leon N. Tolstoi. Translated from the Russian by Charles Johnston. Philadelphia, Henry Altemus, 1898. /298/

that the main part of Tolstoi's discussion really lies. The book is a sermon on art, in the course of which many of the deepest problems of esthetics are touched on or treated at length.

Now, a sermon should appeal to our emotions, and should stimulate us to richer and loftier purpose. Viewed in this aspect, Tolstoi's book is hardly success-ful. Instead of the power that wins and persuades, Tolstoi's strength in many parts of this work takes the form of mere violence. One is reminded that the author is old. Lecturing from the mount of threescore and ten, he has none of the errors of young theorists, nor at the same time has he the enthusiasm of youth, which often atones splendidly for error; he shows rather the irascibility of old age than its tempered wisdom. Though he has a great height from which to view the world, his eyes are bad; and for all the contagion of good will and brotherly love which he preaches, his own heart is not warm enough to make us forget in the fervor of his belief the fallacies contained in it. Neither the truth nor the error of his teaching stirs us very deeply. The reaction on his doctrines is cold, and the very incitement to better things which he preaches as the great glory of true art fails to beat in the blood. This failing, almost pathetic to one who has felt the astonishing power of Tolstoi's earlier writings, would not be so noticeable were it not the very shortcoming for which he condemns what we call art. In "What is Art?" the genius, though still wonderful, is broken and scattered, not masterful like the genius of the great artist who in a time of supreme intellec-tual vigor gave us "Anna Karénina." The power of the man holds our interest, but does not bring us irresistibly to his conclusions. The thought comes to us many times in reading the book that Tolstoi has outlived his power. Where he should command and inspire, he irritates the reader or leaves him cold, and the sermon fails.

But one is not left in an indifferent state /298/ of mind. The reaction on the book, though perhaps cold and judicial, must be strong. Interesting questions are raised and discussed in an interesting manner. Tolstoi's book is an important utterance on important problems.

Before passing to these problems, however, let me first call attention to certain general biases and limitations which must affect Tolstoi's work, and then dispose of certain minor things in the essay, which, though he spends many pages in their development, are only incidental to his principal thought, and grow like excrescences out of the crotchety side of his doctrine.

One bias is evident: Tolstoi is a Russian. In Russia class distinctions are cruelly manifest, and Tolstoi's socialism and hatred of aristocracy are too sec-tional to form the basis of a universal theory of art. Russian art, moreover, with notable exceptions in fiction and music, does not rank with the best art of modern Europe, and the narrow range, marked by the special works of art which Tolstoi selects to praise or to blame, makes one question whether he is well enough acquainted with the art of other countries. The accidents of time and place cramp his view and distort his theory.

Tolstoi's greatest limitation is one partly of temperament, partly of educa-tion. He is not a wise student of philosophy. A philosopher he certainly is, perhaps a great one in the untechnical sense; but he does not see the value of metaphysics, which lifts its head above the paltry pursuits of men and which sees God as the religious consciousness of the common man cannot see him. Tolstoi will not admit that one can find more in the universe than God the Father and men the brothers. Great world-formulas, which spell Beauty with a capital letter and forget king and peasant, may not be such fatuous nonsense as he thinks. Tolstoi invites adverse criticism by calling attention repeatedly to his weak spots.

This he does fatally by uttering heresies against the demigods of art. Some of our gods may be of putty, but not all. To have our love of Greek statues condemned as immoral is staggering. This effect soon gives way to a sense that one is listening to a monomaniac, when, one by one, nearly all our great artists become objects of Tolstoi's attack. It is doing Tolstoi an act of overjustice to pass by these things as unimportant. If he exposes his breast, it is right to strike him, but one prefers to win scientifically. Therefore I shall not argue with him if he condemns the symbolists and the decadents; personally, I agree with him at this point. But if we are right in considering them bad, it is not because we are somewhat mystified in reading them, not because their ideas are not morally good for humanity, but for some purely "artistic" reason (*not* as Tolstoi understands the word), such as lack of unity, of coherence, of beauty of expression, of sincerity. He may be right when he insists that Goethe's "Faust" does not produce "a true artistic impression," but the reason for such a doubtful conclusion is not that "Faust" is "based on borrowing." Perhaps one may complain justly of its lack of unity, but the life of genius awakens it from dead imitation. When Tolstoi brands Greece as "a half-savage, slave-trading little nation, which could nicely depict the nakedness of the human body and construct buildings pretty to look at," and stigmatizes the "production of Sophocles, Euripides, Æschylus, and especially Aristophanes," as "wild, coarse, and meaningless," it is generous to keep silent. Let him think that Michelangelo's "Last Judgment" is foolish, that Beethoven's later period is futile, that Ibsen, Wagner, Strauss, and the rest are mere imitators. Maybe Wagner's operas have their silly movements; but it is hard to sit calm and hear a critic say, "All this beauty is of the lowest type."

It is necessary to mention these things, because they are the rubbish which must be cleared away before one can get to the good of Tolstoi's work. To treat them as the peevish impotence of a man with a hobby uncontrolled is to help Tolstoi to keep his feet. Unless one separates these sweeping condemnations from the cooler discussion of the book, one cannot do justice to what is sane.

II

According to Tolstoi, art is an important activity which costs an incalculable amount of labor and ruins millions of human lives. What is there to justify this great expenditure of work? Is art, that is, what is commonly called art, worth what it costs? The usual answer is that art awakens and preserves one's sense of beauty, that it is food for a natural esthetic hunger within us which must be satisfied. As a matter of fact, few persons get the pleasure which art pretends to furnish. The toiling millions, whose life-blood runs red on the altars of Art, never feel the soothing touch of her hand. Nor is art an end in itself, like truth and honor, to which enormous sacrifice should be paid un- /299/ questioningly. Art, like other good activities, is a means to a wider, better, more brotherly life; in other words, the life of socialism.

Criticism and esthetics, continues Tolstoi, have tried to make the function of art the search after the beautiful. But beauty is only another name for pleasure of a selfish, unworthy sort. If I say that a certain poem is beautiful, I mean simply that it pleases me; and my neighbor, who finds no pleasure in it, says truly that it lacks beauty. Beauty is the vitiating factor in art. Tolstoi's syllogism runs thus: There is no standard of pleasure; beauty is pleasure; therefore beauty cannot be the standard of art. The truth of this conclusion is enforced by the fact that writers on esthetics have always tried to frame their definitions of art to include the productions that have appealed to them or have been recognized in their time.

How, then, he asks, shall we define art?

Art is transfer of feeling. The action of art consists in "calling up in one's self a feeling once experienced, and conveying this feeling" by means of symbols, "so that other people are affected by this feeling and live it over in themselves." By means of art, the individual not only experiences again, in a higher form, his own emotions, but becomes a partner in the experience of the race. True art thus prevents isolation, and brings about a common brotherhood. It lifts our view of life from the personal to the universal. Now, the universal is represented in any given race and period by the prevailing religious consciousness, and it is this religious consciousness which the best art most clearly and most forcibly expresses, for it is the highest understanding of life. Whenever, as is the unhappy case of the educated to-day, the religious consciousness grows dim and faith goes out of the temple, art, Tolstoi maintains, is prevailingly bad, because people have nothing left to measure it by except personal pleasure.

Rooted in a false conception of art, esthetics, which calls itself the science of the beautiful and falsely pretends to have arisen among the Greeks, has tried to make a holy trinity of goodness, beauty, and truth. These three qualities, when stripped of metaphors and misleading associations, are found to have nothing in common, to lead, in fact, in quite different directions. To follow beauty is to depart from good; and truth, being destructive of delusion, annihilates the prime condition of beauty.

Such false esthetic theories have made art an exclusive pursuit of the elect; while the masses, who are true judges of real art, are considered by the artistic cliques as not being educated up to high appreciation of fine productions. Except for a few works which teach broad religion and a wide-armed humanitarianism, little has been created in art which the honest literate workman, the great model of manhood, can enjoy. Only the rich, whose sense of art is atrophied, can take pleasure (and that a debilitating, immoral pleasure) in the modern novel, which is, with few exceptions, a morbid study of the loves of the upper classes; in the symbolists and the decadents; in complex, highly technical music; in Wagner; in Beethoven of the second period. Corresponding to the prevailing cliques in art, spring up schools of imitation of approved masterpieces and schools of criticism which foster this imitation.

Thus, Tolstoi complains, a great organ of human progress, art, which should be the great means of communication between men's hearts and souls, is diseased and impotent. Callous to the true contagion of art, and feeling only a tinge of artificial rapture over fine technic or clever novelty, the upper classes live without the softening effect of true art, and drift away from morality. The common people waste labor in works of false art, and grow corrupt by continual contact with it. Morality is weakened by the unwarranted confounding of good and beauty.

What, then, according to Tolstoi, are the conditions of true art? Real art is contagious; it produces mental union with the author and, through him, with the spectators. The stronger the contagion, the better the art; that is, independent of the worth of the feelings it carries. To make good art, these feelings must be good; that is, all art depends for its value on the goodness of the subject-matter. This subject-matter must have as its essence the religious consciousness of the time. The purpose of Christian art should be to bring man nearer to God; the feelings must accordingly be universal, common to men, and must be expressed with clearness and sincerity. Ideas that make for religion and humanitarianism must be presented so that the ordinary man may feel them as he contemplates a work of art. The artist must work for love, because he has a message, not because he is skilful with words or musical symbols, and can make money selling exhibitions of his skill. With simplified media of expression and a higher education among the poor, distinction in class /300/ will vanish, and the hidden artists among the people will come forth with the truths they have to tell. The good can produce good art and the good can enjoy it. Aristocracy, says this great peasant-count, will fall when the true art comes. In his vision of the true art some day to be, Tolstoi might have quoted Kipling:

No one shall work for money and no one shall work for fame.

Nor shall "the joy of the working" count either, except that the real art-worker shall be promoting the common happiness, and so be happy himself. Art for art's sake and all the superrefined taste of the falsely educated must disappear before something larger and finer when moral socialism brings true Christian art.

III

It is well just here to admit in part the justice of Tolstoi's arraignment of modern art, since most of my criticism is opposed to his teachings. It is a sad fact that millions of dollars and thousands of human lives are devoted to false, useless art; nay, to art which is worse than useless, which debilitates and perverts the people who feed their senses on it. The only questions are, whether any educated people pretend that this is art; whether the most fastidious of Tolstoi's "atrophied" critics and connoisseurs are not as bitterly opposed as he to lascivious operas, "Frenchified" novels, nude atrocities in flesh and paint; and whether the same honest workman, who toils with such heroic patience for his family, does not enjoy these cheap yellow corruptions more than the pampered child of culture. Is it not the ruddy-cheeked peasant who, as soon as he comes to town, makes straight for the beer-saloon adorned with wicked women who lie in suggestive postures in frames of gilt? The crime is there. Are the super-refined to blame for it? I shall say more of this when I come to discuss the qualified judge of art.

Pointing much nearer the breast of the cultured is the charge that art has parted company with life; that novels of refined sexual love imitate one another in their independence of truth and of naturalness; that the cultured dilettante has a lust for production, which breeds bastard books and abortive pictures. It is true that some critics seem to care more for form than for substance, that to them anything is artistic which is technically skilful, that good structure and good style cover a multitude of sins against God's truth and man's welfare. Not content with deifying mere good workmanship, critics form exclusive and hostile schools, and pretend to solve the mystery of how genius manifests itself. It is a bitter fact that the study of recognized masterpieces is carried to such an extent that imitations multiply beyond count. Unnatural tastes are created for certain styles of art, and thousands of hacks set to work to imitate what has pleased, and so to please again. It must be confessed that certain critics isolate themselves from the intelligent public and take pleasure in admiring what few others can enjoy, and admiring it for that very reason. The false note struck half in fun by Lowell, when he said that he wanted Chaucer for himself and a few friends, jars everywhere in modern criticism. The supreme contempt of critics who make Walter Pater a fetish, for those who dare to dislike his fine intricate form for its own sake, is an example of this scornful exclusiveness, which says, "I am holier than thou." And in so far as Tolstoi preaches as a cure for these diseases a wider sympathy with men, unflinching sincerity, independence of critical idols and codified forms of worship, simplicity of style, and decency of subject-matter, he is a good teacher. One wishes that some good might come from his stinging rebuke of literary snobs who erect fences between themselves and "Philistines," their name, apparently, for all sensible, healthy people. There is a tendency among certain modern writers to estimate supersubtle indirectness of expression above anything else on either side of the heavens. The idea embodied counts for nothing so long as it be set forth in language which shows, to use the jargon of later-day criticism, "sensitiveness to word-effects." If Tolstoi can pull such people into the sunlight, his book will not be in vain.

IV

The chief noun in esthetics is beauty. Since Tolstoi rules beauty out of art entirely, his work is not so much a treatise on esthetics as an attack on the very existence of this branch of philosophy. "There is no objective definition of beauty," he says; and again, "All attempts to define what taste is can lead to nothing, and an explanation why one thing is pleasing to one person and not to another . . . does not and cannot exist." "All esthetic theories consist in recognizing certain productions as good because they please us, and then establishing a theory of /301/ art . . . such as to embrace all these productions." These statements deny psychological esthetics and metaphysical esthetics, leaving only dogmatic criticism and history. Now, although it is true that no esthetic theory is more adequate than any other theory which man has ever tried to formulate, although no one has succeeded by any method, psychological or metaphysical, in telling us exactly what beauty is, yet it is destructive of all esthetics, destructive of artistic and literary criticism, to say with Tolstoi that, because beauty is only a kind of pleasure, it has no place in art. The true relation between beauty and pleasure is this: We associate with things the degrees and kinds of pleasure they give us, and say that the quality by virtue of which we derive pleasure from them is their beauty. That beauty expresses merely the value of the thing to us. To try to find its value independent of ourselves is nonsense. This I shall develop presently.

First, however, it is necessary to separate esthetic pleasures from other pleasures. The pleasure one takes in the beautiful comes from the keenest exercise of the perceptive senses, and is not to be confounded or classed with pleasures, like those of eating and breathing, which attend the discharge of function in other organs than those by which we perceive. This line of division is obvious, yet Tolstoi confusedly associates with the enjoyment of perceptions the bad reputation that, in ethics, hangs about the animal pleasures. Past the age when the lust for life is strong, Tolstoi has a moralistic prejudice against pleasure; so the very fact that beauty pleases, vitiates it. Furthermore, recognizing that pleasure is subjective, that the beauty of a poem varies with the person who reads it, Tolstoi concludes that beauty cannot be a standard.

These fallacies are due to Tolstoi's lack of training in philosophy. He does not see that the same subjectivity that destroys for him the value of judgments about beauty holds in all the judgments we make. Like beauty, all things that men think about and believe in—God, goodness, truth, all the conclusions of science, religion, ethics—depend on the biased individual. The whole world of thought and experience is subjective, and to destroy esthetics on the ground that its judgments are based on personal pleasure is to destroy equally all branches of thought. This is a commonplace in modern philosophy, and does not need to be enlarged on here.

The fallacy which rules out pleasure as the register of anything good and true misses the meaning of half of human life and is in strange contradiction to Tolstoi's very definite statement that art is transfer of feeling. Feeling is the key-note, and Tolstoi, like some other moralists, has not had a sure ear for its hum in the gamut of things human. Man is primarily an emotional creature. His rationality is an after development. Now, as Mr. Santayana shows in his chapter on the nature of beauty,[1] all values depend on emotional consciousness. Without the sense of pleasure or pain, there would be no such thing as appreciation, weighing of values. Our sense of preference depends on our feelings in both ethical and esthetical experiences. Pleasure is the register in us of what an object means for us. Therefore, not only is Tolstoi wrong in saying that judgments about art must not depend on our pleasures, but if he understood psychology, he would see that his own theory, his book, all that he writes, is an expression of his pleasure, his personal sense of value, the very sort of ground which he would draw from under the structure of esthetics.

The difficulty into which Tolstoi has fallen is a natural danger to one who does not watch thought closely. The rational side of human thought has a deluding soundness of aspect which makes one forget that the stuff with which the reason builds is selected according to our preferences.

Moral preferences, moreover, on which ethics is constructed, being based on remoter pleasures, which concern rather the whole of life than the emotions of the hour, set up for themselves and lose sight of the emotional choices which underlie all morality. For this reason morality, which looks askance at pleasure, whereas esthetics openly avows it as the ground of its being, seems to have an independent right to exist, free of personal judgments, and draws its white skirts away from esthetics.

With preference, then, based on pleasure, esthetics confessedly deals, and sees in art the activity which tries to separate and preserve what pleases us from what is ugly, that is, unpleasant. To justify esthetics on this ground would be as useless as to try to prove that there ought to be a science of ethics. It is enough to have shown that the reason for which Tolstoi has tried to separate art and beauty—namely, that beauty can be traced back to mere pleasure or pref-/302/ erence—is a fallacy, which, if insisted on, is fatal to all the rest of human thought.

V

The trouble with Tolstoi's approach to questions of art is that he comes to it as a moralist. It is significant that, of all writers on the philosophy of art, the three who have dealt with it in the least satisfactory manner, Plato, Ruskin, and Tolstoi, have been primarily interested in ethics, in sociology, and in economics. To Tolstoi, as we have seen, all art which does not make for two great moral principles, devotion to God and universal brotherhood, is bad. He would correct art. Plato, on the contrary, would reject art, with a few exceptions, on the ground of two charges against it, one metaphysical, the other ethical.

Art, says Plato,[1] deals with the appearances of things, which are, in turn, only the imperfect images of ideal reality; art is, therefore, twice removed from truth. Moreover, art deals largely with unworthy passions,[2] and represents

[1] "The Sense of Beauty," by George Santayana, pp. 14–23. /302/
[1] "Republic," Bk. X. /303/
[2] "Republic," Bk. II, IX, X. /303/

the gods as beings in the flesh; therefore it excites in men the base emotions which it depicts, and falsifies religion. The first theory is hardly a live one in modern times, and perhaps needs no refutation here. But it may be said that Aristotle and Schopenhauer are sounder. Aristotle believes[3] that art comes nearer to expressing the idea which nature but imperfectly embodies in matter. "The illusions which fine art employs do not cheat the mind; they image forth the immanent Idea which cannot find adequate expression under the forms of material existence." For Schopenhauer, art is an escape from miserable personality to the universal, and so to larger truth.

The bearing of this metaphysical discussion on Tolstoi is a bit remote, but it suggests how completely he fails to see one great value of art, its attempt to perfect something, if it be only the human form. The finest sense men have is a love of the flawless. Our conception of God is an expression of this love, but God is invisible to the senses, which seek perfection in more tangible form through art. Art tries to take a little section of life or nature and rid it of flaws and excrescences until it expresses one idea, unhindered, free from what is irrelevant. This is the meaning of Beauty with a capital letter, which Tolstoi sneers at as a vague, meaningless abstraction of metaphysicians. Both Tolstoi and Plato think of works of art too narrowly as mere pictures of things, and accordingly go astray in judging the value of the picture by the value of the thing depicted. They make unfair demands that art shall justify itself by its subject-matter alone.

This leads to the second charge of Plato that art represents base passions. One phase of this idea Tolstoi brings out strongly in his arraignment of the novel of sexual passion, which is too often the production of a man "suffering from erotic mania," and which stimulates morbidly our sexual desires. There is truth in this. How many novels are there which make vice attractive! In this the French are great offenders. Masterly in style, fine in construction, delicate in the handling of extremely dangerous subject-matter, with a subtle skill in touching the feelings and at the same time in dealing opiates to the sense of moral distinctions, too many of the French *nouvelles* and *romans* during the last thirty years tend to lure us into bad air, where the dimness of the light makes the smut show less black. Some of them, it is true, like a few of Guy de Maupassant's stories, deal with problems of sex in a healthy manner and are good for the right minded adult; but there is little in the modern French story of that love of purity and the sure understanding of it, through which the artist gives us at once the fascination of vice for men and its loathsomeness, so that the reader experiences a revulsion against it, and a purification of the emotions, of which Aristotle makes so much! Although, to be true to life, the novelist must deal with vice, he need not revel in it. In the preface to one of his novels, Théophile Gautier says that Virtue is a wrinkled grandmother and Vice a pretty girl who shows her ankles. The Frenchman is to blame for thinking so, and cannot afford to laugh at the Puritan for loving the grandmother and asking the pretty girl to wear longer skirts. Fortunately, there is little hypocrisy about the indecent novel. It cannot cheat the man with his eyes open. Even the scientific school of Zola, the "subjectivists," who pretend to "study" vice as an excuse for painting it luridly, cannot sow bad seed except in bad soil. Here is the great answer to Tolstoi. Art bad in subject-matter cannot hurt the moral man so much as Tolstoi thinks. The worst art could do little harm if morality did its work.

So we cannot agree with Plato in ruling /303/ out of art the expression of any but high and lofty ideas, or with Tolstoi, who confuses a bad idea with a bad ideal, yet we can agree that the subject-matter of art should be cleaner than it

---

[3] Butcher, "Aristotle's Theory of Poetry and Fine Arts," p. 160 ff. /303/

is, for art would sacrifice nothing and would free itself from the charges of the rigid moralist.

But all rigid moralists do not condemn art as we know it. According to Ruskin, whose moral esthetic theory is an odd mixture of sober thought and irrational prejudice, art is man's instrument for the glorification of God. In this sense art has a moral function, but it is not, like the useful arts, subservient to life and the problems of existence. It is an end in itself which we pursue because it broadens the vision and opens the view to "Him in whom [we] rejoice and live." This, I take it, is another way of expressing the attempt of art to get through matter to idea, the function of art which Tolstoi ignores and which Plato denies.

To get at a moral theory of art, Tolstoi discards the notion of beauty. Ruskin deifies it, and makes all ideas of beauty essentially moral.[1] The very love of God which is cardinal in Tolstoi's theory, Ruskin makes a secondary consequence of enjoyment of beauty. He agrees with Tolstoi that the sense of art may be atrophied by association and long habit; but, unlike Tolstoi, he holds that true beauty is the soul of art, its presence is recognized by the highest senses of the pure in heart, and it embodies or typifies in human life God's infinity, divine comprehensiveness, divine permanence, divine justice, and divine energy. The faculty which perceives beauty is the *theoria,* the power of seeing, which finds its perfect state in charity, unselfishness, and justice of moral judgment. Immoral qualities in art destroy beauty. The lion is more beautiful in a state of kingly repose than when snarling over a dead carcass. Only love can produce the ideal form, and objects of moral hatred cannot become objects of great art.

This theory of the moral essence of beauty is certainly sounder than Tolstoi's doctrine as a working hypothesis by which to judge art. Although open to serious objections, it deals better with the relations between the moral and the esthetic sides of man than Tolstoi's absolute exclusion of beauty. It at once invites art to a full life and arrives at moral conclusions which Tolstoi might accept. "Divine Providence," says Ruskin,[2] "which leaves it open to us . . . to abuse this sense [the sense of sight, beauty, art, etc.], like every other, and pamper it with selfish and thoughtless vanities as we pamper the palate with deadly meats, until the appetite of tasteful cruelty is lost in its sickened satiety, incapable of pleasure, unless, Caligula-like, it concentrates the labor of a million lives into the sensations of an hour, leaves it also open to us, by humble and loving ways, to make ourselves susceptible of deep delight from the meanest objects of creation, and of a delight which shall not separate us from our fellows, nor require the sacrifice of any duty or occupation, but which shall bind us closer to men and to God, and be with us always, harmonized with every action, consistent with every claim, unchanging and eternal." If Tolstoi should read Ruskin, he would see that there is at least one other writer on art who moves in the same general direction, though by a more attractive road.

In all these moralistic theories of art there is a truth and there is a misconception. The truth is a great one, easy for the writer on esthetics to overlook, that in life the hardest and most important thing men have to do is to lead good lives. Our moral task is so great that it overshadows everything else. No matter whether one's ethical theory depend on divine command or expediency or abstract principle or what not, all else in life shrinks into nothingness when the problems of morality press hardest. Lovers of art as we are, we should be willing to sacrifice art if the gods would take from us the curse of wickedness. Better

---

[1] "Modern Painters," Vol. II, Part I, pp. 15, 16. /304/
[2] Ibid., p. 26. /304/

a dull, gray world which is good than an interesting, bright-colored life where sin festers in the soul, even while the eyes are feasting on beauty. I put this strongly in order to go as far as possible with our moral writers on esthetics. One can understand thus why Plato banished the poets so calmly. He was ready to sacrifice a lesser good to a greater good; and if his charges against the delightful arts are true, then, we consent, let them by all means be exiled. If art is immoral, we can see why Tolstoi wants it completely regenerated, and we can sympathize with the almost agonized struggle of Ruskin to save art and morality together.

But the misconception back of this is as great as the truth. Except Plato, who limits and undervalues art, these moralists expect art to do more than it possibly can. It is right to require of art that it shall not hinder morality, but it is folly to expect art to put its shoulder to the moral wheel. Indirectly, /304/ by enlarging our knowledge and our sympathies, by covert didacticism, by the general purifying and stimulating of the emotions, art may help morality, even as a man may do good because it is an immediate pleasure. But the play of art must not, cannot, be turned into the work of morality. Art decorates the house which morality tries to keep sound, but the decorator is no carpenter. If morality could do its work finally, the play of art would still go on. As it is, men must work and play too. So long as the work is first and most important, and so long as it is imperfectly done, the play must be somewhat restricted; but the play has its own place in life and need not be suspended or called by any other name. Perhaps, however, the name "play" connotes the trivial and the unessential. As Mr. Santayana says,[1] some people take the word in its frivolous sense and condemn the thing. But play means really all activity that is not forced on us by the necessity of adjusting ourselves to the conditions of life. It means not what is fruitless, but what is spontaneous, an activity for its own sake, in which, but for our imperfect adjustment to surroundings, which it is the business of work to correct, man finds his true happiness. We speak of the "play" of the senses, the "play" of the imagination, and so on. Thus art, being the product of the genius and the imagination, is play, and has its value in itself. It is a thing for man to pursue for its intrinsic worth. So long as art does not mean immoral art, "Art for art's sake" is a true and living maxim. Work is activity against hindrances; art as play, being unhindered, goes into the regions which slow-footed, plodding morality cannot reach.

As I have said, art may do work, and it is the occasional willingness of art to be of practical use that has made our moralists wish to press her forever into the service of morality. There is often, too, an element of artistic pursuit in the necessary work we do. The work of the artist himself is largely play. As Stevenson says,[2] "The most profitable work is that which combines into one continued effort the largest proportion of the powers and desires of a man's nature, in which he will know the weariness of fatigue, but not that of satiety, and which will be ever fresh, pleasing, and stimulating to his taste. . . . This is what his art should be to the true artist, and that to a degree unknown in other and less intimate pursuits." Here is indeed the pleasant element that makes a play of work; but play, as such, must not be expected to identify itself with work.

So Tolstoi has mistaken the nature of art when he has given it such a binding and special task to perform. He may ask art to be of great and serious value to man, and indeed it is and should be so, but he has not the right to expect art to help always in the drudgery of morality.

---

[1] "The Sense of Beauty," p. 27. /305/
[2] "Familiar Studies of Men and Books," Henry David Thoreau, p. 129. /305/

VI

After all this discussion of the nature and relations of art, how shall we determine what good art is and who is qualified to judge it?

It has been said that a good piece of literature is one that·has been enjoyed by many people for many years. This is definite enough for the art of the past; for recent works, we can find no infallible standard by which to weigh and classify them. There are schools which, like the old Edinburgh Reviewers, set up standards and throw to the rubbish-heap whatever in literature fails to comply with them; but there is nothing about a work of art in itself which, like the birthright of a prince, gives it immediate title to distinction. It rather undergoes a democratic election which has to be ratified from year to year before its place is assured. This, I believe, Tolstoi indirectly teaches, and his attacks on a too limited and exclusive enjoyment as the test of art are largely just. Unless, sooner or later, a large majority come in and support the individual judgment, the greatest critic in the world cannot say what shall be added to, or subtracted from, the list of the elected masterpieces. He may give reasons a-plenty for his decision, but the reasons themselves will depend on his personal like and dislike, and will stand or fall with his conclusion unless agreed to by others. A man always has a right to say, "For me, this is great art." To him, then, great art it is, and no one shall gainsay it. But when a man expresses the opinion of the majority through the ages, he can omit the "for me," and his statement becomes an impersonal fact. The decision lies with the many, not with the few. So far Tolstoi is on the right track, although his use of the word "exclusive" is paradoxically wide, and seems to apply to all the rich and cultivated taken together.

The question, then, arises, Who is eligible to help decide whether a work is good or not—who is the qualified voter? /305/

Defining art as the transfer of feeling, Tolstoi makes the supreme assumption that any sane human being can feel again the expressed feelings of another. "Good art," he says, "is always intelligible to every one." Here is a great error. Art cannot suggest to a man a feeling which he has not had before. The previous experience of a reader, his capacity in general, determines how much he shall receive of emotional pleasure or of moral stimulus from the work of a great artist. We take our little cups to the fountain of beauty and get them filled, and our cups vary in size from the littleness of ignorance and inexperience to the greatness of full appreciation. Socialism reduces us all to one caliber, and in this it falsifies the great fact of human diversity and unlikeness. It is untrue that "the great objects of art are great only because they are accessible and intelligible to all," "because the relation of every man to God is one and the same." Every man who thinks (and all men do think in some degree) has a special view of man and of God, and to him appeal only such parts of art as touch feelings possible in him kindred to those which the artist expresses. The same Book of Job, the story of Joseph, the Psalms, "Uncle Tom's Cabin," and other works that Tolstoi cites as good, mean more to one than to another, according to his temperament, his experience, and his attitude toward life.

The necessary diversity of judgment among men is the foundation of disputes about the relative values of artistic productions—disputes which Tolstoi attributes to various sorts of perverted and exclusively trained taste. As I have said, the only possible way to decide the worth of works of art is to see where there is greatest unanimity of opinion. But all who have eyes to see and ears to hear are not equally able to judge.

Who is the normal and truly qualified critic? Surely not, as Tolstoi says, the toiler of the people, although a few genuine poets may have their hands on the plow, or their shoulders under the hod. There is something so inevitable about the expression of genius, and the tendency of the man who can recognize real genius to assert himself, that no amount of hardship inflicted by the rich, no degree of corrupt culture among aristocrats, could keep the people down, if they were as pure and genuine lovers of art and poets potential as Tolstoi holds them to be. A voice from the people like Burns is a rare phenomenon. I speak here of production and enjoyment of production together, because it is true that it takes a poet to understand a poet; and, though not true of individuals, it is true of classes and of castes, that where art is appreciated, there art is produced. It has a fine sound, but it strikes wide of the truth to say that "to simple uncorrupted toilers of the people . . . the very highest is intelligible."[1] Tolstoi commends "Adam Bede." Well, I hold that it means more to a hundred callow sophomores than to a gang of horny-palmed laborers. Tolstoi brings it against our modern light opera that the honest literate workman stands agape at it. Well, so he stands agape at "Hamlet," at an oratorio of Handel, or at Homer. From the Book of Revelation he gets wild prophecies and promises which, in his ignorance of metaphorical language, his lack of historical and poetic sense, he takes with stupid literalness. I would not for a minute underrate the moral worth, integrity, and manly dignity of Tolstoi's ideal peasant, but it is absurd to think (unless he chance to be a genius clad in homespun) that he can have the finest feelings or begin to understand the highest in the very art which Tolstoi admits to be good —"Les Miserables," Dickens, the Bible, Dostoyevsky, and so on. "The highest world-concept of his time" is not present to the consciousness of the simple day-laborer; neither, on the other hand, does it dwell in the heart of the warped critical consciousness that feeds on caviar; but it is found in the cultivated man who, with his eyes open, has been out of his own village, has seen much, felt much, worked much, and tried to make the best of himself. We have thousands of such men who enjoy books and pictures—doctors, merchants, bankers, professors, lawyers; they know the world, they know as much as any one does of heaven, and they can tell what art is good more surely than the simple, "uncorrupted workman," more surely, too, than the professional critic who dwells in art until he forgets how it looks from the outside.

For a cultivated audience, it is hardly worth while to make a long argument against Tolstoi's sublimated workman as an appreciator of art; but, remember, we are all atrophied and exclusive and must let the uncorrupted toiler into our sanctuaries of art to see what he enjoys. Granted he enjoys a good deal, but can he tell a chromo from a Turner, Homer's "Iliad" from a book of fairy-tales? Probably not. Our taste may be atrophied, but he has none at all. Not to /306/ speak of works of art, does he enjoy the very country he lives in? Does he ever watch a sunset? Two summers ago I spent a month in the Susquehanna valley and made a point of asking about thirty different farmers if they did not think the valley beautiful. Yes, they usually replied, but the tobacco business wasn't what it used to be before so much was imported from Havana. A Pennsylvania farmer is surely as fine as a Russian peasant, yet he has little enough eye for things good to look at. To make him enjoy the view from his cottage door, you must educate him, teach him to use his esthetic faculty, open his mind to what is beautiful. If he cannot see the beauty of a sunset, what business has he with art? The true judge of art is the man of experience, who has been enjoying art for a long while and learning much about the life art deals with. His judgment in art, like his judgment in morals, in politics, in all wide and vital subjects, sur-

---

[1] "What is Art?" p. 148. /306/

vives the dicta of schools, because the final majority of his fellows are with him. To set the unschooled workman, whose faculties are undeveloped, above this man of general culture, not to speak of the man of preëminently high sensibility, is to destroy the highest criterion of artistic values. /307/

❧ ART CRITICISM

T. S. Knowlson

"In spite of the pretences of our democratic philosophies,
the classes whose backs are bent with manual labour are æsthetically inferior to the others."
Amiel's Journal, p. 141.

It is not at all surprising to find that Tolstoy men have been greatly interested in the problems that concern the philosophy of art. As a literary artist of the first rank, the question *What is art?* must have presented itself to him at an early stage in his career; and when one remembers that his mind is eminently philosophic in character, it becomes evident that such a question clamouring for solution could not be lightly set aside: an answer would have to be found sooner or later. In the present instance the answer was "later," for Tolstoy had more pressing matters to deal with than the underlying principles of art. He allowed himself fifteen years' study and reflection before publishing *What is Art?*

After a preliminary grumble at the conditions under which dramatic art is carried on, Tolstoy /129/ addresses himself to the real subject by drawing attention to the startling disagreements among authorities as to the essence of all art expression. In this he is quite correct: from Baumgarten to Sully and Grant Allen there has been a veritable Babel of conflicting definitions. Hardly two writers agree as to the meaning of the word Beauty. In these circumstances Tolstoy decides to eliminate the offending word altogether, and substitute the idea that art is a means of intercourse between man and man. . . . /130/

. . . Art is the expression of human feelings with a view to infect others with like feelings, and the feelings themselves may be good, bad, or indifferent. The only doubt arises out of the last clause. Good art we know, and indifferent art we know, but what is bad art? It is the clever and effective expression of debasing feelings, but it is still art, for the greatest gifts of expression may be defiled by the choice of an ignoble subject. Is there, then, no rule which lays down the legitimate subject-matter of art? Tolstoy is ready with an answer. The rule enacts the transmitting of "the highest feelings to which humanity has attained, those flowing from the religious perceptions." And what is a religious perception? It is "an understanding of the meaning of life which represents the highest level to which men of any period of society have attained, — an understanding defining the highest good at which that society aims."² Lest a narrow meaning should still be attached to the phrase "religious perception," it may be wise to add the testimony of Mr. Aylmer /132/ Maude, concerning whose Introduction to *What is Art?* Tolstoy is enthusiastic. Mr. Maude says the subject-matter of what we in our day can esteem as being the best art, is of two kinds only: —

(1) "Feelings flowing from the highest perception now attainable by man, of our right relation to our neighbour and to the source from which we come. Of

---

"Art Criticism," in *Leo Tolstoy: A Biographical and Critical Study* (London and New York: Frederick Warne and Co., 1904), pp. 129–142.

² *Ibid.* [*What is Art?*], p. 156. /132/

such art, Dickens's *Christmas Carol*, uniting us in a more vivid sense of compassion and love, is a ready example.

(2) "The simple feelings of common life, accessible to every one, provided that they are such as do not hinder progress towards well-being. Art of this kind makes us realise to how great an extent we already are members one of another, sharing the feelings of one common nature." Tolstoy's "religious perception" is consequently something more than the phrase would connote to the average English mind; it includes elements that are social and humanitarian — in the popular sense of the word. This is well stated in Tolstoy's concluding chapter. "The destiny of art in our time is to transmit from the realm of reason to the realm of feeling, the truth that well-being for men consists in being united together, and to set up in place of the existing reign of force that kingdom of God — *i.e.* of love — which we all recognise to be the highest aim of human life."[2] /133/

Such is the Tolstoyan conception of art. How does its author defend it? As might be expected, he defends it with considerable ingenuity and acuteness. That art should unite all men together, seems at first sight a plea without much to be said in its favour, but Tolstoy's breezy criticisms of "upper class art," with its exclusiveness and intolerable inanity, are not only good reading, but serve as real guides to the man who, in art, is trying to work out his own salvation. It is contended, and not without truth, that scepticism — or narrow-mindedness — has impoverished the subject-matter of art, diminished the scope of its audience, and deprived the artist of his first claim to attention, — sincerity. Many pages are devoted to evidences said to support his threefold indictment. There are palpable weaknesses in the chain of argument, notably the attempt to pick out instances of good art. Tolstoy selects Schiller's *The Robbers*, Victor Hugo's *Les Misérables*, Dickens's *The Tale of Two Cities*, Stowe's *Uncle Tom's Cabin*, Dostoievsky's *Memoirs from the House of Death*, and George Eliot's *Adam Bede* as samples of the best work; and after pouring contempt on the productions of many a great name in music, painting, and poetry, he adds the following damaging confession: — "I attach no special importance to my selection; for besides being insufficiently informed in all branches of art, I belong to the class of people whose taste has by false training been perverted. And there- /134/ fore my old, inured habits may cause me to err, and I may mistake for absolute merit the impression a work produced on me in my youth. My only purpose in mentioning examples of works of this or that class is to make my meaning clearer, and to show how, with my present views, I understand excellence in art in relation to its subject-matter. I must, moreover, mention that I consign my own artistic productions to the category of bad art, excepting the story *God sees the Truth*, which seeks a place in the first class, and *The Prisoner of the Caucasus*, which belongs to the second."[1] This passage is thoroughly Tolstoyan in its courage, the courage which despoils fine creations about whose message and meaning it stands in doubt, and the courage which does not hesitate to demolish the claims of *Anna Karenina* to a place in the temple of fame. But such courage argues the lack of a faculty that is *par excellence* the test of critical values, — discrimination; and Tolstoy by the confession just quoted not only exhibits his own poverty of judgment, but weakens the foundations on which his criticism of art is built.

To enter the lists against Tolstoy might appear to be an action demanding as much courage as that shown by the Russian prophet himself, but a survey of the whole position will give the reader the required confidence. Take, first of all, the arguments adduced to prove that professionalism /135/ in art is the cause of

[1] Introduction to *What is Art?* p. xvii. /133/
[2] *What is Art?* p. 211. /133/
[1] *What is Art?* p. 170. /135/

perverted taste. Tolstoy does not believe in men living on an income derived from producing objects of art: the need of an income compels them to create stories, novels, and poems which lack the note of sincerity, or to paint pictures and compose music similarly defective. There is enough truth in the remark to keep it from sinking, but if it really means that the greatest art was never paid for, whilst third-rate stuff always fetched its price, one cannot but disagree. Shakespeare was an artist and a man of business who made his profession remunerative, and Sir Walter Scott loses nothing of his reputation because he wrote for money. In view of Tolstoy's sense of the importance of art,[1] it is a little surprising that he will allow no man to be set apart and ordained to that work, but further reflection brings to mind the fact that a separate consecration to art would disarrange the social scheme whereby it is decreed a living must be obtained by the work of one's hands. In Tolstoy's world the artist is required to be a layman. And as for the *art critic*,—well, he is exterminated. "If a work be good as art, then the feeling expressed by the artist—be it moral or immoral—transmits itself to other people. If transmitted to others, then they feel it, and all interpretations are superfluous."[2] This is a hard knock for both artist and critic. If the artist has not made his meaning clear and needs the help of a /136/ professional expositor, it is very bad for the artist; and if the expression of feeling is plain even to the simplest, it is equally bad for the critic, inasmuch as his services are quite unnecessary. But after all it is only Tolstoyan art that needs no interpretation: *Uncle Tom's Cabin* to wit. To select an audience of peasants and express feelings so that they will appreciate them without assistance of any kind, is to produce art that the educated folk will certainly understand; but will they or ought they to be satisfied with it? The question will come up again later on, when the main thesis is discussed. Let it be sufficient here and now to say that there is too much affectation and something that is a good deal worse about the art criticism of the day, and it is easy to endorse the verdict of Ossip Lourié, one of Tolstoy's disciples: "Mais le critique déploie plus souvent son propre *moi* que celui de l'artiste."[1] But even Ossip Lourié does not crawl on all-fours after his master. He says, "On croit généralement que le critique doit montrer ce que le poéte ou l'artiste n'a pas assez montré, il doit ouvrir ce qui n'est qu' entr' ouvert, il doit déployer."[2] The artist *par excellence* often builds better than he knows,—Tolstoy in his *Anna Karenina* for example,—and it is part of the critic's function to interpret art products in relation to their creators, to products of a similar character, and to the surrounding life. /137/

Schools of art fare no better than art critics. Technique occupies little place in Tolstoy's rigid scheme. If a man can't write or paint, no school can teach him, —he says. True, but it can teach him much that is helpful. No school can impart quality and power to a voice, but it can educate the gifts of nature, and thus justify the sole object of its existence.

The main thesis of Tolstoy's *What is Art?* is this,—that every work of art should be of such a nature that everybody coming in contact with it will instantly receive the artist's feeling, and be the better for it. There is an amplitude of brotherhood in this idea, but there is not much else. It is an attempt to force the world of art by the power of pure arithmetic. Why should mere numbers of themselves decide so important an issue? If five hundred farmers dislike a pic-

---

[1] *What is Art?* p. 51. /136/

[2] *Ibid.,* p. 119. /136/

[1] *La Philosophie de Tolstoï,* p. 174. /137/ ["But the critic more often unfolds his own self than that of the artist."]

[2] *Ibid.,* p. 174. /137/ ["One generally believes that the critic ought to show what the poet or artist has not shown enough of, he ought to open what is partially open, he ought to unfold."]

ture, or see nothing in it, and five other men praise it highly, does the larger number carry the day apart from the principles of art criticism? To the discerning mind neither the five hundred nor the five mean anything at all apart from the reasons they give for approval or disapproval. And yet the bulk of mere votes is part and parcel of Tolstoy's method of valuation. "The only advantage," he says, "the art I acknowledge has over decadent art lies in the fact that the art I recognise is comprehensible to a somewhat larger number of people than present-day art."[1] If this be the only /138/ advantage, we cannot but see on how flimsy a basis the whole superstructure is made to rest.

In furtherance of his contention that art should be understood by those who follow manual pursuits, Tolstoy says, "For the great majority of our working people, our art, besides being inaccessible on account of its costliness, is strange in its very nature, transmitting as it does the feelings of people far removed from those conditions of laborious life which are natural to the great body of humanity."[1] But can these far-removed people help having different feelings from working men? Of course in a Tolstoy world there would be no such people at all; but, granting their existence, it follows as a necessary consequence that variety of life and occupation will evolve variety in feeling and expression. The best answer to Tolstoy is furnished by a luminous article from the pen of Mr. A. E. Fletcher, of whom it is not too much to say that he is on other matters most strongly in sympathy with Tolstoy. In criticising the views expressed by Mr. E. J. Dallas in his *Gay Science*, Mr. Fletcher admits that "undoubtedly art is for all, and no man has the shadow of a claim to the title of great poet unless he is possessed of the enthusiasm of humanity, and hears in his soul the music not only of 'earth in its woods, and water in its waves,' but of 'man in his multitudes.' But it is simply because art is for all that few only can /139/ appreciate it at first, for the majority of men are the victims of ignorance and prejudice and selfishness; and it is impossible, therefore, that they can appreciate that which is great by reason of its freedom from these characteristics, until at least their nobler instincts have been awakened by the contemplation of perfection. Christianity is for all, but the greatest Christians are just those who during their lifetime are least appreciated in this world. 'Not this man, but Barabbas,' howled the mob in the judgment hall of Pilate, when the choice was given them of deciding for the Founder of Christianity Himself or for a notorious robber."[1] And did not Christ Himself recognise the right of selecting an audience? "Cast not your pearls before swine." Incapacity to receive this message was no detriment to an apostle; it ascribed no direct blame to the hearer, neither did it suggest the weakness of the gospel message. It is thus with the message of art. If a great artist expresses himself in poetry, in painting, in fiction, or in marble, and the multitude do not understand him, what then? Let the multitude wait. A great soul needs a great interpreter,—this is really why we have a place for the true critic in our midst. The multitude waited for Shakespeare to be revealed, and for Browning and Wordsworth to create a taste for themselves.

The working class—the peasantry—those whose /140/ mental density Tolstoy has so mercilessly portrayed in *Resurrection*—do not exert claims for a first place in the artist's thought: they have more sense than that. It is the anxiety of the socialist system-maker to effect a harmonious body of doctrine which is responsible for such jejune proposals. Tolstoy has much to say of Ruskin that is good, and they are both agreed on the abomination of railways. Let us therefore hear Ruskin: "It is an insult to what is really great in art or literature to suppose

---

[1] *What is Art?* p. 20. /138/
[1] *What is Art?* p. 71. /139/
[1] "The Philosophy of Art," *The New Age*, 30th Dec. 1897. /140/

that it in any way addresses itself to mean or uncultivated faculties. No man can be really appreciated but by his equal or superior. . . . The question of the merit of artwork is decided at first by a few, by fewer in proportion as the merits of the work are of a higher order."

To sum up. Tolstoy is to be congratulated on the vigorous way in which he clears the ground at the beginning of *What is Art?* We were more than weary of a hundred different kinds of "beauty," of "ideals" and "theories" and "manners." Consequently it was refreshing to come across a simple definition, viz. that art is the expression of human feelings with a view to infect others with like feelings,—the feelings themselves being good, bad, or indifferent. There is little to quarrel with, so far; but when Tolstoy begins to expound his position, we soon find cause to dissent. How are we to distinguish good art from bad art? By "religious /141/ perception," which signifies an understanding of the meaning of life; in other words, a knowledge of the highest good. Any picture, poem, or statue that fails to minister to this end is bad art. Perhaps so, but much depends on the accuracy of the words as here used. The "meaning of life" and the "highest good" are elastic terms, and novels which to our mind minister to both would be condemned by Tolstoy. The plain truth is that with him good art is an exploitation of the sense of brotherhood and mutual helpfulness, and all else is bad art. If a man has a feeling to transmit to his fellows, he is bound by the law of the greatest number, that is, he must simplify his feeling and rob it of every trace of personality so as to make it plain to those who are most numerous,—the working classes. In itself the aim is morally commendable, but it is impossible of accomplishment, and for that reason is absurd. An art whose sole advantage lies in its being appreciated by the greatest number of people is not an art that is likely to live; it is against facts as we know them. Moreover, it is hardly the kind of doctrine that should come from a man who elsewhere speaks of "the narrow-minded people who compose the multitude."[1] And if these people are the best critics, where is there one among their number who can write an analysis like Tolstoy's *Guy de Maupassant?* /142/

⌘ TOLSTOI ON ART

Arthur Symons

I

The theory which makes feeling the test of art, and an ennobling influence upon the emotions the aim of art, has never received so signal a discomfiture as in the book by Tolstoi, called "What is Art?" in which that theory is put forward as the only possible one, and carried, in the most logical way, to its final conclusions. Tolstoi, as it seems to me, is more essentially a man of genius than any writer now living. He has carried the methods of the novel further into the soul of man than any novelist who ever lived; and he has at the same time rendered the common details of life with a more absolute illusion of reality than any one else. Since he has given up writing novels, he has written a study of the Christian religion which seems to me, from the strictly Christian point of view, to leave nothing more to be said; and he has followed out his own conclusions in

[1] *Vicious Pleasures,* p. 25. /142/

"Tolstoi on Art," in *Studies in Prose and Verse* (New York: E. P. Dutton and Co., 1904), pp. 173–182.

life with the same logic as that with which he has carried them out in writing. He is unique in our time in having made every practical sacrifice to his own ideal. Everything he writes, therefore, we are bound to receive with that respect which is due alike to every man of genius and to every man of unflinching sincerity. It is impossible that he should write anything which is without a value of its own, not necessarily the value which he himself attaches to it. It may scarcely seem, indeed, that Tolstoi has much more of the necessary equipment for writing a book on art than, let us say, Bunyan would /173/ have had. Yet if Bunyan had sat down to write a book on art, in which he had given us his real opinion of Milton in the present and Shakespeare in the past, such a book, if it had told us nothing worth knowing about Shakespeare and Milton, would still have been well worth reading, for the sake of Bunyan himself and of the better understanding of that Puritan conscience which Bunyan embodied. In the same way this book of Tolstoi's, trying as it is to read, and little as it tells us about the questions it sets out to enlighten, has an undeniable value as the utterance of Tolstoi, and as the legitimate *reductio ad absurdum* of theories which have had so many more cautious and less honest defenders.

Tolstoi is not an abstract thinker, a philosopher by temperament, though he has come finally to have a consistent philosophy of life, not, as with Nietzsche, a mere bundle of intuitions. His mind is logical, and it is also that of a man of action: it goes straight to conclusions, and acts upon them, promptly and humbly. He desires, first of all, to become clear himself, to "save his own soul"; then he will act upon others by the instinctive exercise of his goodness, of what he is, not by some external reform. All his reforms would begin with the head and with the heart; he would "convince" the world of what to him is righteousness, taking it for granted that men will naturally do what they see ought to be done. Thus he has no belief in Socialism or in Anarchism, in any mechanical readjustment of things which is not the almost unconscious result of a personal feeling or conviction. To Tolstoi the one question is: What is the purpose of my life? and his answer, explains the interpreter, is this: "The purpose of my life is to understand, and, as far as possible, to do, the will of that Power which has sent /174/ me here, and which actuates my reason and conscience." Preferring, as he tells us, to seek goodness "by the head" rather than "by the heart," to begin with the understanding, he has none of the artist's disinterested interest in "problems," as Ibsen, for instance, has. When Ibsen concerns himself with questions of conduct, with the "meaning of life," he has no interest in their solution, only in their development, caring only to track the evil, not to cure it. They are his material, from which he holds himself as far aloof as the algebraist from his *x*. Now Tolstoi is what he is just because he has been through all this, and has found himself compelled to leave it behind. He is a personality, and the artist in him has never been more than a part of his personality. Tolstoi first lived, then wrote, now he draws the moral from both careers, working upon life itself rather than upon a painting after life. His final attitude is the postscript adding a conclusion to his novels. As a novelist he had kept closer to actual life, to the dust of existence, than any other novelist; so that "Anna Karenina" is perhaps more painful to read than any other novel. It gives us body and soul, and it also gives us the clothes of life, society. There are none of the disguises of the novelist with a style, or of the novelist with a purpose. It is so real that it seems to be speaking to us out of our own hearts and out of our own experience. It is so real because it is the work of one to whom life is more significant than it is to any other novelist. Thus the final step, the step which every novelist, if he goes far enough, may be impelled, by the mere logic of things, to take, is easier, more inevitable, for him than for any other. The novelist, more than any other artist, is concerned directly with life. He has to watch the passions at work in the world, the shipwreck of ideals, the action /175/ of society upon man, of man upon society. When he is tired of considering these things with the unimpassioned eyes of the artist, he begins to concern himself about them very painfully: he becomes a moralist. Perhaps he has been one: he becomes a reformer.

Tolstoi's theory of art, then, is this: "There is one indubitable indication distinguishing real art from its counterfeit, namely, the infectiousness of art. If a man, without exercising effort and without altering his standpoint, on reading, hearing, or seeing another man's work, experiences a mental condition which unites him with that man, and with other people who also partake of that work of art, then the object evoking that condition is a work of art. . . . And not only is infection a sure sign of art, but the degree of infectiousness is also the sole measure of excellence in art." Art, thus distinguished, is to be divided into two classes; first, religious art, and secondly, universal art. "The first, religious art—transmitting both positive feelings of love to God and one's neighbour, and negative feelings of indignation and horror at the violation of love—manifests itself chiefly in the form of words, and to some extent also in painting and sculpture: the second kind (universal art), transmitting feelings accessible to all, manifests itself in words, in painting, in sculpture, in dances, in architecture, and, most of all, in music."

Now here is a theory which, in the cautious hands of most critics, would produce but one result. We should be told that, judged by such a standard, modern writers were all wrong and older writers all right; that Verlaine, Huysmans, Manet, Liszt, Rodin, had departed from the "obvious," or the "well-recognised," or the "inevitable," or the "classical" lines of religious and universal art, while Shakespeare, Goethe, Raphael, Bach, Michelangelo, remained, perfect in their several /176/ ways, to show us by their perfection the laws which our uncouth and extravagant generation had broken. But this is not at all what the theory really means, and Tolstoi shows us what it really means. Tolstoi shows us that on this theory we have to get rid of the "rude, savage, and, for us, often meaningless works of the ancient Greeks: Sophocles, Euripides, Æschylus, and especially Aristophanes; of modern writers, Dante, Tasso, Milton, Shakespeare"; in painting, Michelangelo's "absurd Last Judgment," and "every representation of miracles, including Raphael's 'Transfiguration' "; in music, everything but "Bach's famous violin *aria,* Chopin's nocturne in E flat major, and perhaps a dozen bits (not whole pieces, but parts) selected from the works of Haydn, Mozart, Schubert, Beethoven, and Chopin." On the other hand, we are to accept "as examples of the highest art, flowing from love of God and man (both of the higher, positive, and of the lower, negative kind)," in literature: "The Robbers," by Schiller, Victor Hugo's "Les Pauvres Gens" and "Les Misérables," the novels and stories of Dickens, "The Tale of Two Cities," "The Christmas Carol," "The Chimes," and others; "Uncle Tom's Cabin," Dostoieffski's works, especially his "Memoirs from the House of Death," and "Adam Bede," by George Eliot; in painting, a picture by Walter Langley, in the Royal Academy of 1897, "a picture by the French artist Morlon," pictures by Millet, "and, particularly, his drawing, 'The Man with the Hoe,' also pictures in this style by Jules Breton, L'Hermitte, Drefregger, and others"; all of which Tolstoi has seen only in reproductions.

Here, then, is what the theory really leads to; and it cannot be said that Tolstoi is less emphatic in his condemnation of contemporary art than of that art which /177/ we are accustomed to call classical. Wagner is "only a limited, self-opinionated German of bad taste and bad style"; Baudelaire and Verlaine were "two versifiers, who were far from skilful in form and most contemptible and commonplace in subject matter"; some of Kipling's short stories are "absolutely unintelligible both in form and in substance"; his own works are all bad art, except two short stories, "God sees the Truth," and "The Prisoner of the Caucasus"; and in one of his lists of "spurious counterfeits of art," we are scornfully told that "people of our time and of our society are delighted with Baudelaires, Verlaines, Moréases, Ibsens, and Maeterlincks in poetry; with Monets, Manets, Puvis de Chavannes, Burne-Joneses, Stucks and Böcklins in painting; with Wagners, Liszts, Richard Strausses, in music; and they are no longer capable of comprehending either the highest or the simplest art." A good deal of this is what we have so often heard, from such very different lips. But never before has any one been keen-sighted enough, and honest enough, to see and admit how logically one-half of this condemnation depends on the other. Our critics have condemned Wagner for the qualities by which they have come to praise Beethoven; Verlaine for the innovations which they applaud in Hugo; Rodin for the imagination which they adore in Michelangelo. It is only Tolstoi who sees that all these artists are obeying, in their various measures, in their various ways, the same laws; that to condemn one is to condemn all the others as well: and he condemns all.

II

Tolstoi's theory of art, which we have found to lead to what is practically the entire condemnation of art, /178/ with a few arbitrary exceptions, is based on a generous social doctrine of equality, a conviction of the "brotherhood of man," and a quite unjustifiable assumption that art is no more than "an organ of progress." To Tolstoi it seems astonishing that any one at the present day should be found to maintain the conception of beauty held by the Greeks; that "the very best that can be done by the art of nations after nineteen hundred years of Christian teaching is to choose as the ideal of their life the ideal that was held by a small, semi-savage, slave-holding people who lived two thousand years ago, who imitated the nude human body extremely well, and erected buildings pleasant to look at." Yet he himself selects as examples of "good, supreme art" the "Iliad," the "Odyssey," the stories of Isaac, Jacob, and Joseph, the Hebrew prophets, the Psalms, the Gospel parables, the story of Sakya Muni, and the hymns of the Vedas; and I do not think he would contend that his list of modern works of art (Dickens, Dostoieffski, George Eliot, "Uncle Tom's Cabin," and the rest) shows any artistic or spiritual advance upon those masterpieces of the very earliest ages. If, then, the only modern works which he admits to be written on sound principles cannot for a moment be compared with the ancient works to which he gives the same theoretic sanction, what room is left for astonishment that an ideal of art, divined two thousand years ago, should still remain essentially the highest ideal of art?

Closely linked with this confusion of art with progress is another application of Socialistic theories to questions of art, not less demonstrably false. "A good and lofty work of art," he tells us, "may be incomprehensible, but not to simple, unperverted labourers (all that is highest is understood by them)." And he declares that the "Iliad" and "Odyssey," the Bible narratives, /179/ including the Prophetic Books, and the other masterpieces of ancient art of which I have given his list, are "quite comprehensible now to us, educated or uneducated, as they were comprehensible to the men of those times, long ago, who were even less educated than our labourers." But such a statement is absolutely unjustifiable: it has no foundation in fact. The "Iliad," to an English labourer, would be completely unintelligible. Imagine him sitting down to the simplest translation which exists in English, the prose translation of Lang, Butcher, and Leaf; imagine him reading: "Upon the flaming chariot set she her foot, and grasped her heavy spear, great and stout, wherewith she vanquisheth the ranks of men, even of heroes with whom she of the awful sire is wroth!" To the English labourer the Bible comes with an authority which no other book possesses for him; he certainly reads it, but does he read with an intelligent pleasure, does he really understand, large portions of the Prophetic Books? It is as certain that he does not as it is certain that he does read with pleasure, and understand, the Gospel parables and the stories of Isaac, Jacob, and Joseph. But does this fact of his understanding one, and not understanding the other, set the parables higher as art than the Prophetic Books, or the stories of Isaac, Jacob, and Joseph higher than the "Iliad"? On Tolstoi's own theory it would do so, but would Tolstoi himself follow his theory to that extremity?

To such precipices are we led at every moment by the theory which makes feeling the test of art. Tolstoi tells us that he once saw a performance of "Hamlet" by Rossi, and that he "experienced all the time that peculiar suffering which is caused by false imitations of works of art." He read a description of a theatrical performance by savages, and from the mere description /180/ he "felt that this was a true work of art." Is this quite fair to the instincts, is it not a little deliberate, a choice decided upon beforehand rather than a simple record of personal feeling? Even if it is a preference as instinctive as it is believed to be, of what value is the mere preference of one man, even a man of genius; and of what value in the defining of a work of art is it for any number of people to tell me that it has caused them a genuine emotion? Come with me to the Adelphi; there, in no matter what melodrama, you shall see a sorrowful or heroic incident, acted, as it seems to you, so livingly before you, that it shall make you hot or cold with suspense, or bring tears to your eyes. Yet neither you nor I shall differ in our judgment of the melodrama as a work of art; and Tolstoi, if he were to see it, would certainly condemn it, from his own point of view, as strongly as you or I. Yet it has answered, in your case or mine, to his own test of a work of art; and certainly, to the quite simple-minded or uneducated people there present, it has been accepted without any critical afterthought as entirely satisfying.

No, neither the uneducated judgment nor the instincts of the uneducated can ever come to have more than the very slightest value in the determination of what is true or false in art. A genuine democracy of social condition may or may not be practically possible; but the democracy of intellect, happily, is impossible. There, at all events, we must always find an aristocracy; there, at all events, the stultifying dead-weight of equality must for ever be spared to us. In material matters, even, in matters most within his reach, has the labourer ever been able to understand a machine, which he will come in time to prize for its service, until it has been laboriously explained to him, and, for the most part, forced /181/ upon him for his good? How, then, is he to understand a poem, which must always continue to seem to him a useless thing, useless at all events to him? Tolstoi, throughout the whole of this book on art, has tried to reduce himself intellectually, as, in practice, he has reduced himself socially, to the level of the peasant. And, with that extraordinary power of assimilation which the Russians possess, he has very nearly succeeded. It is a part of the Russian character to be able to live a fictitious life, to be more western than the Westerns, more sympathetic, out of indolence and the dramatic faculty, than one's intimate friends. And Tolstoi, who is in every way so typically a Russian, has in addition the genius of the novelist. So he is now putting himself in the place of the peasant, speaking through the peasant's mouth, in all these doctrines and theories, just as he used to put himself in the place of the peasant, and speak through the peasant's mouth, in his stories. The fatal difference is that, in the stories, he knew that he was speaking dramatically, while, in the doctrines and theories, he imagines that he is speaking in his own person. /182/

※ TOLSTOY

L. William Flaccus

> *Why, where but in the sense and soul of me, Art's judge?*
> *Browning.*

In 1880 Turgenief on a visit to Yasnaya Polyana found Tolstoy much changed: feverishly at work making himself over, pondering God and the universe. With this plunge into self-analysis and mysticism he had little sympathy; he referred to it with indulgent cynicism in a letter to a friend: "Every one kills his fleas in his own way." He feared a loss to Russian literature; few appreciated as he did Tolstoy's art, fine in its characterization, healthy in its animalism, and of an epic breadth. Was this "great writer of our Russian land" to turn ascetic and moralist? Three years later Turgenief sent from what proved to be his death-bed an appeal to Tolstoy not to forsake literature.

The appeal went unheeded. Tolstoy unceremoniously bowed himself off the stage of art and definitely became a critic of life and a social reformer. Never afterward did his work escape the cramping coils of moral purpose. He wrote simple stories for /140/ the peasants, philosophical essays, pamphlets and manifestoes on questions of the day: all of them very sincere; some of them very true; none of them from an artistic point of view worthy of his earlier work. Even when he turns to the novel, as he did in *Resurrection*, good material is washed bare of artistic possibilities by too strong a moral corrosive.

There are many who deplore this change — this bending to the moral yoke — and look with a great deal of distrust on the great crisis in Tolstoy's life. Conversion, they hold, may possibly be good for the man, but assuredly is fatal to the artist. A distorted view of life, they say, has reacted unfavorably on Tolstoy's art and view of art. It is easy to see some grounds for such criticism; if a theory is no stronger than its weakest dictum or application, little can be said in favor of Tolstoy's political, moral, and æsthetic theories; and least of all can be said in favor of his views on art. What can be held of a man who regards King Lear as a mere clutter of improbabilities and denies Shakespeare grasp, sense of measure, and true characterization; of one who rejects Dante and Michael Angelo nonchalantly, and shows as little understanding of the trenchant intellectualism of Ibsen as he does of the elusive art of Maeterlinck or Baudelaire and the rich art of Boecklin, Beethoven, and Wagner? These erratic views are expressed in two essays: *What is Art?* published in 1898, and *Shakespeare*, /141/ in 1906. They cannot be set to the score of old age, for nothing could be more virile than Tolstoy at eighty; besides, letters, diaries, reminiscences prove that many of them extend back to ripe manhood. For years Tolstoy tried to force Shakespeare on himself, always without success. "I invariably

"Tolstoy," in *Artists and Thinkers* (New York: Longmans, Green, and Co., Inc., 1916), pp. 140–160.

underwent the same feelings: repulsion, weariness, and bewilderment." It would be quite as unfair to set aside because of them Tolstoy's whole theory of art, and to ask: Why consider a blind man's theory of color? To deny that a great artist like Tolstoy has some understanding at least of the essentials of beauty, is too much like going at things with a scoop. Limited in range his feeling for art certainly is, for he could not enjoy verse and its music, and so misjudged the Symbolists utterly. When he tests King Lear by means of retelling the plot in the baldest possible prose, he overlooks the meaning of poetic pitch of character and incident. Highly complex forms of art he could not appreciate, but within this range and its racial, personal and cultural limits his appreciation of art is genuine and in the main convincing and sound; and what is true of his art holds also of his judgment of art: it is truest when nearest the soil. That is why he has such a fine feeling for Homer and for the rich, earthy art of folk-song and folk-epic. Nor is it safe to regard the crisis for which *My Confession* stands as a sudden wrenching free which ever after /142/ left a moral twist. Some influence must be admitted; some warping of judgment and some estrangement from the artistic as such. But, after all, Tolstoy's art, at its earliest and even at its best, has a moral strain to it. The problem of the reshaping of character is not peculiar to *Resurrection;* it appears in *Anna Karenina* and still earlier in terse and virile form in *The Cossacks;* the question of the meaning of life, which Tolstoy came to use as the test of art, haunts Besuchoff in *War and Peace* and Levin in *Anna Karenina,* and figures prominently as far back as 1852 in the unfinished novel *Youth.* In view of this it is absurd to say that Tolstoy's attitude toward art at some definite time came within the deep shadow of a moral eclipse.

The truth of the matter seems to be this: Back of Tolstoy's art criticisms is a definite and thoughtful theory of art and its relation to life, a theory worked out gradually and unevenly. Erratic as it is, it is much stronger than its weakest link. True or false, it is at least vital; partly because it is himself—his personality caught in one of its sincerest expressive movements—and reflects the directness, massiveness, and liveness of his interests; partly because it comes from a creative genius; partly because it is a cultural theory of art: a peculiarly earnest attempt to connect art with life and to see the values of art in relation to whatever else of value a /143/ fixed will and a hungry imagination can snatch from life. It is therefore entitled to a hearing.

Tolstoy's essay on Guy de Maupassant, written in 1894, gives interesting matter. We are told that in 1881 Turgenief brought him the *Maison Tellier* collection of stories. It was an ill-chosen moment. "That particular period, the year 1881, was for me the fiercest time of the inner reconstruction of my whole understanding of life, and in this reconstruction those employments called the Fine Arts, to which I had formerly given all my power, had not only lost all their former importance in my eyes, but had become altogether obnoxious to me owing to the unnatural position they had hitherto occupied in my life, and which they generally occupy in the estimation of people of the wealthy classes." Maupassant did not escape this general disfavor. His workmanship was admired, but much of his material found repellent, and his attitude towards life, ill-defined. Later when he came back to Maupassant and read *Une Vie* his estimate changed. Here he saw what he had thought lacking and what he was fast coming to regard as the essential of good art. The essay reflects this juster estimate, and in it are to be found Tolstoy's four tests of good art.

The first of these four art tests is *genius*, that is, "the faculty of intense, strenuous attention, applied according to the author's tastes to this or that /144/ subject; and by means of which the possessor of this capacity sees the things to which he applies his attention in some new aspect overlooked by others." There must, in short, be a close and fresh view of things. Again, there must be *beauty of expression.* The third quality demanded is *sincerity:* an earnestness burnt into its material. The fourth is "*a correct, that is, moral relation of the author to his subject.*" All these he finds in most of Maupassant's work.

These four tests, with the emphasis thrown sharply on the fourth, give the key to Tolstoy's theory of art, but only if they are understood in their psychological sources and in the drift of their logic. With the first three this is a simple matter, for it is not difficult to understand and to justify genius, sincerity, and clearness and beauty of expression as tests of good art. Nor is the problem of source difficult: they reflect much in Tolstoy's character and are in turn reflected in his art. Nothing could be more earnest, surer in touch and bolder in design than some of his character studies; in his descriptions no detail is too minute for a sharp, searching, vitalizing imagination. The snowstorm in *Master and Servant* is wonderfully true; so are the descriptions of dumb animals, the battle canvases and gambling scenes in *War and Peace.* Nothing escapes him: he is equally at home in the hot life of the steppes and in the jaded life of the salon. He catches with /145/ photographic accuracy the homely doings of peasant life and the unobtrusive panorama of nature—soil, wind, and weather. As for the source from which these three demands spring, it is to be found in the quality of directness which marks Tolstoy the man above all else. The desire to live earnestly and to see clearly was with him almost an obsession; so downright and energetic is he in his search that he often fails to judge cautiously and sanely; revealing a most perplexing blend of idealist and straight, none too subtle, common-sense thinker; and yet this directness in its good variants marks what is best in his art, in shaping his studies of peasant character, for instance.

The fourth art test is, however, the one most heavily staked. An author is to have "a correct, that is, moral relation" to his subject. Two questions immediately shake themselves free: What is meant by a right, or moral relation? What is considered a right, or moral relation?

As to the first question, one set of clues is given by the essay itself. Maupassant's short stories are praised because they bring out so sharply the awful disillusionment of animal love. This might suggest moralizing and a "wages of sin" idea. Nothing is more congenial to the Anglo-Saxon and more distasteful to the Frenchman. It would be idle to deny that Tolstoy often moralizes in just this way, in his later short stories especially. It is the peasant's greed or /146/ his shiftlessness and love of vodka that is the distressingly obvious moral lesson of such tales as *How much Land does a Man Require?* and *How the Little Devil Atoned for the Crust of Bread.* But here Tolstoy has something else in mind. "An artist is only an artist because he sees things not as he wishes to see them, but as they are." That is the voice of the great realist who by the mere relentless handling of cause and effect gives the shattering of Anna Karenina's life impressively and objectively with no attempt at moralizing. What Tolstoy means is that art must be rooted in a *Weltanschauung,* a life attitude, and that this, and not character or plot, is the true principle of unity in a novel or a play. Life is thought to have an inherent moral quality; this the true artist is to give intensely and objectively. If he takes life piecemeal his art becomes false and insignificant. Just as there is one position from which an object of sense yields itself most fully, so there is one point of view from which life is held to disclose its meaning. So we are to ask the artist: "From what standpoint will you illumine life for me?" Discussing a young Russian writer of great promise, Tolstoy said that while he admired the artistic quality of his work he failed to find in it a definite philosophy of life.

True art then must give a clear, undistorted reflection of life and its meaning. An artist must first of all understand life in all its elemental force and in all /147/ its puzzling reaches. All this might be mere phrase or pose; and there are many with whom philosophy is either or both. Not so with Tolstoy, for with him the problem of life is an urgent, pressing one; it is the very hunger of his existence. He comes back to it again and again; his letters and diaries are full of self-analysis, confessions, self-damnings. Curiously intent on living earnestly and seeing clearly, he jots down his master faults, maps out studies and methods of discipline, launches and questions all manner of thoughts; and all this with little or no trace of the morbid, and in the midst of much riotous living. But life for many years proved too sweet in the living for more than mere foreshadow-ings of that great spiritual crisis of which *My Confession* gives so intense and sincere an account. No one who fails to see the significance of that crisis can understand the high seriousness of his view of art. Tolstoy was in his forties, in good health, happily married, a successful writer, successful in the experi-ments in peasant schooling he had tried on his estates, when the craving for a rational view of life caught him full sweep and drove him to the very edge of despair.

> "My life had come to a sudden stop. I was able to breathe, to eat, to drink, to sleep. I could not, indeed, help doing so; but there was no real life in me. I had not a single wish to strive for the fulfilment of what I could feel to be reasonable. If /148/ I wished for anything, I knew beforehand that, were I to satisfy the wish, nothing would come of it; I should still be dissatisfied."

> "I knew not what I wanted, I was afraid of life; I shrank from it, and yet there was something I hoped for from it.
> "Such was the condition I had come to, at a time when all the conditions of my life were preëminently happy ones, and when I had not reached my fiftieth year . . . Moreover my mind was neither deranged nor weakened; on the contrary, I enjoyed a mental and physical strength which I have sel-dom found in men of my class and pursuits: I could keep up with a peasant in mowing, and could continue mental labor for ten hours at a stretch without any evil consequences."

All this doubt and this anguish, as of a man starving, crystallize about the question: Is Life "an evil and absurdity"? which is the problem of *My Confes-sion*. Curiously enough it at first takes on a selfish cast. "What am I with all my desires?" Why set mind to purpose or hand to work when the outcome must be decay and death? Tolstoy, to whom by temperament the aspect of death was horrible, had come to feel that the thought of this fleetingness and decay would embitter every joy and cripple every aim. "I, like Sakya Muni, could not drive to the pleasure ground when I knew of the existence of old age, suffering and death." It is the world old cry of anguish in the presence of change and of death, /149/ the great denier. But another question appears in a passage like the following: "Why do I live? — The question was, why should I live, i.e., what of real and imperishable will come of my shadowy and perishable life — what meaning has my finite existence in the infinite universe?" Nothing could be sharper than the contrast between this question and the one originally asked: that was a problem of satisfaction; this is one of service. In the one I ask life to justify itself to me; in the other I ask of myself a justification at the bar of life; in the first I assume that life ought to be sweet to the taste and am routed in the midst of my pleasures by the death's head of change and decay at the banquet; in the second I challenge this assumption and think of life, not as an invitation to enjoy, but as a demand to work. The first problem does not hold Tolstoy, he pushes on to the second. Assume that satisfaction of desires defines the meaning of life, and you are caught in the swirl of unreason, but the unreason is in you, not in life. You have put things wrongly. Is life devoid of reason because it rejects an irrational demand? In this way Tolstoy by shifting the emphasis forces the prospect of a solution of the problem of life. Life seems too large and sane to be cast aside on account of the disappointed pleasure-seeker's despair; thousands seem to find a meaning in it; they seem to live strongly, clearly, happily; their point of view seems vital; their faith, sustaining. Why then not turn to this /150/ simple, strong life of the masses for guidance? This Tolstoy did resolutely.

> "I renounced the life of my class, for I had come to confess that it was not a real life, only the semblance of one; that its superfluous luxury prevented the possibility of understanding life, and that in order to do so I must know, not an exceptional parasitic life, but the simple life of the working classes, the life which fashions that of the world, and gives it the meaning which the working classes accept. The simple laboring men around me were the Russian people, and I turned to this people and to the meaning which it gives to life."

The message Tolstoy gets from the masses is that the only rational life is a life of faith, work, self-denial, humility, kindliness, and charity. The meaning of life is found in social service and in an ideal of self-culture built about energetic self-discipline and sincere religious aspiration.

It is from this point of view that Tolstoy studies and condemns modern culture, and develops a cultural theory of art. His criticisms on modern art must be viewed in the light of his attitude toward modern culture. Our culture, to his way of thinking, wrongly assumes enjoyment to be the meaning of life, and exhausts itself in the pursuit of material comfort, in a restless craving for luxury and the sources of pleasure. Pessimism and *mal de vie* are too often /151/ only the expression of pleasure-seeking thwarted or gone wrong. Again, modern culture is exclusive. It is built on the slavery of the masses, and exacts heavy sacrifices in time, labor, and suffering of the many for the benefit of the few. Why, asks Tolstoy, should they that are nearest to life and an understanding of it, they to whom life is not a plaything or a morsel for the senses, but something concrete, earnest, vital, of social purpose—why should they be sacrificed in order to strengthen the pleasure-seeker in his wrong position? Why should there be this deplorable sacrifice of life and character? "But how wonderfully blind we become as soon as the question concerns those millions of workers who perish slowly and often painfully, all around us, at labors the fruits of which we use for our convenience and pleasure!"

Modern art Tolstoy considers no less wasteful and exclusive than modern culture. It is selfish, exclusive, and costly. It exacts the toll of work from the many and yields pleasure and profit to the few. In its complex forms, grand opera, for instance, it is accessible to few, intelligible to fewer still, and costly out of all proportion to its value. There is much crude fun and not a little malice in Tolstoy's description of a grand opera dress rehearsal at St. Petersburg. This wastefulness of modern art is tragic because the drudges of art, the printer, the stagehand, the musician, caught in a deadening routine, get nothing of the glamour of art, and because there is such a /152/ favoring of soft-living artists at the expense of really useful material. The drudge, the artist and the art patron alike miss the true meaning of life: the first because he is a drudge, the others because they are pleasure-seekers. Here lies the root of the evil: art instead of being a cultural force is becoming an instrument of pleasure in the hands of the moneyed and leisured classes. Small wonder then that it revels in a complex technique, loses itself in symbolism and cryptics, and glorifies passions and impulses over which the common man shakes a puzzled head. Ingenuity is gained, for what could be more ingenious than the court pastoral, the sonnet, the ode, the symphony? But it is gained at the expense of force and breadth. At its worst this exclusive art, always within easy reach of the decadent, expresses the abnormalities of a mind out of focus; at its best it reflects shallow class ideals and surface vanities. These class ideals are: sense of honor, or pride, blatant patriotism, and amorousness. They are parasitical developments of life and lack the vigor, freshness, and massive pressure of the elemental. To Tolstoy with his intense hunger of life such ideals seemed vapid. He caught at the life of the peasant—in his work at Yasnaya Polyana, in his talks and comradeships of the open road, in his pilgrimages to Optin monastery; in such a life close to the soil he thought he detected an unmatched strength and intensity, spiritual and artistic. In peasant life he /153/ saw at least the promise of a wisdom that is not mere cleverness, and an art that is not a mere toying with sounds, colors, and feelings.

This line of reasoning might suggest an onslaught on art as such, but that is certainly not Tolstoy's purpose. He is not to be ranked as an enemy of art; he is not a scoffer, but a critic; a critic whose concern for true art gives the sharpest possible edge to his attack on what he considers bad art. To him true art is a cultural force of immense importance, but easily sent astray—made, as in the mass of modern art, to serve a false ideal of life, and selfish, exclusive, costly interests.

What then is true art, art not culturally perverted? "Art is one of two organs of human progress. By words man interchanges thoughts, by the forms of art he interchanges feelings, and this with all men, not only of the present time, but also of the past and the future . . . To evoke in oneself a feeling one has once experienced, and, having evoked it in oneself, then, by means of movements, lines, colors, sounds, or forms expressed in words, so to transmit that feeling that others may experience the same feeling—this is the activity of art. Art is a human activity consisting in this, that one man consciously by means of certain external signs hands on to others feelings he has lived through, and that other people are infected by these feelings and also experience them," Such passages prove that Tolstoy regards /154/ art as self-expression, and essentially transference of feelings. It is here that he gets his test of true art: the excellence of any work of art depends, first, on whether or not it conveys feelings effectively, second, on the worth of the feelings conveyed.

The contagiousness of art in turn depends on three things: the novelty and originality of the feeling, the clearness with which it is expressed, and the sincerity of the author. Good art must be *striking, luminous,* and *convincing.* Thus in the technique of the drama Tolstoy demands "a true individuality of language, corresponding to the characters; a natural, and at the same time touching plot; a correct scenic rendering of the demonstration and development of emotion; and the feeling of measure in all that is represented." Of the three essentials of transference of feelings sincerity is the most important. "It is always complied with in peasant art, and this explains why such art always acts so powerfully; but it is a condition almost entirely absent from our upper-class art, which is continually produced by artists actuated by personal aims of covetousness and vanity."

Passing to the second test of good art: how are we to judge of the worth of the feelings conveyed? At any particular stage of social development there is a certain amount of religious perception and feeling. Art draws on this, and good art draws on it most fully. The religious consciousness of any given time /155/ is the judge of the worth of the feelings conveyed—it is this startling assertion that Tolstoy's thought arrives at. But he interprets religious consciousness as "an understanding defining the highest good at which that society aims; it is nothing else than the revealing of a new creative relation of man to the universe." This earnest and penetrative wisdom is strong in the choice spirits of an age, and at work in the life of the masses. Life is freshened by this source of new, forceful, and communicable feelings, and art is the gainer, for there is "nothing so old and stale as gratification" and "nothing so new as the feelings which flow into the religious consciousness of a given time." Hebrew and Greek art are cited to point the argument. While false art is continually impoverishing itself, true art draws on the richest possible soil. Tolstoy in this way connects the tests of novelty, clearness, and sincerity with that of worth of content.

Tolstoy is quite aware that religious feeling and perception are different in different ages, and that in order to judge of the worth of present-day art it becomes necessary to get the tone and temper of the present-day religious consciousness. This, Tolstoy holds, is summed up in two things: sonship in God and brotherhood of men. "The religious consciousness of our times, in its widest and most practical application, is the consciousness that our well-being, material and spiritual, temporal and eternal, is included in /156/ the brotherly life of all people, in our living union with each other."

Stripped of all church ceremonial and theology, Christianity is for Tolstoy nothing but a very simple but immeasurably strong combination of the ideas: sonship in God and brotherhood of men. They in turn are the great fresheners and sustainers of what is best in modern art. If art is directly religious, giving what is best in religious perception and giving it simply and convincingly, it is of the very best; if it turns against anti-social feelings, it is on a slightly lower plane; if it expresses certain simple, fundamental feelings, such as gaiety, tenderness, grief, it is still, though indirectly, religious art, for it fosters the sense of human kinship. Tolstoy with an honest avowal of fallibility classes among good art: Millet's *Angelus,* the novels of Dickens, Victor Hugo, Dostoevsky, Mozart, Weber, and part of Chopin and Beethoven—and folk-poetry. His own art he condemns with the exception of two stories: *God Sees the Truth* and *The Caucasian Prisoner.*

Such, for good or ill, is Tolstoy's theory of art. In its results it is beyond a doubt disappointing in a great many ways. Its heresies and gross lapses of insight stand out, but in and of themselves they would not be strong enough to condemn it. The fault lies deeper: it is Tolstoy's onesided, narrow interpretation of culture that spoils his theory of art. Any theory of art as frankly cultural as Tolstoy's is made or /157/ marred by the conception of culture that carries it; a flaw in that counts tenfold against it. Here is where Tolstoy is weakest, for as a social thinker he often lays himself open to the charge of being crude, rash, and narrow; he turns to large problems, looks at them intently, impatiently, but not always largely. One searches in vain for sound judgment of essentials and for a finely discriminative strain of thought: fitful flashes of truth in a Cimmerian darkness, that is all there is, instead of an even, luminous flooding of social problems. He demands that life swing back to simple archaic forms and that art express the strength, the directness, the simplicity of this genuine culture—which amounts to casting aside intellectual achievements and forcing art to move within the confines of peasant thought and peasant feeling. There lies the damning fact, in this stultification of art, in the failure to see that art as well as life is constantly becoming a richer and a more subtle thing, and that with its ever increasing range of expressiveness it must find a place for the subjective, the complex, the elusive, the abnormal. It is all the richer for a Maeterlinck or a Baudelaire. Over against a fresh, simple, strong peasant art Tolstoy sets the danger of pose, affectation, and sickening self-exploitation; he has no eye for other possibilities. Peasant life may be simple and strong, but it is often dull or gross, and popular art often shares this dulness or grossness; Tolstoy himself became the victim of that /158/ dulness when on reading one of the most touching scenes of his *The Power of Darkness*, a play based incident for incident on an actual criminal case among peasants, to a group of peasants, he was greeted with unexpected laughter. Again, artistic *finesse* need not mean a mannered or a sickish art.

But if Tolstoy's theory of art is disappointing in results, it is not disappointing as a problem. All sorts of questions spread from it like a fan. Does the Thinker crowd out the Maker? Can the philosophical impulse develop only at the expense of the artistic? Or if there is war between the two, is it not rather the direction taken by either that is responsible? That in Tolstoy the moral interest seriously endangered his art and his interest in art there can be no doubt. The philosophical tinge to his earlier work deepened to the problem, How ought I to live? What is the meaning of life? Questions like these ought to be an artistic asset; they ought to make art richer, more searching—and they do it in Hardy, in Anatole France, in Gorky. What of *Jude the Obscure* and *The Gods are Athirst*? No one has seen more sharply than Gorky the tragedy of a soul lost in the tumult and social unreason of modern life. His characters, hungry for life and an understanding of it, but crippled, entangle themselves in their own thoughts and purposes or else face life with the dumb agony of an animal at bay. If in Hardy, Anatole France, and Gorky, why not in Tolstoy? Is it because he /159/ puts the problem too reflectively, too self-consciously; because his philosophy is stark naked? Is it perhaps because a solved problem is artistically a dead problem? Or does the flaw lie in the nature of Tolstoy's solution? Are there greater possibilities for art in regarding life as a cruel joke or a senseless jumble than as a purposive, man-centered system? Is it because under Tolstoy's hands the problem shrinks from a cosmic to a moral one, leaving nature outside? Tolstoy was a keen observer of nature, but not a philosophical interpreter of her changes, laws, and moods. Hardy's cruel, blunt analysis and Anatole France's comments, at once sympathetic and caustic, run the problem of man into the problem of nature. Maeterlinck's art owes much to his interest in nature; the individual's life, steeped in mixture of the delicate, the smooth, the fantastic, turns to a richer, more aromatic blend of character and destiny. But Tolstoy destroys what color it has by washing it in moral brine.

There is much meat for argument in all these questions; and there is not a little that is perplexing in Tolstoy the Artist and the Thinker. /160/

❈ TOLSTOI'S THEORY OF ART

Lafcadio Hearn

. . . His conclusion is this: "If art be the means of expressing and convey-ing emotion, then the noblest art must be that which expresses and conveys the noblest form of emotion. Now the noblest emotions are emotions shared by all men; and true art should be able to appeal to all men, not to a class only. The proof that modern art is not great art, the proof that it is even bad art, is that the common people cannot understand it."

We now come face to face with two serious objections.

First, you may say that the reason common people can not understand great art is simply this, that they are stupid and ignorant. How can they com-prehend a great work of literature when they can not understand the language of literature? They can read only very simple things; to read /293/ a great poem or a great work of fiction requires a knowledge of the language of the educated. Common people, not being educated, of course cannot understand.

Very bravely does Tolstoi face this objection. He answers that the so-called language of the educated ought not to be used in a great work of art. A great work ought to be written in the language of the people, which is really the language of the country and of the nation, whereas the language of the edu-cated is a special artificial thing, like the language of medicine, the language of botany, or the language of any special science. And he tells us that he thinks it selfish and wicked and unreasonable to make literature inaccessible to the people by writing it in a special idiom which the people can not understand. Moreover, he says that the greatest books of the world have never been written in a special literary language, but in the common language of the common people. To illustrate this he quotes the great religious books and great religious poems, the Bible and the books of Buddhism which, in the time of their composition, must have been produced in the living tongue, not in a special language. What reason can possibly be offered except a reason of prejudice for making literature incomprehensible to the masses? It is no use to say that with common language you can not express the same ideas which you are in the habit of expressing through literary language. If you think you can not utter great thoughts in simple speech, that is because of bad training, bad habits, false education. The greatest thoughts and the deepest ever uttered, have been written in religious books and in the language of the people. In short, Tolstoi's position is that the whole system of literary education is wrong from top to bottom. And this statement is worth thinking about.

Let me give you a quotation, showing his views about the incomprehensi-bility of art:

"To say that a work of art is good, and that it is never- /294/ theless incom-prehensible to the majority of men, is just as if one were to say of a certain kind of food that it is good, but that the majority of mankind ought to be careful not to eat it. The majority of men, doubtless, may not like to eat rotten cheese or what is called in England 'high' game—that is, the flesh of game which has been allowed to become a little putrid—meat much esteemed by men of per-verted taste; but bread and fruits are only good when they please the taste of the majority of mankind. And in the case of art it is just the same thing. Per-verted art cannot please the majority of mankind; but good art should of neces-sity be something capable of pleasing everybody."

From "Tolstoi's Theory of Art," in *Life and Literature* (New York: Dodd, Mead and Co., 1929), pp. 288 299.

Now let me give you an interesting quotation which illustrates the degree to which what is now called great art seems unnatural to common people:

"Among people who have not yet become perverted by the false theories of our modern society, among artisans and among children, for example, nature has created a very clear idea of what deserves to be blamed or to be praised. According to the instincts of the common people and of children, praise rightly belongs only to great physical force"—as in the case of Hercules, of heroes, of conquerors—"or else to moral force"—as in the case of Sakya-Muni, renouncing beauty and power for the sake of saving man, or the case of Christ dying upon the Cross for our benefit, or as in the case of the saints and the martyrs. These ideas are ideas of the most perfect kind. Simple and frankly honest souls understand very well that it is impossible not to respect physical force, because physical force is a thing that of itself compels respect; and they also can not help equally respecting moral force—the moral strength of the man who works for the sake of good; they feel themselves attracted toward the beauty of moral force by their whole inner nature. "These simple minds perceive that there actually exist in this world men who are more respected than the men respected for physical or moral force—they perceive /295/ that there are men more respected, more admired, and better rewarded than all the heroes of strength or of moral good, and this merely because they know how to sing, how to dance, or how to write poems. A peasant can understand that Alexander the Great or Genghis Khan or Napoleon were really great men; he understands that because he knows that any one of them would have been able to annihilate him and thousands of his followers. He can also understand that Buddha, Socrates, and Christ were great men, because he feels and knows that he himself and all other men ought to try to be like them. But how is it that a man can be called great merely for having written poems about the love of woman? That is a thing which, by no manner of means, could he ever be made to understand."

Elsewhere he gives a still more amusing illustration. The common people, he says, are accustomed to look at statues of divinities, angels, saints, gods, or heroes. They understand quite well the reason for such images. But when they hear that a statue has been set up to honour a man like Baudelaire, who wrote poems of lust or despair, or when they hear of a statue set up in memory of a man who knew how to play the fiddle, that appears to them utterly monstrous. And perhaps it is.

I have thought of a second strong objection to Tolstoi's position, an objection which he himself has not dwelt on—a philosophical objection. It is customary now-a-days to consider superior intelligence as connected with a superior nervous system. Many persons, I am sure, would be ready to say that the common people cannot understand high art, because of the inferiority of their nervous system. Compared with educated and wealthy people, they are supposed to be dull, therefore incapable of feeling beauty. They live, in Europe at least, among miserable conditions of dirt and bad smells. How could they appreciate the delicate fine art of civilization? I say that many persons would argue in this way, but no clear thinker would do so. As /296/ a matter of fact, in modern Europe the best thinkers, the best artists, the best scholars, really come from the peasant class. Some farmers have been able with the greatest difficulty to give their children a better education than the average. Even in the great English universities some of the highest honours have been taken by men of this kind, proving as Spencer said long ago that the foundation of a strong mind is a strong body. I know what Tolstoi would say about the aesthetic refinement of the nervous system. He would simply say that what is called exquisite nervous sensibility is nothing more than hyper-aesthesia—that is, a diseased condition of the nerves. But leaving this matter aside, let me seriously ask a question. Is a common peasant of the poorest class really insensible to beauty? Or what kind of beauty shall we take for a test? The European stand-ard of art holds the perception of human beauty to be the highest test-mark of aesthetic ability. Is the common man, the most common and ignorant man of the people, insensible to human beauty? Is he less capable, for example, of judging the beauty of woman than the most accomplished of artists? Now I do not know what you will think of my statement; but I do not hesitate for a moment to say that the best judge of beauty in the world is the common man of the people. I do not mean that every man of that class is better than others; but I mean that the quickest and best judges of either a man or a woman are the very same persons who are the quickest and best judges of a horse or a cow.

For after all, what we call beauty or grace in the best and deepest sense, represents physical force, with which the peasant is much better acquainted than we are. He is accustomed to observing life, and he does it instinctively. Beauty means a certain proportion in the skeleton which gives the best results of strength and of easy motion in the animal or the man. Suppose again that we consider the body apart from beauty; what does it mean? It means the /297/ economy of force; that is, a body should be so made that the greatest possible amount of strength and activity is obtained with the least possible amount of substance. To say that a man accustomed to judge an animal cannot judge a human being is utter nonsense. Such a man, in fact, is the best of all judges, and seldom makes a mistake. Now history of course has curious instances of the recognition of this fact by great princes. In the time of the greatest luxury of the Caliphs of Bagdad, when the Prince wished to find a perfectly beautiful woman to be his companion, he did not invariably go to the governors of provinces or to the houses of the nobility in search of such a woman. He went to the wild Arabs of the desert, to the breeders of horses, and asked them to find the girl for him. A memorable example is that of Abdul Malik, the fifth Caliph of the house of Ommayad; he asked a common horse trader how to choose a beautiful woman, and the man at once answered him, "You must choose a woman whose feet are of such a form, etc."—naming and describing every part of the body and its best points exactly as a horse-trader would describe the best points of a horse. The Caliph was astonished to discover that this rude man knew incom-parably more about womanly beauty than all his courtiers and his artists. The fact is that familiarity with life, with active life, gives the best of all knowledge in the matter of beauty and strength. Once in America I had a curious illustration of what such familiarity can accomplish in another way. At a certain meeting of men from many parts of the country, there came into the assembly a common man of the poorest class who could tell the exact weight of any one in the assem-bly. You must remember that every man was fully dressed. All agreed to pay him something for proof of his skill, for it is very difficult to tell the weight and strength of a man in Western clothes. Well, the man took a little box, put it on the ground, and asked each person present to step over it. As each person stepped, he cried out the /298/ weight; and the weight was almost exactly as announced in every case. Afterwards I asked him how he did this extraordinary thing. He answered, "When you lift your leg to step over the box, I can see the size and the line of the front muscle of the thigh, and from that I can tell any man's weight." There is a good example of what natural observation means.

But to return, in conclusion, to the subject of this essay. I think it will give you something to think about; and certainly it confirms the truth of one thing which I have often asserted, that the sooner Japanese authors will resign themselves to write in the spoken language of the people, the better for Japanese literature and for the general dissemination of modern knowledge. I think this book is a very great and noble book; I also think that it is fundamentally true from beginning to end. There are mistakes in it—as, for instance, when Tolstoi speaks of Kipling as an essentially obscure writer, incomprehensible to the people. But Kipling happens to be just the man who speaks to the people. He uses their vernacular. Such little mistakes, due to an imperfect knowledge of a foreign people, do not in the least affect the value of the moral in this teaching. But the reforms advised are at present, of course, impossible. Although I believe Tolstoi is perfectly right, I could not lecture to you—I could not fulfil my duties in this university—by strictly observing his principles. Were I to do that, I should be obliged to tell you that hundreds of books famous in English literature are essentially bad books, and that you ought not to read them at all; whereas I am engaged for the purpose of pointing out to you the literary merits of those very books. /299/

✖ TOLSTOY'S ESTHETIC DEFINITION OF ART

Israel Knox

Tolstoy's philosophy of art consists of two distinct elements: the first is esthetic in purpose and meaning, and defines art as the infectious communication of emotions; the second is socio-religious, and is concerned with the moral value of the emotions or experiences transmitted by means of art. Unhappily, critics have concentrated completely upon the moral passion in his view and its incidental prejudices. It is therefore very proper to grant full autonomy to that part of Tolstoy's theory which is purely esthetic and to examine it in the light of recent thought.

Tolstoy's esthetic definition of art is as follows: "To evoke in oneself a feeling one has once experienced, and having evoked it in oneself, then, by means of movements, lines, colors, sounds, or forms expressed in words, so to transmit that feeling that others may experience the same feeling—this is the activity of art. . . . Art is a human activity, consisting in this, that one man consciously by means of certain external signs, hands on to others feelings he has lived through, and that other people are infected by these feelings, and also experience them."[1] Briefly, Tolstoy's definition may be summarized in one sentence: "Art is the infectious communication of emotions." Three concepts are involved in this definition: That art is communication; that it is infectious communication; that it is the infectious communication of emotions. The three words "communication," "infectious," and "emotions," are focal in Tolstoy's esthetic approach to art and their meanings and implications must be closely considered.

The controversy as to whether art is essentially expression or communication seems to me entirely fortuitous. The solution is simple and lucid: art is expression for the sake of communication. When John Stuart Mill wrote that the poet never thinks of a listener,[2] he gave utterance to an inadequately partial truth. It may be that at the moment of impelling inspiration, in the fiery enchantment of

"Tolstoy's Esthetic Definition of Art," *Journal of Philosophy,* 27 (1930), 65–70.
[1] Tolstoy: *What Is Art? and Essays on Art,* tr. by A. Maude, p. 123 (Vol. 18 in Tolstoy Centenary Ed.). /65/
[2] Mill: *Dissertations and Discussions* (Am. Edition), Vol. I, p. 97. /65/

an absorbing mood, in his vision of the glamorous quality of a thing and his feelings about it, the poet becomes oblivious of the /65/ world and of men and is concerned only with the music and the imagery of his poem. Surely this is a psychological factor that enters into every human activity. In every task the spirit of creation descends upon the loving performer and his attention and passion become riveted to the thing itself. This is true of any creative process because somewhere in the soul of the maker there is a profound intuitive awareness of the ultimate function and purpose of the fulfilled dream, of the accomplished task. The urge to express, to find a final and inevitable form for a feeling or thought, flows directly out of that consuming hunger that all men possess for spiritual communion. Art is expression for the sake of communication. It is an objectification of an experience for the sake of a beholder; it is addressed to his imagination. Art is a communicable expression; the two terms are inseparable; the one is the complement of the other.

It is in his insistence upon the communicability of art that Tolstoy differs from Véron. To Véron art was essentially expression; the external manifestation of the emotions felt by men. Tolstoy points out the insufficiency of such a definition very succinctly: "A man may express his emotions by means of lines, colors, sounds, or words, and yet may not act on others by such expression, and then the manifestation of his emotions is not art."[3] For art must be shared; it must be perceived and felt by a beholder; it must act on others who become keenly aware of its existence and power. The flowering of art is communication: the wafting of a vision, the revelation of an experience to humanity.

In an essay published in this JOURNAL[4] Professor Ducasse affirms the correctness of the view held by Véron. He believes that Tolstoy failed to discern the intrinsic nature of language. He cites as evidence the very specific fact that his own paper—the paragraph which contained the critique of Tolstoy—would remain a perfect expression of his thoughts, even if it were not read by anyone, and consequently could not perform that transmitting or communicating function which Tolstoy postulated as fundamental to language. This seems to me fanciful. Professor Ducasse creates an artificial situation and endows it with circumstances which are psychologically inconceivable. The truth is that when Professor Ducasse wrote his essay, there was no doubt in his mind that his thoughts would be shared and his words would be read. The desire to express was imperceptibly and inextricably blended with a deeply-rooted urge to transmit and to communicate—its single result constituted the written paper. And yet Professor Ducasse can not fully do away with this problem of communication; he forbids it to enter /66/ through the door, but permits it to flutter in through the window. He can not deny the transmitting phase in art, therefore he attributes it to the gregarious impulse, which he describes as different and separate from the impulse to express. Is it really true that in the artistic activity it is possible to make a sharp and definite cleavage between the two impulses? Is it not their coalescence, their union that stimulates, provokes, and brings forth into the world that genuine work of art which can be shared, enjoyed, and comprehended? If Professor Ducasse is right, why should the artist wish to externalize his expression in a recognizable medium? Art as expression needs no external manifestation; its aim is achieved in the sheer intuition. Once this theory is acknowledged only one possible conclusion follows: Croce's doctrine that art is internal expression consummated even before the act of exteriorization has begun. But this is an evasion of the real problem: the essence and function of art as a dynamic human activity, as a profound social phenomenon. The

---

[3] Tolstoy: What Is Art? p. 120. /66/
[4] Vol. XXV, pp. 181–186, March 29, 1928. /66/

social force and significance of art is rooted in its communicability; this communicability clearly means the transmission and revelation of feelings and thoughts. Whether this is due to the exteriorized intuition or to a gregarious impulse, is a different problem; what remains indisputably clear is the fact that art becomes art only when it is shared and perceived and appreciated by others, when it is a genuine expression for the sake of an effective communication. Tolstoy did not, as Professor Ducasse would have us believe, propound a theory of language; he did not even directly and peremptorily deny that the art process in the strictest psychological sense may not perhaps be analyzed to be an expressive activity without any ulterior interests. What he did defend was the thesis that art in the matrix of social life could have its only discoverable value when it speaks the language of the human heart in a way that can be understood and shared by many. Véron's theory is at best incomplete; the outward expression of feelings remains an invisible sun until its warmth and shimmer pass into the being of a beholder; more, somewhere in the spirit of the artist is a glowing desire to make this expression a thing of strength and sweetness, of lovely and bejeweled passion so as to render it more communicable to a beholder. It is not essential to the truth of Tolstoy's conception of art to prove that even psychologically it arises out of the wish to transmit,[5] rather than merely to express. Still it is immensely important to note that both Grosse and Hirn in their anthropological studies of the origins and beginnings of art unite in their verdict that "an individual art is nowhere demonstrable"; that "art ap- /67/ pears as a social manifestation";[6] that "the artist's presentation needs for its completeness to be complemented by the beholder's conception";[7] that "without a public—in the largest sense of the word—no art would ever have appeared."[8]

The meaning of Tolstoy's concept of communication becomes even clearer when it is noted that he always stressed that element in it which he called infectiousness or contagiousness. To tell a tale is not enough for art; it must sear the soul of the contemplator, or delight it, with the feelings and experiences of the artist. The dearest quality in art to Tolstoy was its power of union—that wonder by dint of which hearts and minds estranged from each other in the artificial market-places of the world are reunited in the strong and simple love of their common understanding of their common humanity. It was perhaps this that Shelley had in mind when he condemned egotism as the colossal obstacle to the writing of good poetry and attributed all great poetry to Love.[9] Art communicates; it does more: it unites. It is a form of communion in which the spirit participates.

Doubtless Tolstoy was more concerned with the moral or spiritual significance of the infectiousness of the artistic communication. He was, however, also cognizant of its sheer esthetic and psychological importance. It is worth while to note that the contagiousness of art was emphasized in some manner or other by a number of thinkers in the history of esthetic thought. It is already implied in the principle of catharsis which Plato faintly intimated and which Aristotle formulated. In fact Aristotle already had a real glimpse of the modern notion of the relieving power and function of art. It is clearly evident in Croce's doctrine of the identity of genius and taste. Croce sees the high peak of art in that supreme moment when the vision of the artist and the beholder is blended in

---

[5] Or more precisely, out of the blended, out of the *inextricably blended* wish to express-and-to-communicate, i.e., art is expression for the sake of communication. /67/

[6] E. Grosse: *Beginnings of Art*, p. 50. /68/

[7] E. Grosse: *Beginnings of Art*, p. 26. /68/

[8] Y. Hirn: *Origins of Art*, p. 25. /68/

[9] Shelley: *Defense of Poetry* edited by Prof. A. S. Cook, p. 14. /68/

the same intuition, when the boundary between genius and taste disappears, when both clasp the same concrete image. This is Tolstoy's contagiousness of art; the very sentence in which he speaks of this union is similar to Croce's language.[10] It is corroborated by Hirn from the /68/ anthropological viewpoint; he sees in primitive as well as in all art the great reliever for overpowering feelings in the artist as well as in the contemplator; he accounts in great measure for the enjoyment of pain through its enhancement and accentuation of feelings. To do all this art must infect.

The conception of art as contagious communication solves an additional problem which baffled Bosanquet. He was displeased by the prevalent impression that the process of contemplation was a recipient one, a passive attitude, that there was a wide discrepancy between genius and taste.[11] But if infectiousness is one of the preëminent signs of art, it appears that the difference is in degree only and not in kind, in quantity and not in quality, that there is a depth of experience and an immensity of feeling that can be kindled to a living passionate intensity from soul to soul by the light that is art. The contemplative process is not a vague passive reaching out to a distant shining star; it is an active surging creative participation in a sharable human emotion; it is a throbbing of this emotion in one's own blood.

The degree of infectiousness is the sole measure of excellence in art, and Tolstoy enunciates three conditions upon which it depends: The originality of the feeling transmitted, the clearness with which it is transmitted, and the sincerity of the artist's own feeling. A work of art must be the authentic articulation of a feeling the artist has divined, personally or vicariously. It will achieve universality only when it possesses the seal of the individuality of his own soul. The feeling should be rendered with a maximum of clearness so as to evoke in the receiver a sentiment of spiritual union, a pleasant realization that the artist has expressed for him what he has already long known and felt. But the *summum bonum* in all art, the supreme ineluctable quality, the condition in which everything else is summed up, is the sincerity of the artist, the force with which he himself feels the emotion he transmits. Every work of art must emanate out of the depths of the maker's being. It must be his autobiography, and it will in turn become, by the fact of contagiousness, the autobiography of the contemplator, of the beholder. Art is the infectious communication of emotions; the stronger the infection, the better is the art; individuality, clearness, and sincerity in the feelings expressed and transmitted are the means by which this high destiny of art may be fulfilled.

There remains to be noted the third focal term in Tolstoy's esthetic definition of art; that art is the infectious communication /69/ of *emotions*. The significance of sheer feeling can not be underestimated in the domain of art; it is the concomitant of all intellection, of all ideation, of all thought; at no point can it be disregarded. And yet one is loathe to apotheosize Tolstoy's schematic division of life into the realms of thought and feeling, of mind and heart. It is too simple; the influence of his adored Rousseau is too evident. The reality of great art consists in the perfect blending of inspired thought and inspired

[10] *Tolstoy:* "The recipient of a truly artistic impression is so united to the artist that he feels as if the work were his own and not someone else's—as if what it expresses were just what he had long been wishing to express." (*What Is Art?* p. 228.)

Croce: ". . . But in that contemplation and judgment, our spirit is one with that of the poet, and in that moment we and he are one thing." (*Æsthetic:* p. 121, Eng. tr. by D. Ainslie.)

No attempt is made here to imply that there is any fundamental kinship between the theories of Tolstoy and Croce. These citations are brought merely /68/ to show that even such antipodal thinkers on art as Tolstoy and Croce find themselves in agreement on this specific problem. And this despite their different terminologies. /69/

[11] Bosanquet. *Three Lectures on Æsthetic*, p. 31–33. /69/

emotion, in the luminous intuition which the imaginative reason fashions into a concrete, vivid communicable image. It is fallacious to attempt to dissociate feeling from reflection. What is true is, that in the realm of art, an idea may not be analyzed as an abstract detached speculative problem, but must be planted in a living heart and chronicled as an emotional experience. It would be better therefore to substitute for the word "emotions" in Tolstoy's definition the word "experience," and to interpret experience as that spiritual synthesis of thought and feeling which constitutes the stuff of life. When experience is so defined, art may be truly stated as the infectious communication of experience. /70/

NOTES ON THE MORALISTIC THEORY OF ART: PLATO AND TOLSTOY

Israel Knox

Tolstoy has not been the first in the history of culture to look askance upon a goodly portion of the fine arts, and to consider art, in general, both a menace and a might, either an instrument of evil or a powerful spiritual influence for good. "Thou shalt not make unto thee a graven image, nor any manner of likeness of any thing that is in heaven above, or that is in the earth beneath," is not only the injunction of Moses but also of Plato. Plato and Moses, both prophets of the eternal and the immutable, the one naming it Yahveh, the other calling it the Idea of the Good, could not help but see in art a shadow, a phantom, a distorted reflection of that which is divinely perfect, ineffably beautiful, and consequently inimitable, and can be experienced only in those single moments of mystical intuitive rapture, when the soul is farthest in its flight from the body. And therefore Moses, when the passion to *experience* God becomes unendurable, leaves the tents of Israel for forty days and nights, and in the intensity of his ecstasy fails to appear at the promised time; likewise Plato in the *Symposium* desirously longs after that final stage of universal love and beauty, when the soul has passed by stepping-stones from earth to heaven. To Plato art was the imitation of things and actions in a world itself the passing apparition, the transient shadow of a luminous sun, of the reality of the empyrean of Ideas. This does not mean that Plato thought of art as an imitative activity in the literal sense of the term. It is possible that he meant very much the same thing that Aristotle did when he spoke of epic poetry, and tragedy, and comedy, and the music of the flute and the lyre as modes of imitation. Aristotle did not use the word in a derogatory sense; his conception of the mechanism, of the actual creative aspect of art, was very lucid: Sophocles does not make a real *Oedipus Rex;* he represents, pretends, imitates. The world of art, therefore, is an imaginative one, a realm of pretense, an imitative activity. This might also have been Plato's definition of art, but his inferences could not accord with Aristotle's. To Plato art was pretense in a theater of pretense; to Aristotle art was imaginative pretense, a creative process, a Poesis, in the theater of real life, making for us pretenses of the intrinsic, the universal, the spiritually coherent and true in the emotions, actions, and characters of men in this theater of life. To Aristotle the pretense of art is a penetration to the core of life; it is more philosophical than history which is an imitation of /507/ what did empirically and isolatedly happen in the collocation of events in time.

"Notes on the Moralistic Theory of Art: Plato and Tolstoy," *International Journal of Ethics*, 41 (July, 1930), 507–510.

It is fairly evident that Tolstoy agrees on this single point with Aristotle and not with Plato. And this is true despite his remark to Gorki on the inventiveness of the arts, on their sporadic nature. Tolstoy probably would not concur in Aristotle's conclusion that the aim of poetry is to give pleasure. That is a different matter. He accepts, however, the need and reality of art in a real world. He does more: he considers it one of the indispensably necessary conditions of human life. He endows it with a unique and immensely important function. He could not, as Plato did, exile all the poets from his republic. Not for him this brilliant paradox. He needed them, he wanted them, the true and good poets, in his Kingdom of Heaven on earth, to send shafts of light and love into the hearts of men. This cardinal theoretical distinction between the two prophets must be emphasized. To Plato art was an irresponsible creation, a fantastic dream, a land of shadows; to Tolstoy, it was a real and necessary human activity.

It is in the concreteness of their socio-ethical considerations that Plato and Tolstoy approach each other across the ocean of twenty-three centuries. Strange as it may seem, the metaphysician of the Ideas was one of the most consummate sociologists in the history of thought; he whose vision was given to the contemplation of eternity, busied himself as few men did, with the ordeals, trials, and needs of humanity in the cave, of men in their temporal terrestrial existence. Not that the sage of Yasnaya Polyana and the philosopher of Athens find themselves in tune on this problem. Tolstoy postulates the inviolability of the spirit in men and the unqualified equality of all mankind. Plato is more concerned with the chemistry of the soul and constructs his ideal commonwealth in the form of a timocracy. But this they have in common: an insatiable hunger for universal human happiness, a passionate yearning for the enthronement of the Good Life. Towards this one purpose they bent all the energies of their intellects and kindled all the flame of their spirits. They were well aware of the social function of the imagination in shaping and controlling conduct; they wished to harness the power of its appeal in the service of the Good Life. And their opinions meet at a number of points.

Plato anathematized not only the heritage of Homer, but also the poetry of the social visionary and prophet Hesiod, and he consigned to the graveyard the imperishable tragedies of Aeschylus and the colossal art of the Periclean Age. He found in them a thousand vices he could not condone. Tolstoy repudiated the art of the Renaissance and renounced the greater part of the artistic creations of modern Europe, not sparing Shakespeare, Goethe, Beethoven, and Ibsen. Both set up an extraneous criterion for /508/ the value of a work of art: is it true or false? And they did not base their question on artistic or psychological grounds, nor on the intrinsic ethos of the soul (which is the same thing), but on an external, premeditated and predetermined moral code. Both were interested in fettering the imagination to the chariot of morality and both failed to perceive that the imagination is most moral when it is the free, spontaneous criticism of life. Santayana observes that Plato's strictures upon the fine arts are so relentless because he himself possessed the most delicate aesthetic sensibilities, and therefore overestimated its influence on character and affairs. That is equally true of Tolstoy. What wonderful joy melody must have evoked in the soul of Plato that he felt constrained to limit it in the Republic to the strong martial strain; and we know for a fact that Tolstoy touched to tears by music, often fled from it, saying, "What does it want of me, what does it want of me?"

The final concrete conclusions of the two masters differ a little. Plato is seduced by his own logic. He is superbly consistent. Not only is art an imitative activity. Not only does it divert men's minds from the exigencies of life, but poetry harms even the good. And why? Because poetry does precisely what

Tolstoy wishes it to do: It communicates experiences; it is the language of the heart. We restrain our sorrow and laughter in the market-place, whereas under the influence of poetry, we allow freedom and lassitude to our feelings. Poetry feeds and waters the passions; she bejewels them with fascinations. Hymns to the gods and praises of famous men are the only poetry that ought to be admitted into the good state. Tolstoy, too, restricts the subject-matter of art, and decries the greater portion of it for being the charming expression of a limited range of sensual, lustful emotions experienced by a small coterie of society. But he reaffirms its necessity in human life and eulogizes it as the communication of universally felt emotions. Only that these emotions be conducive to the moral improvement of man. He does not wish to stimulate the martial fortitude of the state, nor to sustain the myth of the god-ordained division of its population into three classes; therefore he fears neither laughter nor sorrow, knowing too well that these are means of union among men. And yet how much difference is there, in principle, between a poetry that consists of hymns to the gods and praises of great men, and an art that preaches the brotherhood of men (in a definite moral sense, for in its larger meaning, good art has always done this) and transmits only those feelings indisputably intelligible to all?

Plato and Tolstoy criticized art on moral grounds. In this, they were right. To look upon art in the light of the larger socio-spiritual life is to pay it the most glowing compliment. In a world of suffering and frustra- /509/ tion, where our purest gladness is not unalloyed with pain, where "our sweetest songs are those that tell of saddest thought," where man himself in the tragedy of his spiritual blindness has erected so many obstacles to his happiness and emancipation, art, too, must concern itself with the ethos of the soul, with the problems of humanity. In such a world, it is not meant for the good and great artist to play the rôle of a delicately refined clown, of a performer of amusing tricks for a small and select élite. He must be Prometheus. He must bring light. He must express for us that which becomes frozen upon our own lips or withers in our own hands when we attempt to render it comprehensible and communicable. If he does this, his creations will be beneficent, and will be ranked higher or lower in the estimation of mankind in proportion to the clarity and insight with which he reveals our experiences. To make such art is to lessen the sorrow under the sun, is to liberate the mind, is to bring a little happiness into life. To make such art, is a supreme moral achievement. Had this been the view of Plato and Tolstoy, at least one dissident voice would have remained silent. But their view is really a negation of the moral function of art. They would compel it to distort experience, to evaluate it before its objectification. It has been the lot of Man in his wonderfully strange path across history to know and to love both anguish and exultation. He has learned to cherish these; they have become holy and inviolate to him. No prophet is great enough to exclude any of their nuances from the realm of art.

If the inspiration of the artist is a happy one, if he has really succeeded in transmuting an experience into creative form and vision, he has given humanity not only a thing of truth but also of delight. To stress the spiritual significance of art does not mean to deny that ineffable ecstasy, that feeling of patterned harmony which it affords its lovers. The two are wedded. Art becomes art in their indistinguishable union. Such art is rare and precious, and there is not too much of it in the world. But what we have of it is greatly to be treasured. /510/

TOLSTOY'S IDEAS

✠ ART IS COMMUNICATION

Sidney Finklestein

To understand art, we must know not only the individual works of art but the cultural life of which they are a part. Works of art come into being through artists' imagination, thought, and labor. Cultural life, however, is created by society. Whether an artist shows a meager or a full comprehension of his times, whether he accepts the dominant cultural values of his age or is aware of the contradictions within that culture, his work is shaped by that cultural life.

We can see art simply as a means of enjoyment. A great many treatises on art are written from the standpoint of the pleasure that works of art can give to us. Such discussions ignore the complex relations between artist and audience, and the role of society in providing the basic conditions of communication. For an explanation of art they fall back upon the idea of abstract beauty, which to them is a purely aesthetic emotion, opposed to the emotions and sense perceptions of everyday life.

Such treatises have often been of value in expanding the reader's sensitivity to the sensuous qualities that are the open door to the appreciation of art. But their approach, leaning upon the idea of abstract beauty or the aesthetic emotion, fails to explain why the methods of art creation change so drastically from one age to the next, and even differ within the same age. Surely if art is the creation of abstract beauty apart from the living world, its principles could have been standardized after the passage of centuries. Yet any attempt to recreate a typical art /9/ work from the past is doomed to failure. The product is inevitably dead. It is common, on the other hand, for a simple popular work—a story, cartoon, or dance tune—to contain more of the quality of art than a finished product of the conservatory which happens to be based upon the most intense study of the methods of the great masters. The reason is not that our concept of what is beautiful has changed. A work out of the past can continue to give us intense pleasure. The reason is that art is not a thing, but an act; not an object, but a communication. Being a communication, it involves not only an artist, the creator, but an audience, and a language familiar to both. This language is a product of society, rather than of the individual, who at best makes a small, if important, addition to it. Since this is so, the language changes as society changes. All efforts to call a halt to the change of language have inevitably failed, whether in the realm of words, which we usually think of as

"Art Is Communication," in *Art and Society* (New York: International Publishers, 1947), pp. 9–13.

language, or the realm of sound, rhythm, line, color, and shape, which are the language of music and the graphic arts. Thus, a contemporary communication has a quality not found in one from the past, and the power of a work of art is measured by the effectiveness of its communication rather than by the model it follows.

The languages of communication which are so integral a factor of art did not arise for the purpose of providing material for artists. They arose out of the need of men to live together and expand their relationships. They developed as the changing and growing organization of mankind that we call society provided new material for them and made new demands upon them. Just as society became an organization involving man's emotional relationships, in which his physical needs were clothed, so these languages of communication took on a content of emotional and human relationships. Over the passage of centuries these languages, passed down from one generation to another, have come to embody the history and experiences of the past, as well as the changing aspects of the day, and have become rich fabrics capable of the most subtle and elaborate manipulation. As we have come to know more about ourselves, our fellow men and the world, this knowledge has come to be included in our languages. The /10/ aesthete's concept of the artist as someone who takes dead matter and breathes life into it is only a half-truth. This combination of human emotion with dead matter is truly the character of a work of art, but it is not the artist alone who has worked the miracle. Language as created by society has done it for him. That is the artist's necessary starting point.

It is this presence of emotion within language, essentially due to the fact that language is saturated with human relationships and human perceptions of nature, that rouses the aesthetic emotion so beloved by philosophers of art. The special excitement or feeling of beauty in a work of art is due to the fact that art is not an emotion of the artist, or a collection of materials that exists outside of him, but a combination of both. There is an intense pleasure in finding the mark and character of a human being in what is apparently abstract sound or dead matter; the pleasure of all social communication given concentration by the craft of the artist, who is a master of communication. Because the languages used by art have so rich a human content, it is possible for some people to go further and make art partly a substitute for the real world and for real human relationships. It is even possible to find satisfaction in a past world of art as a flight from the present. But this is an aberration rather than, as some would have it, a path to an explanation of the fundamental character of art.

Art being communication, what then can we say is the difference between art and ordinary communication, such as the casual words we speak every day? There is no impassable barrier between the two. In the most general sense, just as all art is communication, so all communication is art. We think of music and picture as closer to art than the word, but actually man communicated by sound before he had the spoken word, and by picture before he had the written word. But there is a difference in kind and degree of communication, so much so that the artist for several centuries has become a recognized specialist. To understand the differences that arose in communication, so that we can understand the place of art in the world, we must add to our concept of language the concept of form.

Form exists in a rudimentary sense even in our casual speech. /11/ If we analyze our speech, we find that we do not simply put together words as symbols for various things, but repeat familiar phrases, images, and even rhythmic patterns. These groupings of words and sounds, handed down to us rather than invented by us, are simple forms, and we use them because as a pattern they contain feelings, thought, and ideas not found in the individual words themselves. This is art form at its simplest. A melody is such a form, its whole embodying a feeling not found in the notes themselves that make up the melody, and so is a line, or arrangement of lines, that suggests something from nature or life.

It is best not to use the word "art" to describe these simple patterns of language, because the complexities of modern society have given a special meaning to the creation of works of art. But it is important to see the quality of art in these patterns, for without art in this most simple form, there would be no art at all. It is important to remember in this connection that many works are now accepted as fine art which were not conceived at all in modern terms of what an artist is and how he works. Examples are cave drawings, Indian pottery and blankets, Chinese bronze vessels. In fact a story which someone may tell us as part of an ordinary conversation may, if written down, be recognized as having the quality of a work of art. A child's drawing may have a similar quality, putting on paper a real memory or perception. Unfortunately while modern society permits us to develop our handling of words with sensitivity and imagination, it allows similar possibilities with line or sound to die away.

Form may be defined as a pattern of language that embodies a perception or emotion not found in the separate language elements. As society developed, with its growing conquest of nature and its changing means of production of goods, methods arose of giving communication an extension in time and space. Such methods were the carving of stone and working of metal, the use of paints, the invention of writing. Through these means a communication could remain long after the moment of its conception, or it could be reproduced and repeated in places far removed from one another. This development influenced, likewise, the kind of ideas and emotions that were put into these more /12/ permanent and far-reaching forms. Out of these activities, becoming so important a part of the institutions of society and given in turn so great a complexity by a society growing more complex, forms arose of a far more elaborate kind than the simple patterns of language. Such forms are the oration, the historical chronicle, the religious prayer, the temple, and the public celebration. They involved the kind of craftsmanship with language that we now associate with art. They were not art forms as we like to think of art forms today, however. Yet what is left to us of such forms rank with the greatest achievements of art, such as the Bible, the architecture and sculpture of ancient Egypt, and the Greek drama.

With more complicated and varied means of production the craftsman came into being, and then divisions arose among the craftsmen themselves. Out of the craftsmen came the modern conception of an artist. But even with the appearance of the artist, recognized as such within society, the definition of art cannot be a law laid down for past, present, and future. It must rather be a description of the different places the artist held in society at different times, whether he was known as an artist or not, and of the role he played as society divided into landowner and slave, into feudal lord and serf, into owner of the means of production and workman.

Art, then, consists of a language of communication and of forms through which this communication attains a complexity of meaning, a permanence of existence, and an extension in space so that it can be addressed to all the members of a society. The creation of works of art has always been one of the functions of society, sometimes allied to its institutions of government, law, and religion, binding people together; sometimes allying itself to new institutions that arose to replace outmoded ones. The study of art is a study of these languages and forms. Through a study of these elements we will be able to see how even when the artist considers himself an individual dissociated from society, his work is a part of its complex life. It is a part of its culture, which is a record of the customs, the ways of life, the morals, the human relationships, and the ideals and practices of each age. /13/

✸ KHRUSHCHEV HITS "DONKEY" ART

The Soviet press today picked up Premier Nikita Khrushchev's ridicule of abstract art and turned it into a plea for a return to a "realism" that can serve communism.

Khrushchev, who like Prince Philip and former President Eisenhower definitely knows what he likes about art, touched off the storm Saturday night by attending an exhibition by Moscow artists.

He told one group of artists and sculptors their work is so abstract that they looked like they were "daubed by the tail of a donkey."

Armed with this colorful criticism, the Communist Party newspaper *Pravda* today told Soviet artists what they may and what they may not paint.

Pravda criticized "the pseudo-innovation and incorrect trends which have appeared in the work of certain artists and writers."

"The Leninist Party of Communists," it said, "has, by directing the development of literature and art to serve the people in the spirit of the great ideals of communism, established conditions making possible an unprecedented burgeoning of artistic creativeness."

The editorial hailed the "mighty power of Lenin's principles of ideology, national roots and realism and the unbreakable ties between the work of the artist and the life of the people."

It urged a return to the "glorious traditions of our realistic art" and scored artists who "chase unthinkingly after western fashion, spending their time in pathetic imitation of the corrupt and formalistic art of the bourgeois world."

Khrushchev had told the artists that good art should "give a truthful picture of the life of the people, inspire . . . cultivate noble sentiments and a deep understanding of the beautiful."

It was not known what effect this would have on Soviet art, which was severely restricted in earlier years to a rigid "realism" that favored representational paintings of tractors or peasants in the field.

It was learned that the works which Khrushchev panned Saturday night would be returned to the artists. And an exhibition of abstract art, due to open here Thursday, was canceled at the last minute without explanation.

Tass, the Soviet news agency, said at the time that the artists thanked Khrushchev for his "constructive comments," but "mumbled" when the Soviet leader asked them to explain their work.

Pravda, in a review of the exhibition, said more than 100,000 persons had seen the picture Khrushchev panned. It said the people "warmly approve" the pictures Khrushchev liked, but "sharply and justly criticize works in which formalistic tendencies appear."

"Khrushchev Hits 'Donkey' Art," *The Ann Arbor News,* Dec. 3, 1962, p. 6.

It singled out three works—"The Naked Women" and "Still Life" by Falk and the sculpture "Motherhood" by Pologova—for special criticism.

The newspaper expanded its theme on painting into a general condemnation of western tendencies in art as a whole and attacked "unthinking imitation of western examples" in music.

"This imitation-disease manifests itself most vividly in the jazzomania which, in recent times has engulfed sections of our musical life," it said. /6/

⌘ COMMUNICATION *VERSUS* EXPRESSION IN ART[1]

Lascelles Abercrombie

A good deal of the recent interest in æsthetics must be due to Benedetto Croce; for by his restatement of the æsthetic problem, he has restored it to the condition of being *arguable.* For theories of art which began by evoking such unruly mysteries as *beauty* and *idealisation*—theories which then found that, instead of being guided by friendly powers, they had started on a series of battles with invisible demons—for these confusions Croce substituted a simple tactical movement, and quietly showed logic the way in: the theory of art became the logic of expression. This was so refreshing that it was hailed as a revolution: and Benedetto was indeed the right name for its author. Historically, as he himself might say, it was certainly the readjustment required; but of course it was not new, and he would be the last person to claim that it was final. A further readjustment has been suggested, and this again will prove to be nothing new; for to make, as strictly as Croce does, æsthetic theory the theory of expression has revived the question whether the *theory of art* should not be a limitation of general æsthetic theory—whether, that is to say, art does not require a closer specification than *expression.* Ought not, perhaps, the *theory of art* to be some theory of *communication?* (To the implied distinction between art and æsthetic I shall come later.)

Those who think (I am one myself) that this would take the theory of art a step beyond Croce, may usefully be reminded that it is a step which Aristotle took almost without noticing it, as a matter of course. But the importance and significance of a move forward in philosophy is not so much in arrival as in departure: not so much in the place we get to as in the direction we have come, and why we have come.

The first and, for some things, still the best treatise on these studies also approached art from the side of expression. It was natural for Aristotle, as a Greek, to assume that art must be, in some way, *a mimesis.* The notorious dangers of translation have allowed this technical term of his to obscure one of his greatest services to æsthetics. But he is himself /68/ to blame, for he does not always use the word in the same sense. *Mimesis* is, I suppose, sufficiently translated, as it is commonly used in Greek, by 'imitation'; and there are some passages in the Poetics in which this is right enough. They are all passages which not only are unnecessary to the main structure of his theory, but which

"Communication *versus* Expression in Art," *British Journal of Psychology*, 14 (1923), 68–77.

[1] Read to the Æsthetics Section of the British Psychological Society, January 29, 1923. The paper supposes some acquaintance with the arguments so brilliantly sustained in Croce's *Estetica come Scienza dell' Espressione* and *Breviario di Estetica.* /68/

flagrantly contradict it. He is not the only philosopher who has tried to extend his argument by slightly dislocating the meaning of his terms. For outside these occasional and anomalous passages, the word *mimesis* is always used by Aristotle in a special connection, which imposes on the word a special sense: a sense which our word 'imitation' is not accustomed to bear. Thus, if we translate literally (that is, with a false rigidity of verbal equivalence, and therefore incorrectly), Aristotle is made to say that tragedy 'imitates' a certain kind of action: and the whole process of his argument shows this action to be something that cannot actually occur: it can only occur as an idea. Clearly, this is the sort of imitation which he postulates in music and dancing; it is, in fact, not what we call imitation at all: it is expression. Indeed, to translate literally sometimes makes Aristotle's *mimesis* yield mere nonsense: as when poetry "imitates men better than they are." He must mean formalised or idealised imitation, say some commentators: that is, imitation which is precisely not imitation. Others say, he is simply thinking of the heroes of legend; but how can poetry imitate men who are not there to be imitated? Some of Aristotle's followers have encouraged this confusion by sticking to what they conceived to be his terminology, though they saw clearly enough what he meant. Thus Sidney, with no intention of startling us, says the sacred poets "imitate the inconceivable excellencies of God"; and in a passage which crystallises the real sense and the apparent paradox of what I may call Aristotelian imitation, Sidney contrasts "the meaner sort of painters, who counterfeit only such faces as are set before them," with "the more excellent," whose work he typifies by a picture of Lucretia, wherein the artist "painteth not Lucretia whom he never saw, but painteth the outward beauty of such a nature"; this, he says, is to imitate, but adds that such an artist, in order to imitate, "borrows nothing of what is, hath been or shall be." Sidney does not mean that the artist does not borrow the elements of his technique from nature; his argument has sufficiently provided against the imputation of such absurdity. He means that the finished work as a whole imitates something which does not exist in nature. Where does it exist? It exists ideally, until it is imitated in art—that is, expressed.

I elaborate the Aristotelian meaning of imitation in art, not merely /69/ because that meaning is expression, but also just because it was on this very word, the word for imitation, that this special sense was imposed. Plato had taken the usual line that art *begins* by imitating objects. Aristotle's argument is not really concerned with how art begins. The chapter in which he perfunctorily accepts, with Plato, the commonplaces about art's origin in mimicry is quite unnecessary as a starting-off place for his argument, quite at variance with his main thesis, and quite untrue. It is a mistake which we may legitimately ignore. It is indifferent to Aristotle's theory how the artistic impulse arises; though for one art—tragedy—he describes keenly and with profound insight the form the impulse must take in order to be expressed. The first importance of his argument is that it brings in *mimesis* at a *later stage* of the genesis of a work of art. *Mimesis*, for Aristotle, comes when the artist has to find, in the medium he is using, an equivalent to his impulse, his idea, his intention, etc. This, once stated, was decisive, both against Plato and for the true theory of art. Plato called the *conception* of a work of art a *mimesis*: Aristotle called the *technique* of a work of art a *mimesis*. That is to say, out of the vague popular notion that art is imitation, which Plato made into ingenious nonsense, Aristotle drew the essential doctrine that art is expression.

But he still called it imitation! What justification can there be for that? A very good one, if language would allow it, as Greek apparently did but English hardly can. For by speaking of artistic expression as imitation, Aristotle makes it impossible for us to forget that artistic expression must be *recognisable*—that is, universally recognisable. It must not only be good as expression—expression in which the impulse is satisfied: it must be good in the opposite direction—as revelation of the impulse. To call expression in art imitation was Aristotle's way of implying that expression in art is also communication.

No doubt he thought it enough to imply a thing so obvious; but his theory as a whole certainly required that it should at least be implied. For Aristotle also assumed that art has a function, which he described as *katharsis*. His whole theory may be summed up as *katharsis* by means of *mimesis*—expression which necessarily has a function. Now if art has a function it cannot be confined to the artist. It cannot be a function which *stops short*; for to speak of the function of art is to speak of its peculiar effective relation to life in general. And whatever we may think of *katharsis* as an adequate or even intelligible account of art's function, it at least applies equally to the artist and to his audience. Aristotle indeed hardly attended to the function of art in the artist; and perhaps /70/ no one did until Goethe took it so seriously. What interested Aristotle was the function of art in the artist's audience; and this, he says, takes place by means of expression. An artist creates by expression a work of art, and this effects in its audience that for which it had throughout been designed. What else can this mean but that the expression which creates a work of art is an expression which is necessarily also communication?

If so, art is an expression of the same kind as language; and it is in fact an almost irresistible metaphor that an artist, whatever his medium, *says* something. Now a man who speaks evidently expresses himself; but it is an expression which would not be language unless it were communicable. It does not exist, of course, in the signs and sounds by which it is communicated. It does not exist in the air or on paper, in our mouths or our ears or our eyes. It exists, that is to say, as expression; and just so art is by many said to exist. But it is equally true that language does not exist *merely* as meaning; for to speak of language is to speak of meaning *as conveyed* by signs and sounds. The idea of language is not simply an idea of expression, but of expression which can pass from one mind to another. Language in the speaker's mind is expression, and in the hearer's mind it is expression. The characteristic thing about language is the further fact that the second is the result of the first: that language is communication. Here too the analogy with art seems to hold.

But there is an important refinement in the idea of language which requires to be brought out in order that we may be safe with this analogy. Dante puts it in a compact sentence which, I dare say, many people pass over as a mediocre platitude or a medieval oddity. "It is more human," says Dante, "to be heard than to hear. *In homine sentiri humanius credimus quam sentire.*" That is to say, the nature of language is more concerned with the speaker than with the hearer.

There is first a speaker: on that bare fact we shall all agree. Now, it may be argued, language is for the speaker simply expression; but to the hearer it is communicated expression. Since, therefore, the speaker comes first, language as expression must be ranked above language as communication. And must not this hold good of art too? Must we not say that art is essentially expressive, and only by accident communication? May it not even be (as some seem to think) that communication in art is no more than an epiphenomenon, the presence or absence of which is wholly indifferent to the real fact and essential nature of art—the real fact being simply an intuition, which cannot occur except as an expression? This of course would make an experience of art quite incapable of

/71/ being differentiated from an experience of natural beauty: a conclusion which many not only seem to accept but to welcome.

But what does Dante's characteristically terse and searching remark really mean? For his whole discussion is based on the obvious axiom that language exists as communication or it does not exist at all: the speaker *requires* a hearer. But if a man communicates something to us, he communicates something that is *his own* — something he has made his own; and we accept it as his. Expression is supposed by, and included in, communication. But what expression? Language, says Dante, exists rather by *being heard* than by *hearing;* and this significant antithesis of passive and active means just this: that *another man's expression* is being made to occur in us *as our expression:* the thing of first importance which language effects is not so much that *I understand* as that *a man is understood by me.* Therein lies the essential nature of communicated expression. For all expression is personal; and conscious experience is nothing but personal expression. What I experience I personalise. Now if I experience nature (let me use that convenient word), in that act something becomes the merely passive to the active of my expression; and there is no personalisation in the experience except mine. But in communicated experience, what is given to me is already personalised; what stands as the passive to my active was previously active itself: another spirit has been before me. And I know it. When an expression is communicated to me, what occurs is my way of expressing what has already existed as an expression, and is so accepted by me. Must I therefore say it is my way of intuiting what has already been intuited? I can at any rate say that I intuit it *as* what has been already intuited; for it is given to me in the form of an intuition: unlike nature, which is given to me wholly and *ab initio* to be formed. It makes no difference to allow that, after all, communicated expression exists not by being communicated, but by being expressed: that is, *in me.* That scarcely needs saying; what does need saying is that communicated expression differs decisively from all other kinds: not by the mechanical fact, but by the spiritual fact, of being communicated.

This is the sense in which I would insist that art is communication against those who will only have it to be expression. I would insist, in fact, that expression in art must be regarded as being also communication, because it must necessarily take that form in order to be what we call art; expression succeeds in art when it succeeds as communication. All objections based on the truism that art exists at last as expression fail to take into account the fact that mere expression does not give us the /72/ quality of art; that is only to be found in the spiritual quality of communicated expression. We know that art does not exist in a book or on the stage, in a piano or on canvas: it exists in us. But it exists in us as something communicated, and would not have existed except for its communication. Works of art are made by persons other than ourselves. In the author, art's existence is expression: in us it is the same. But its existence in us is the result of its existence in the author. The mechanical fact of this, however, is important only for the spiritual fact it embodies: the fact that expression in art is not only ours, but the artist's.

"Landscape is art," says Croce. He does not mean a landscape on canvas, but the landscape you see through a window. We must agree with him, if we accept without modification his theory of art as the logic of expression. But suppose I were what is called a landscape-artist: should I merely put on canvas the landscape I *see,* and thus simply fix the *opportunity* for repeating my intuition? By no means: I am reckoned an artist in so far as I manage to fix the intuition itself; and I should do so, not by imitating in paint the landscape seen, but by means of certain qualifications which painters call 'design' or 'composition.' This, to be sure, would be expression. But to what end? How is it judged effective? It is judged effective precisely by its power to compel others to experience what I have experienced; which is assuredly much more than what my eyes have seen. It is effective, that is to say, not merely by its power to express, but (involving that) by its power to communicate; and as it is judged effective, so it is judged as art. When we look at a painted landscape and find it worth looking at, we do not find there what we could have provided ourselves: we do not find simply *a view;* we find there another man's spirit, communicated in terms of landscape, and we find it worth knowing. To equate art with the æsthetic experience of nature, is to give an instance of the familiar process of widening denotation until connotation vanishes. The word loses its meaning; and we must turn to and find another word to label those things which hitherto we have called art. Labelled they must be, for they are different from anything else, and especially different from nature. They differ precisely in being communicated experiences — in the spiritual quality which that implies.

We require two sciences, with two distinctive titles. Adopting words already in use, we require to be quite clear what we mean by æsthetics, and what we mean by the theory of art. Closely related though they are, their subjects should be kept distinct. The general study of experience as such — of intuition and expression — is the large topic of æsthetics. /73/ This, among other things, would propose to account for, or at least, to investigate, our admiration for and delight in nature, with, no doubt, such discriminations of the naturally *sublime* and *beautiful* as would prove necessary. But the theory of art would study the communication of this, — of whatever can occur under the heading of æsthetics, that is, the communication of personal experience; the conditions and means of its communication, and the spiritual significance, not to be paralleled in nature, of communicated experience, with the special qualities (which nothing can replace) of the artistically sublime and beautiful. Let me admit here that the value of art is the value of the artist; but I am not to be manœuvred from this admission into admitting further that I value art simply because I find there in an unusual degree (owing to the artist's superior faculties) the sort of experience I have in nature. The value of art and the value of nature are incommensurable. Only by confusing the topics of æsthetic science and of the theory of art could one be set above the other. No sane man could wish to live wholly in art; and if he did wish it, he could not possibly do it: like Caliban, he must eat his dinner. But we rightly value art for something we can never get in nature: for the satisfaction of some 'desire of the mind' which can only come under the peculiar spiritual condition of communicated experience. The elucidation of this should be the aim of any theory of art.

That art is communication we should, of course, be able to assert on better grounds than the authority of former theories or the analogy of language. So far I have endeavoured to explain precisely what is meant by saying that art is communication. But if I have succeeded in doing so, no more should be needed now than to glance at the fact of art in one or two of its aspects in order to see if communication, in the sense I have described, really does hold good there. It is said, for example, that all people have the experiences of artists. This is not true, for all people have not the experience of making a work of art. But your out-and-out expressionist pays scant attention to that, regarding it as a sort of adjunct, extrinsic to the real fact: if you want it, you have only to want hard enough, and you will get it. But leaving out this most important contribution to the special quality of art — a contribution only to be accounted for in the view that art is communicated expression — let us allow that all people have the sort of experiences which impel artists to make works of art. Does that make everyone an artist? It has been argued that it does; and I find it difficult to regard this as anything better than philosophical sharp practice. But the logic of art as expression requires it. Art is intuition; everyone has intuition; so everyone is an artist. But the /74/ man who calls himself an artist and has never made a work of art in his life, is he not a notorious figure of fun? And why? Because the non-practising artist is a contradiction in terms. Let everyone have the same intuitions as artists; nevertheless a person is only called an artist when his intuitions become works of art: when he makes *his* experiences available for *others* to experience. If you do not call him that you must call him something else; for he is an exceptional person, who requires to be classified for the mere convenience of talking about him. Why not keep the word which everywhere means precisely this person? But if you abolish the notion of communication in art, you empty the meaning out of the word artist, and must find another word to contain that meaning: *"the man who can publish his experiences."*

And he *must* publish them. Until he has published them he is a man frustrated. Now if expression were all he wanted, by the mere fact of *possessing* his experience he has it. But we know that the artist is precisely the man who is not content simply to possess his experience. He is not content until he has also made it communicable: in a work of art. And note this also. He must *learn* how to communicate it, and in order to succeed he must devote himself to labour at it. Justly, if art is communication, we speak of a *work* of art: the phrase is a superfluous compliment, if expression by itself (that is, the happy event of an intuition) will account for art. Either Beethoven and Milton, in their prolonged struggles to perfect their art, were wasting their time; or their furious industry was *needed*: and in that case their art is not to be accounted for simply as expression. It was the communication of expression they were labouring to perfect. For to do so, they had to translate intuition into the medium of their art — into the instrument which could communicate it; since intuitions themselves are clearly incommunicable. They had, in the Aristotelian sense, to *imitate their experience:* the word well expresses the process of making one set of things *represent* another — an essential part of the fact of art. It needs no elaboration, and the expressionist theory can only evade it. If a poet wishes to kiss a girl, he may do so and write a poem about it; or not do so and write a poem about that. The girl may be real or imaginary; but in any case the affair, which ever way it went, did not take place in words. As æsthetic man, the experience itself would suffice him. As poet, it would not; he would have to find the words for it — the words which, intuited by us, would make his experience ours. Then art — poetry — would have occurred; expression would have taken the form of communication.

This process, which is nothing but the *technique* of art, and may be /75/ summed up as symbolic representation, holds good everywhere: not more in music and poetry than in those arts, such as landscape painting, which are erroneously supposed to be in some special way representative. All art is representative of spirit: no art is representative of nature. For the thing submitted to us to be experienced in art is already in the form of an experience, completely organised and isolated into coherent unity of expression. But that expression, which is art, occurs in us because we have translated it out of the artist's *technique* of communication, and could not occur unless it had been so communicated: that fact gives it its special quality as art. The law which governs artistic technique is obvious and universal. It is that the effective is also the expressive — or rather the communicative, remembering that we take communication to include expression. If A can be relied on to effect B, then clearly in order to communicate B we can use A. This shows the importance of those studies in æsthetic psychology which investigate, to the amusement of the expressionists, our reactions to certain shapes, colours, tones, etc. It shows, for example, what Lipps has contributed to the better understanding of art. Such studies will never give us the nature of art; but they will give us the means available to the *technique* of art — what the artist can rely on for the communication of his experience.

Let me correct beforehand a possible misinterpretation. I called *technique* symbolic representation; and the phrase must be taken exactly. That is to say, there is not first the communication, and then the expression in our minds: the communication does not unburden itself of a message, which we then appreciate; we do not have to extricate a meaning from *technique*. Art (whatever emphasis we may lay here or there for polemical purposes) is not to be regarded as communication effecting expression: but rigidly and always as *communicated expression* — expression which cannot occur except as and when communicated. There is no question of *technique* being fitted on to content, as there might be if it were the mechanical fact of communication which mattered. What matters is the spiritual fact of communication: that the expression which is art cannot occur in us except as communicated by sensible *technique* — which cannot but mean, in the form already of a perfected experience: not requiring us to make (as in our everyday life) our usual more or less successful spiritual conquest of nature, but requiring our own personalisation of a conquest already won. The assurance of significance which gives to art its irreplaceable and inestimable value is to be derived from this very fact. But to discuss that would take me too far from my immediate topic. I mention it to show how vital, in my view, the idea of communication is to the true theory of art. /76/

Two common objections may be briefly met here. If art is communication, how does it differ from other communications — *e.g.* language? This is not serious. Art communicates not instruction, information, argument, persuasion: it communicates experience. And it communicates this whole: not the object of it nor opinion about it nor feeling for it, but experience itself, which includes all these. Hence the many-sidedness of artistic *technique;* and hence its formality. For experience, an incommunicable unity, must disintegrate as it passes into its complex communicable representation in *technique*. But this must, in every moment of it, provide for a final complete re-integration into artistic *form*, which by exhibiting itself as self-contained answers to the original unity.

But if an artist labours to make his expression communicable, must that not mean that he composes for his audience, not for himself? I have very little patience with the notion that Shakespeare put in his vulgar passages in order to tickle the mob. I personally enjoy these passages, and I naturally assume that Shakespeare, though he knew they would 'go down,' put them in because he liked them. But the objection is simply a misunderstanding, which may be cleared up on the analogy of language as Dante's trenchant phrase sums up its nature. Language exists primarily not because men want to hear but because men want to be heard. The motive comes from the speaker, but is directed to the hearer. Speech does not exist for the sake of the hearer, but it is necessarily accommodated to the hearer. If a man has something to say, he takes care to say it intelligibly; for otherwise he does not say it at all. So art does not exist for the sake of the audience; but it does not exist at all if the audience cannot take it in. Art is governed by the requirement of the artist; but he would not be an artist unless he required to be understood. His expression, as an artist, necessarily takes the form of communication. And the more successful his communication is as an appeal to his audience, the more he has his audience at his mercy — the more they must submit to *his* experience. The supreme artists are the supreme masters of communication. /77/

✸ THE CONCEPT OF ARTISTIC EXPRESSION

John Hospers

III

. . . To say that a work of art expresses something is . . . to say that the artist has communicated something *to* the listener by means of his work. Expression is not just something evoked in us, it is something which the artist *did* which he then *communicated to* us. . . . Let us pursue this line of thought a little. /332/

The typical kind of view here is one hallowed by tradition; we might describe it roughly as follows: The artist feels a powerful emotion which he expresses by creating a work of art, in such a way that we, the audience, on reading or seeing or hearing the work of art, feel that same emotion ourselves. Whether the artist did this by intent—*i.e.* whether in creating he wanted us to feel this emotion, which is what Collingwood denies that a true artist will do—or whether he was working something out within himself without thinking of an audience, does not matter at this point; the important thing is that, whether by intent or not, whether he created with an audience in mind or only to express what he felt, the artist put something into his work which we, the audience, can get out of it; and what we get out is the same thing that he put in. In this way whatever it is that he put in is communicated to us who get it out. Expression is thus a "two-way deal" involving both the artist and his audience.

The language used just now in characterising the view is deliberately crude, for I do not know how else to describe it with any accuracy. Indeed, this is the very feature of it which makes it, on reflection, extremely difficult to defend. Nor is it easy to remedy it by employing a more sophisticated language in formulating it, for the sophisticated terms usually turn out to be metaphorical. Yet these metaphors seem to be basic to the theory.

For example, it is said that the artist, by means of his work, *transmits* his emotion to us. But what is meant by "transmit" here? When water is transmitted through a pipe, the same water that comes into the pipe at one end comes out at the other; this is, perhaps, a paradigm case of transmission. When we speak of electricity as being transmitted through a wire, there is not in the same sense something that comes in at one end and out at the other, but at any rate there is a continuous flow of electricity; or, if the word "flow" is too metaphorical, it is, perhaps, enough to remark that at any point between its two ends the wire will affect instruments and produce shocks. When /333/ we transfer this talk about transmission from these contexts to works of art, we may tend to imagine a kind of wire connecting the work of art with the artist at one end and with the audience at the other; or, if we do not actually have such an image, at any rate the term "transmit" takes its meaning from situations such as we have just described; and the question arises, what does it mean in the very different context of art? If it is not like these orthodox cases of transmission, what makes it transmission? What is one committing himself to when he says that in art emotion is transmitted?

A metaphor that seems to do better justice to the theory is that of deposition. The artist has, as it were, *deposited* his emotion in the work of art, where we can withdraw it at any time we choose. It is somewhat like the dog burying a

From "The Concept of Artistic Expression," *Proceedings of the Aristotelian Society,* 55 (1954–1955), 313–344.

bone, which another dog digs up at his own convenience. But, of course, the artist has not literally buried or deposited emotion in his work; he has, rather, with or without the divine agonies of inspiration, painted in oils or written a complicated set of notes on paper. It is true that, on seeing the one or hearing the other performed, we may feel certain emotions; but in no literal sense has the artist *put* them there in the way that we put money into the bank to withdraw at a later time. Moreover, the bone that is dug up is one and the same bone that was previously buried; whereas the emotion which we feel (I shall not say "extract") when we hear or see the work of art is not, and cannot be, one and the same emotion as the one which the artist felt (I shall not say "put in").

Let us, then, substitute the metaphor of *conveying*. Whatever it is that the artist is said to be conveying to his audience, of what does such conveyance consist? One person conveys the ball to another by throwing it; the postman conveys letters from the post office to one's door. Is a material continuum necessary for conveyance—the postman between the post office and the house, the moving-conveyor belt for trays or machinery? If something dis- /334/ appeared at one place and reappeared at another, would this be called conveying? If the emotion ceases in the artist and turns up in the audience when they examine his work, has the artist's emotion been conveyed? Again it is not clear exactly what is involved in the talk about conveying. And even if the emotion ceased in the artist and occurred in the audience, would it be the same emotion that occurred in the two? In all the cases of conveyance—the ball, the letter, the water—it is one and the same thing that is conveyed from the one person or place to the other. This condition is not satisfied in the case of emotion. One and the same emotion could no more occur in both artist and observer than the same pain can be passed along from one person to another, even by each person in a row successively pricking his finger with the same pin.

Though the language of the expression theory often leaves the impression that it is one and the same emotion which occurs in both artist and observer, on the analogy with the other examples, this is surely not essential to the theory; perhaps it is enough that they be two emotions of the same kind or class. It may be enough that the artist in composing may feel an emotion of kind X, and the observer on seeing it may feel another emotion of kind X. This probably occurs often enough. But suppose it does; is *this* sufficient for saying that X is conveyed from the one to the other? Is this watered-down formulation really what the theory means when it says that art expresses emotion?

Let us, then, speak simply of "communication". The word "communicate" is somewhat more elastic than the previous ones—people can communicate in person by wireless, and perhaps telepathically—but it is also more vague and difficult to pin down. We could spend many hours discussing criteria for communication. Since we cannot do this, let us take an example in which we would probably agree that communication had occurred. A student summarises the contents of a difficult essay, and the author looks at the summary and says, "That's it /335/ exactly!". Similarly, one might say that an emotion had been communicated if the listener to a symphony described a movement as "haunting, tinged with gentle melancholy, becoming by degrees hopeful, ending on a note of triumph" and the composer said, "Exactly so! That's just what I meant to communicate".

I have some doubts about whether even this would satisfy us as being a "communication of emotion". But, so as not to spend more time tinkering with the highly vulnerable terminology of the expression theory (in the form we are considering in this section), let me state some objections that could be raised to any formulation of it known to me.

1.   There are many experiences which the artist undergoes in the process of creation — the divine agonies of inception, the slow working through of ideas to fruition, and the technical details of execution — which the audience need not and probably should not share. This part of the artist's creative activity need in no sense be communicated. For example, much of the creative process may be agonising or even boring, but the audience on viewing or hearing the work of art should not feel either agonised or bored. At most, then, it is only a selection of the artist's experiences in creation that should be communicated. One should not speak as if somehow the artist's whole experience (including emotion) in creation were somehow transferred bodily to the observer or listener.

2.   Even for the part that the artist wants to communicate to his audience, it is not necessary that he be feeling this at the time of creation, as the theory so often seems to imply. When the artist is under the sway or spell of an emotion, he is all too inclined to be victim and not master of it, and therefore not to be in a good position to create a work of art, which demands a certain detachment and distance as well as considerable lucidity and studied self-discipline. Wordsworth himself said that the emotion should be recollected in tranquillity; and others, such as /336/ Eliot, have gone further and expunged emotion from the account altogether. Perhaps, then, it might be held essential only that the artist *have had* the emotion at some time or other. But if all that is required is that the artist have had some emotion or other of type X, then, since most people of any sensitivity have experienced a considerable part of the gamut of human emotions, including some from type X or any other one chooses to mention, this feature in no way distinguishes the artist, and the theory loses all its punch: it becomes innocuous and, like all highly diluted solutions, uninteresting and undistinctive.

3.   To say that the audience should feel the same kind of emotion as the artist seems often to be simply not true. Perhaps, in lyric poems and some works of music, the listener may feel an emotion of the same kind as the artist once felt; but in many cases this is not so at all. Even when we do feel emotions in response to works of art (and most of the time what we experience should probably not be called "emotions" at all), they are often of a quite different sort: if the author has expressed anger, we feel not anger but (perhaps) horror or repulsion; if he has expressed anguish, we may feel not anguish but pity.

Often it seems quite clear that the audience emotion should be quite different from anything that was or sometimes ever could have been in the mind of the artist. We may experience fascination, horror, or sympathy when seeing *Hamlet* because of what we feel is the oedipal conflict unconsciously motivating his inaction; but this response, a result of Freudian psychology, could hardly have been in the mind of Shakespeare. And why, indeed, should it have been? It is enough that his drama can be consistently interpreted in this way, perhaps even giving it an added coherence; it is enough that he wrote a drama capable of arousing such feelings; it is not necessary that he have experienced them himself.

4.   Epistemologically the most ticklish point for the expression theory is simply this: how can we ever know /337/for sure that the feeling in the mind of the artist was anything like the feeling aroused in a listener or observer? Our judgments on this point, in cases where we do have some evidence, have notoriously often been mistaken. We might feel absolutely certain that Mozart felt joy when he composed the Haffner Symphony, and be amazed to discover that during this whole period of his life he was quite miserable, full of domestic dissension, poverty, and disease. A happy composition does not imply a happy composer. Strictly speaking, the only way we can know how a composer felt is

to ask him, and then only if he is not lying. If he is dead, we have to consult his autobiography, if any, or other written records, if any, and hope that they do not misrepresent the facts and that they do not tell us what the composer or biographer wanted us to think rather than what really was the case. And, of course, they often do this: "Artists who are dead have rarely left satisfactory psychological records, and the difficulties of appealing to living artists, whose motives and intentions are often mixed and their powers of introspective analysis small, are overwhelming". (Osborne, *Aesthetics and Criticism*, p. 153.)

This consequence is fatal if the expression theory is made a criterion of good art. For it would follow that, if we cannot know whether the emotion felt by a listener is of the same kind as that felt by the artist, we cannot know whether or not this is a good work of art. Therefore, in those cases where we have no records or they are of dubious value, we must hold our judgment of the work of art in abeyance. And such a consequence, it would seem, makes the theory in this form pass the bounds of the ridiculous.

"But", it may be said, "we don't have to find out from the artist himself or from written records what emotion the artist felt—we can tell this from seeing or hearing the work of art!" But this is precisely what we cannot do. Though in this area conviction is strong and subjective feelings of certainty run high, our inferences from work /338/ of art to artist are as likely as not to be mistaken. We cannot tell from just listening to the symphony how Mozart felt; the work simply provides no safe clue to this. The best we can do is guess, after hearing the composition, what emotion he was feeling; and then, if the available evidence should point to the conclusion that he actually was feeling so at this time, our inference would have been correct for at least this instance. But once we do this, we are already checking our inference (made from hearing the work) against the empirical evidence, and it is the evidence that is decisive.

We might, in the light of these objections, wish to revise the theory so as not to require that the audience should feel what the artist felt, but only what the artist *intended* the audience to feel. But when this is done, difficulties again confront us: (1) The same difficulties that attend our knowing how the artist felt are also present, though sometimes in lesser degree, in our knowing what he intended. (2) The artist's whole intention may have misfired; he may have intended us to feel one thing, but if even the most careful and sensitive listeners for generations fail to feel anything like this when they hear his composition, shall we still say that we should feel what the artist intended us to feel? (3) The moment we abandon the stipulation that the audience should feel, not as the artist felt but as the artist intended the audience to feel, we seem to abandon anything that could be called the expression theory. For it is characteristic of the expression theory that the artist must have felt something which he wants us also to feel; if he did not feel it, but only tried to make us feel it or intended us to feel it, this is no longer an expression of feeling on his part but a deliberate attempt to evoke it in others—in other words, not expression but arousal.

It may seem that in the last few pages we have been flogging a dead horse; yet if one examines much critical writing he must be aware how far from dead this horse is. Critics and laymen alike are dominated, quite unconsciously, by the metaphors of transmission, conveyance, /339/ and the like, the emotion in the analogy being usually a kind of liquid that is transmitted bodily from artist to audience. Although when made explicit this kind of formulation would doubtless be rejected, it is precisely these metaphors which are at the very roots (to use another metaphor) of the expression theory in the form we have been considering in this section. And the very strong objections to the theory seem seldom to be realised. /340/

✻ BEAUTY IS NOT ALL: AN APPEAL FOR ESTHETIC PLURALISM

W. P. Montague

> *An appeal to artists to supplement their creations of beauty*
> *or objectified joy with creations in which any emotion, even the*
> *most painful and terrible, is objectified, to the end that art may*
> *cease to be a sophisticated affair of the studios and become once*
> *more a power in the life of the people.*

Beauty is defined by Santayana as pleasure objectified, and by Kant as the power of an object to cause pleasure by its intrinsic essence rather than by its existential relation to an observer. The two definitions can be shown to mean the same thing because pleasure is only externalized in an object when it is derived from its essence.

Beauty is generally regarded as the sole aim of most art. But an art which in its content or subject matter objectifies only joyous emotion is sentimental and boring. The justifiable revolt against it takes three principal forms: (1) Moralism, (2) Realism, (3) "Unrealism."

Moralism reduces art to a servile status, making it a means to some ethical or sociological end. In this process the truly esthetic values are in danger of being warped or destroyed.

Realism seeks to imitate nature and to arouse in the spectator the pleasure of recognizing and identifying what is /560/ familiar. This pleasure is pardonable and even innocent, but is not esthetic, though it is often thought to be. Realism is, moreover, too eager to be contrasted with "idealism," and consequently tends to emphasize the disagreeable and trivial aspects of existence.

When challenged for their esthetic irrelevancies, both realists and moralists are apt to defend their claim to be regarded as artists by appealing to the adequacy or effectiveness of their performance. If what is done is not beautiful, it is at least beautifully done.

"Unrealism" is concerned with neither edification nor imitation. It aims directly at beauty of form. And as attention to form must compete with attention to content, the significance of the one requires the insignificance of the other. To achieve this goal of *form at any price*, the subject matter should at least be trivial, and wherever possible it should be altogether meaningless. Unrealism is not confined to painting and sculpture. It has made its way a little into music, a great deal into recent poetry, and in one notable instance even into prose. It is capable of blending to some extent with realism and moralism as they are capable of blending with each other. I suppose that surrealism is but a whimsical and highly piquant blend of realism and unrealism.

Without denying for one moment either the beauty of pure form or the esthetic value of the strange technique by which unrealism seeks to bring it forth, one may be permitted to regret a certain preciosity and exclusiveness that narrows the appeal of the movement and confines it mainly to the studios. Art for art's sake is good, but art for the sake of artists is not so good. It is unfair and a little selfish that those endowed with power to enrich and illuminate the lives of their less fortunate brethren should hug their gifts to themselves and revel in a collectivistic narcissism. Yet so long as purely formal beauty is the one end to be /561/ achieved, a considerable degree of such exclusiveness is inevitable.

Without going back to an optimistic sentimentalism, there is a way for art to recapture that significant *content* which, and which only, in contrast to sig-

"Beauty Is Not All: An Appeal for Esthetic Pluralism," in *The Ways of Things* (New York: Prentice-Hall, Inc., 1940), pp. 560–563.

nificant *form,* can warm the hearts of the esthetic proletarians who, alas, make up the majority of mankind. This is the way of Esthetic Pluralism.

Let us return to the definitions of beauty given by Kant and Santayana and subject them to a simple but momentous extension.

Instead of restricting the realm of the esthetic to objectified *pleasure,* why not broaden it to include objectified *emotion*—and by "emotion" I mean feeling of any kind—the sad, the terrible, and even the horrible? This does not mean that all emotion, still less all expression of any kind, is to be accorded esthetic value. As beauty was not mere pleasure but rather objectified pleasure, so esthetic values are not mere emotions but only such emotions as are objectified. And neither pleasure nor any other feeling is objectified, that is, localized or vested in an object rather than in the conscious subject himself, unless the emotion is, in the Kantian sense, regarded as due to the intrinsic form of the thing and not to its spatio-temporal relations to the percipient. This is what I mean by "Esthetic Pluralism." Beauty is objectified joy, and as such the highest and loveliest of esthetic values. But Beauty is not all—she is a queen, a constitutional sovereign, but not a dictator. And just as hero and heroine shine all the brighter when not the sole persons in the tale, so would the objectified pleasures, if set off and enhanced by objectifications of other emotions, lose the saccharinity and banality that led to the modernistic movements of revolt.

Drama and fiction have, of course, taken this road quite spontaneously without waiting for the sanction of estheti-/562/cians. If the masters of painting and sculpture would do it also and abandon their fixation on beauty either of form or of content as the sole thing that was worth their while, they could make of their galleries macrocosms of the human heart and the totality of its passions. And from these macrocosms not only the aristocracy of connoisseurs and sophisticates but the vast multitude of common men could nourish and enrich their lives. An art thus broadened and freed from its ivory tower might regain, in our own sad days, all and more than all of the power and the glory which pertained to it in the great days of Greece. /563/

⌘ WHAT HAS BEAUTY TO DO WITH ART?

C. J. Ducasse

Almost all writers on esthetics have assumed without argument that beauty is essentially connected with art. The thesis of this paper is on the contrary that there is no essential connection between them. If I am able to give satisfactory accounts of the nature of beauty and of art, and these accounts retain complete logical independence each of the other, that thesis will have been proved. Before attempting to do this, however, I wish to call attention to a fact which already shows that that thesis must be correct. That fact is the existence of ugly art.

Every one already grants that many things which have beauty are not works of art, but natural objects. Conversely, however, there are also many things which are works of art, and which at the same time are ugly. Thus there are ugly designs, ugly color-schemes, ugly paintings, ugly dances, and so on. But a design, for instance, which is ugly, is not on that account any less truly a work of art than a design which is beautiful, for it is born in exactly the same way.

"What Has Beauty to Do with Art?" *Journal of Philosophy*, 25 (1928), 181–186.

Each proceeds from the same sort of impulse, is created through the same processes, and sometimes even by the very same person. And the creator of an ugly work may well admit the ugliness, and insist that he was not concerned to create beauty, but only to express what was in him, and that his work such as it is does just that with complete success. By ugly art I therefore do not at all mean what has been called the ugly in art or the art of pain, namely, the pleasing representation by art of the ugly or painful. Ugly art, on the contrary, is art which displeases. Naturally enough, such art is not much noticed or purchased; for most buyers of art want beauty, and it is nothing to them that a given work successfully expresses what the artist felt, if it is ugly. Beauty, we might well say, is thus almost a condition of the social visibility of a work of art; /181/ but it is not a condition of the existence of one. Ugly art, although easily overlooked or forgotten, nevertheless exists in vast quantities; and therefore art can not be defined in terms involving beauty except by unsound philosophies of art which, confining their view to the highly selected contents of museums and the like, overlook one half of the relevant facts.

That such a thing as ugly art exists proves that there can be no necessary connection between art and beauty. Why there is none will now be made evident by the accounts of the nature of each that I shall submit.

The most widely known attempt to define art in terms not involving beauty is doubtless that of Tolstoi, in his book, *What is Art?* It is true that all the principal esthetic theses of that book were already contained and were found by Tolstoi in the *Esthetique* of Veron, published in Paris in 1878. But in turning them to his own quite peculiar purposes, Tolstoi at the same time rescued them from general oblivion, restated them with new vigor, and gave them such actual influence as they have had. Veron and Tolstoi agree that beauty is wholly accidental to art, and that the essence of art is stated by describing it as *the language of feeling.* At this point, however, their analyses diverge. For Tolstoi a language is essentially a means of communication. Veron, on the other hand, considers primarily not what language is socially good for, nor what needs have shaped its evolution, but rather what language is as a matter of direct introspective observation. And he finds that language is essentially *expression* either of meaning or of feeling—the latter constituting what we call art. Thus he writes: "What properly constitutes artistic genius is the imperious need to manifest externally by directly expressive forms and signs the emotions felt; and the capacity for finding such signs and such forms by a kind of immediate intuition" (p. 35).

There is, I think, no doubt that Veron and not Tolstoi has correctly discerned the intrinsic nature of language. Language is essentially not communication, but expression. For the fact that in writing the present words I am certainly expressing my thoughts in language, would be left quite untouched even if those words were never to be read by any one, and thus were never to perform the transmitting function in terms of which Tolstoi would define language. What is thus true of the language of meaning is equally true of the language of feeling, that is to say, art. The work of art is essentially an attempt by the artist to express objectively what he feels. The displaying to others of his work in the hope that it will transmit to them the feeling objectified in it, is due to quite another impulse, namely, the gregarious impulse. Man dislikes to be alone /182/ not only physically, but also in his opinions and no less in his moods and feelings; but the impulse to share one's feelings is both quite different and separable from the impulse to express them. Art, that is to say, the art activity, may therefore, it seems to me, be accurately defined by saying that it is *the critically-controlled attempt to give objective expression to, i.e., to embody, a feeling.* That it is objective expression that art directly aims at, means that the consideration in the light of which the artist exercises the critical control of his own work is, not the beauty of what he creates, but the adequacy of it as embodiment of his feeling.

In the definition of art just proposed, the provision for critical control rules out expressions of feeling which are not art, such as a child's dancing with joy at the prospect of a picnic. Again, the definition distinguishes art, as objective expression of feeling, from what may broadly be called prose, which is the objective expression of thought, i.e., of meaning. For art as such never expresses thought, but only feeling. What lends a certain plausibility to the contrary opinion is only the fact that often it is in part *by means of* thought or of imagination that art presents to the attention the object which constitutes the expression of feeling; that is, the esthetic object which embodies the feeling often consists of more than is directly presented by the work of art considered purely sensuously.

Again, the word "feeling" in the definition of art given means, not primarily pleasure or displeasure, but emotional consciousness. I use the word "feeling" instead of "emotion," because the latter connotes primarily those few of our feelings which, like anger, love, fear, etc., are connected with recurring typical situations and have therefore received names. But to one feeling which has thus come to be labelled with a name, we have a thousand others just as real which have not, and which therefore easily pass unnoticed.

As a last remark in connection with the foregoing account of the nature of art, I wish to say that the use in it of the word "expression" should not lead to the idea that it has anything in common with the doctrine of Mr. Croce. In the latter, the word "expression" also occurs, but with a meaning which both seems quite peculiar to himself and is left far from clear by the extraordinary statements which he makes concerning it. To point the difference, I may mention that according to Mr. Croce's peculiar terminology Intuition, Expression, and Beauty are only three names for one and the same concept.[1] He also describes expression as "spiritual es- /183/ thetic synthesis," and expressly denies that what he means by that has anything in common with expression in the semiotic or the naturalistic sense. In the conception of art which I have set forth, on the contrary, the word "expression" is taken in the usual semiotic and naturalistic sense. Thus we commonly and properly say that our thoughts are *expressed* by us in words, visible or audible; and it is in the very same sense of the word "expression" that I say the work of art constitutes an expression of feeling. That is to say, the work of art is the objective *symbol* of the feeling. Such a symbol differs from words, which are symbols of meanings, only in that whereas words usually are psychologically conventional and replaceable symbols, the work of art, on the contrary, is always the psychologically predetermined and irreplaceable symbol of the feeling which it expresses.

The characterization of art now given in no way involves the notion of beauty. There remains to characterize beauty independently of any reference to art.

The words "beauty" and "ugliness," I maintain, have no significance in terms of the artist's attitude, which is the creatively practical, but only in terms of the contemplative attitude which is the beholder's, whether that beholder be or not the very man who a moment before was creating what he now contemplates. Space forbids entering here upon a minute analysis of the contemplative or esthetic attitude. But it is indispensable for the present purpose to indicate

---

[1] Expression and Beauty are not two concepts, but a single concept" (*Breviary of Æsthetics*, Rice Institute Pamphlets, p. 263). Also ". . . the false distinction of the indistinguishable, intuition and expression" (p. 229). And in the *Æsthetic* (p. 9), we read that intuition and expression "are not two but one." /183/

briefly its nature. It is to be distinguished from and contrasted with both the inquisitive and the practical attitudes. In these we are interested respectively in gaining knowledge, and in acting upon or about the environment. In the attitude of esthetic contemplation, on the other hand, our interest is in feeling purely for its own sake; as something to be tasted, and as it were rolled under one's emotional tongue. In the esthetic attitude, moreover, we endeavor to sweep ourselves clean of previous feeling, so as to receive without altering whatever feeling the object of contemplative attention will communicate to us. We may thus characterize the attitude of esthetic contemplation as, so to say, a "listening" with our capacity for feeling, for it is to that capacity exactly what listening is to our capacity for hearing.

What takes place when a content of attention is thus esthetically contemplated, is the exact converse of what occurs when an artist objectifies his feeling in a work of art; namely, through esthetic contemplation the beholder extracts from the object the feeling which that object contains *in potentia*. Or, if I may coin the word, he *ecpathizes* the object. Ecpathy is thus something quite different from empathy. Empathy, which anyhow is a misleading name for /184/ what it means, is the psychological process through which *action* (not mere motion) is perceived where it is, or imaginatively ascribed where it is not. But the perception or ascription of action is not of itself esthetic contemplation. The action perceived by means of empathy may, however, be esthetically contemplated, and its import of feeling be thereby extracted from it. Such a case could then be described by saying that we ecpathize the action which we empathically perceive or imagine.

Esthetic contemplation, in the sense now indicated, can obviously be given not only to works of art, but just as well to natural objects. The most that could be said is that works of art are in general easier to contemplate because they do not tempt us to take the practical or the inquisitive attitude as natural objects may do. But in any case, the possession by an object of a potential import of feeling is quite independent of whether that object came into existence naturally or artificially. There is thus no discernible entity, whether real or imaginary, natural or artificial, simple or complex, concrete or abstract, trivial or the reverse, which is not susceptible of being esthetically contemplated, and capable of then yielding to us its characteristic import of feeling.

Bearing in mind what has now been said of esthetic contemplation, we may next formulate the distinction between esthetic and non-esthetic feelings by saying that esthetic feeling is any feeling obtained through esthetic contemplation, and that no feeling is esthetic which is not so obtained. There is thus no kind of feeling which is *a priori* incapable of taking on the esthetic status. Such limitations in kind and degree of intensity as there are to esthetic feelings, are purely empirical, and due to the difficulty of maintaining the esthetic attitude when the temptation to action or to curiosity happens to be strong.

In terms of esthetic feeling we may now characterize beauty. Esthetic feeling is either pleasant, unpleasant, or indifferent. When the feeling is pleasant, the object in the contemplation of which it was obtained is called beautiful; when on the contrary the feeling is unpleasant, the object is called ugly. Beauty is, then, simply the capacity which certain objects possess, of imparting to the esthetically contemplative beholder feelings that are pleasant. The immediate corollary of this is that beauty is a joint function of two factors, namely, the nature of the object and the nature of the beholder. Judgments of beauty are thus objective only in the sense that it is truly of objects, and not of our feelings, that beauty is predicable. They are subjective, however, in the sense that what is predicated of the object is its status in respect of the esthetic pleasure of the individual beholder. Judgments of beauty, and so-called canons of /185/ beauty, have therefore no binding character at all. Such general acceptance as they may meet signifies only that the original or acquired taste of certain more or less numerous beholders happens to coincide.

The brief analysis which has now been given of beauty and of art confirms and explains the essential independence of each from the other which constituted the thesis of this paper, and of which the existence of ugly art already assured us. /186/

✖ THE POETIC PRINCIPLE

Edgar Allan Poe

While the epic mania—while the idea that, to merit in poetry, prolixity is indispensable—has, for some years past, been gradually dying out of the public mind, by mere dint of its own absurdity—we find it succeeded by a heresy too palpably false to be long tolerated, but one which, in the brief period it has already endured, may be said to have accomplished more in the corruption of our Poetical Literature than all its other enemies combined. I allude to the heresy of *The Didactic*. It has been assumed, tacitly and avowedly, directly and indirectly, that the ultimate object of all Poetry is Truth. Every poem, it is said, should inculcate a moral; and by this moral is the poetical merit of the work to be adjudged. We Americans especially have patronised this happy idea; and we Bostonians, very especially, have developed it in full. We have taken it into our heads that to write a poem simply for the poem's sake, and to acknowledge such to have been our design, would be to confess ourselves radically wanting in the true Poetic dignity and force:—but the simple fact is, that, would we but permit ourselves to look into our own /271/ souls, we should immediately there discover that under the sun there neither exists nor *can* exist any work more thoroughly dignified—more supremely noble than this very poem—this poem *per se*—this poem which is a poem and nothing more—this poem written solely for the poem's sake. . . .

Dividing the world of mind into its three most immediately obvious distinctions, we have the Pure Intellect, Taste, and the Moral Sense. . . . /272/

. . . Just as the Intellect concerns itself with Truth, so Taste informs us of the Beautiful while the Moral Sense is regardful of Duty. Of this latter, while Conscience teaches the obligation, and Reason the expediency, Taste contents herself with displaying the charms:—waging war upon Vice solely on the ground of her deformity—her disproportion—her animosity to the fitting, to the appropriate, to the harmonious—in a word, to Beauty.

An immortal instinct, deep within the spirit of man, is thus, plainly, a sense of the Beautiful. This it is which administers to his delight in the manifold forms, and sounds, and odours, and sentiments amid which he exists. And just as the lily is repeated in the lake, or the eyes of Amaryllis in the mirror, so is the mere oral or written repetition of these forms, and sounds, and colours, and odours, and sentiments, a duplicate source of delight. But this mere repetition is not poetry. He who shall simply sing, with however glowing enthusiasm, or with however vivid a truth of description, of the sights, and sounds, and

From "The Poetic Principle," in *The Complete Works of Edgar Allan Poe*, ed. James A. Harrison (New York: Thomas Y. Crowell, 1902), XIV, 266–292.

odours, and colours, and sentiments, which greet *him* in common with all
mankind—he, I say, has yet failed to prove his divine title. There is still a
something in the distance which he has been unable to attain. We have still a
thirst unquenchable, to allay which he has not shown us the crystal springs.
This thirst belongs to the immortality of Man. It is at once a consequence and
an indication of his perennial existence. It is the desire of the moth for the star.
It is no mere appreciation of the Beauty before us—but a wild effort to reach the
Beauty above. Inspired by an ecstatic prescience of the glories /273/ beyond the
grave, we struggle, by multiform combinations among the things and thoughts
of Time, to attain a portion of that Loveliness whose very elements, perhaps,
appertain to eternity alone. And thus when by Poetry—or when by Music, the
most entrancing of the Poetic moods—we find ourselves melted into tears—we
weep then—not as the Abbate Gravina supposes—through excess of pleasure,
but through a certain, petulant, impatient sorrow at our inability to grasp *now,*
wholly, here on earth, at once and for ever, those divine and rapturous joys, of
which *through* the poem, or *through* the music, we attain to but brief and indeter-
minate glimpses.

The struggle to apprehend the supernal Loveliness—this struggle, on the
part of souls fittingly constituted—has given to the world all *that* which it (the
world) has ever been enabled at once to understand and *to feel* as poetic.

The Poetic Sentiment, of course, may develope itself in various modes—in
Painting, in Sculpture, in Architecture, in the Dance—very especially in Music—and very peculiarly, and with a wide field, in the composition of the
Landscape Garden. Our present theme, however, has regard only to its manifestation in words. And here let me speak briefly on the topic of rhythm.
Contenting myself with the certainty that Music, in its various modes of metre,
rhythm, and rhyme, is of so vast a moment in Poetry as never to be wisely
rejected—is so vitally important an adjunct, that he is simply silly who declines
its assistance, I will not now pause to maintain its absolute essentiality. It is in
Music, perhaps, that the soul most nearly attains the great end for which, when
inspired by the Poetic Sentiment, it struggles—the creation of supernal /274/
Beauty. It *may* be, indeed, that here this sublime end is, now and then, attained
in fact. We are often made to feel, with a shivering delight, that from an earthly
harp are stricken notes which *cannot* have been unfamiliar to the angels. And
thus there can be little doubt that in the union of Poetry with Music in its
popular sense, we shall find the widest field for the Poetic development. . . .

To recapitulate, then:—I would define, in brief, the Poetry of words as *The
Rhythmical Creation of Beauty.* Its sole arbiter is Taste. With the Intellect or with
the Conscience, it has only collateral relations. Unless incidentally, it has no
concern whatever either with Duty or with Truth.

A few words, however, in explanation. *That* pleasure which is at once the
most pure, the most elevating, and the most intense, is derived, I maintain,
from the contemplation of the Beautiful. In the contemplation of Beauty we
alone find it possible to attain that pleasurable elevation, or excitement, *of the
soul,* which we recognise as the Poetic Sentiment, and which is so easily distinguished from Truth, which is the satisfaction of the Reason, or from Passion,
which is the excitement of the heart. I make Beauty, therefore—using the word
as inclusive of the sublime—I make Beauty the province of the poem, simply
because it is an obvious rule of Art that effects should be made to spring as
directly as possible from their causes:—no one as yet having been weak enough
to deny that the peculiar elevation in question is at least *most readily* attainable in
the poem. It by no means follows, how- /275/ ever, that the incitements of
Passion, or the precepts of Duty, or even the lessons of Truth, may not be

introduced into a poem, and with advantage; for they may subserve, incidentally, in various ways, the general purposes of the work: —but the true artist will always contrive to tone them down in proper subjection to that *Beauty* which is the atmosphere and the real essence of the poem. /276/

PREFACE TO THE PICTURE OF DORIAN GRAY

Oscar Wilde

The artist is the creator of beautiful things.

To reveal art and conceal the artist is art's aim.

The critic is he who can translate into another manner or a new material his impression of beautiful things.

The highest as the lowest form of criticism is a mode of autobiography.

Those who find ugly meanings in beautiful things are corrupt without being charming. This is a fault. /v/

Those who find beautiful meanings in beautiful things are the cultivated. For these there is hope.

They are the elect to whom beautiful things mean only Beauty.

There is no such thing as a moral or an immoral book. Books are well written, or badly written. That is all.

The nineteenth century dislike of Realism is the rage of Caliban seeing his own face in a glass.

The nineteenth century dislike of Romanticism is the rage of Caliban not seeing his own face in a glass.

The moral life of man forms part of the subject-matter of the artist, but the morality of art consists in the perfect use of an imperfect medium.

No artist desires to prove anything. Even things that are true can be proved.

No artist has ethical sympathies. An ethical sympathy in an artist is an unpardonable mannerism of style.

No artist is ever morbid. The artist can express everything.

Thought and language are to the artist instruments of an art.

Vice and virtue are to the artist materials for an art.

From the point of view of form, the type of all the arts is the art of the musician. From the /vi/ point of view of feeling, the actor's craft is the type.

All art is at once surface and symbol.

Those who go beneath the surface do so at their peril.

"The Preface," *The Picture of Dorian Gray* (New York: Ward and Lock, 1895), pp. v–vii.

Those who read the symbol do so at their peril.
It is the spectator, and not life, that art really mirrors.
Diversity of opinion about a work of art shows that the work is new, complex, and vital.
When critics disagree the artist is in accord with himself.
We can forgive a man for making a useful thing as long as he does not admire it. The only excuse for making a useless thing is that one admires it intensely.
All art is quite useless. /vii/

⌘ PURE ART

Roger Fry

There is such a thing as impure or useful science, and, if you were to analyze that activity, you would find all sorts of biological motives at work, although the fundamental truth-seeking passion of pure science is distinguished precisely by its independence of, and its indifference to, biological necessity.

Similarly there is an impure and, perhaps, useful art (though the use of impure art is not so easily demonstrated as that of impure science); here too, analysis would reveal a number of elements /5/ which really form no part of the essential esthetic activity, and you will make a serious mistake if, after such an analysis, you declare these to be constituent parts of that phenomenon.

If you have a substance which you know to be chemically pure it is clear that you have a right to say that every element which you discover in that substance by analysis is a constituent part of it, but, if you have any reason to suspect an impure mixture, you know that any particular element which the analysis reveals may be due to the impurity and form no part of the substance which you are investigating.

Now that the esthetic activity does mix in various degrees with a number of other activities is surely evident. Take for instance advertisements: many of these show no esthetic effort and do not even try to afford esthetic pleasure; they merely convey more or less inaccurate information about a particular object. You can think of advertisements where not only are the merits of the objects enumerated but the object, let us say a bottle of Somebody's Beer, is depicted. Every detail of the bottle and its label is given so that we may recognize it when we see it in the bar, but there is no sign that in the manner of representation any thought has been expended for our esthetic pleasure. On the other hand I take certain advertisements in American journals, where advertisements are taken seriously and romantically, and I find a very genuine effort, in the proportion and spacing of the letters, in the harmonious consistence of the forms, and in the exact presentation of the object, towards esthetic pleasure. None the less this esthetic appeal is mixed with all sorts of appeals to other feelings than the love of beauty—appeals to our sense of social prestige, to our avarice, to our desire for personal display, and so forth.

Or take again the case of dress—here no doubt there is often a considerable care for pure beauty of line and harmony of colour, but such considerations have continually to give place to far more pressing concerns connected with

From *The Artist and Psycho-Analysis* (London: L. and V. Woolf, 1924).

social rivalry, in fact to all the complicated mass of instincts which go to make up what we call snobbishness.

These, then, are cases of obvious mixtures, in which the esthetic impulse has a part—but you will say these belong to applied art; if /6/ we take pictures which subserve no ultimate use we shall surely be safe. But alas the vast majority of pictures are not really works of art at all. No doubt in most a careful analysis would reveal some trace of esthetic preoccupations, but for the most part the appeal they make is to quite other feelings.

For the moment I must be dogmatic and declare that the esthetic emotion is an emotion about form. In certain people, purely formal relations of certain kinds arouse peculiarly profound emotions, or rather I ought to say the recognition by them of particular kinds of formal relations arouse these emotions. Now these emotions about forms may be accompanied by other emotions which have to do more or less with what I call the instinctive life.

The simplest examples of this can be taken from music. If, as frequently happens, an unmusical child strikes six notes in succession on the piano, the chances are that no one would be able to perceive any necessary relation between these notes—they have been struck by accident, as we say. But if I strike the first six notes of "God Save The King," every one who is not quite music-deaf recognizes that they have, as one would say, a meaning, a purpose. They occur in such a sequence that after each note has been struck we feel that only certain notes can follow and, as the notes follow one another, they more or less adequately fulfil our expectation. *i.e.*, from the beginning the idea of a formal design or scheme is impressed on our minds, and anything which departed violently from that would be not merely meaningless, but an outrage to our sense of order and proportion. We have then an immediate recognition of formal design, of a trend in every part towards a single unity or complete thing which we call the tune.

Now let us suppose that you hear "God Save The King" for the first time; it is possible that you would get an emotion from the mere recognition of that formal system. I do not say it would be a very profound or important emotion, but it might be an emotion, and it would probably stir up no image whatever in your mind, would be associated with no particular person or thing or idea. But those particular notes have become associated with many other things in our minds, so that when they are played we no longer can fix our minds on the form, we are instantly invaded by the associated /7/ feelings of loyalty, devotion to country, boredom from the memory of tiresome functions, or relief that we can now at least leave the theatre. We shall say that that particular formal design of notes has become symbolical of numerous other things with which it has become associated.

Now this simple case presents in easy form some of the problems which confront us in works of art of all kinds. The form of a work of art has a meaning of its own and the contemplation of the form in and for itself gives rise in some people to a special emotion which does not depend upon the association of the form with anything else what ever. But that form may by various means either by casual opposition or by some resemblance to things or people or ideas in the outside world, become intimately associated in our minds with those other things, and if these things are objects of emotional feeling, we shall get from the contemplation of the form the echo of all the feelings belonging to the associated objects.

Now since very few people are so constituted by nature or training as to have developed the special feeling about formal design, and since everyone has in the course of their lives accumulated a vast mass of feeling about all sorts of objects, persons, and ideas, for the greater part of mankind the associated emotions of a work of art are far stronger than the purely esthetic ones.

So far does this go that they hardly notice the form, but pass at once into the world of associated emotions which that form calls up in them. Thus, to go back to our example, the vast majority of people have no notion whether the form of "God Save The King" is finely constructed and capable of arousing esthetic emotion or not. They have never, properly speaking, heard the form because they have always passed at once into that richly varied world of racial and social emotion which has gathered round it.

And what is true of certain pieces of music is even more true of the graphic arts. Here we have forms which quite visibly resemble certain objects in nature, and not unfrequently these objects, such for instance as a beautiful woman, are charged for us with a great deal of emotion. When to this we add that people are far less sensitive to the meaning of visible formal design than they are to audible design, we need not be surprised that pictures are almost /8/ always estimated for qualities which have nothing, or almost nothing, to do with their formal design or their esthetic quality in the strict sense.

To satisfy this emotional pleasure in the associated ideas of images which the mass of mankind feel so strongly there has arisen a vast production of pictures, writings, music, etc., in which formal design is entirely subordinated to the exitation of the emotions associated with objects. And this is what we may call popular, commerical or impure art, and to this category belongs nowadays the vast majority of so called artistic productions. On the other hand in each generation there are likely to be a certain number of people who have a sensitiveness to purely formal relations. To such people these relations have meaning and arouse keen emotions of pleasure. And these people create such systems of formal relations and do not sacrifice willingly or consciously anything of those formal relations to the arousing of emotions connected with objects in the outside world. Their whole attention is directed towards establishing the completest relationship of all the parts within the system of the work of art.

It so happens that these systems of formal relations the meaning of which is apprehended by a comparatively few people in each generation, have a curious vitality and longevity, whereas these works in which appeal is made chiefly to the associated ideas of images rarely survive the generation for whose pleasure they were made. This may be because the emotions about objects change more rapidly than the emotions about form. But whatever the reason, the result is that the accumulated and inherited artistic treasure of mankind is made up almost entirely of those works in which formal design is the predominant consideration.

This contrast between the nature of inherited art and the mass of contemporary art has become so marked that the word "classic" is often used (loosely and incorrectly, no doubt) to denote work which has this peculiar character. People speak of classical music, for instance, when they mean the works of any of the great composers. It is significant of the rarity of comprehension of such formal design that to many people classical music is almost synonymous with "dull" music. . . . /9/

. . . Since most people are unable to perceive the meaning of purely formal relations, are unable to derive from them the profound satisfaction that the creator and those that understand him feel, they always look for some meaning that can be attached to the values of actual life, they always hope to translate a work of art into terms of *ideas* with which they are familiar. . . .

. . . Now I venture to say that no one who has a real understanding of the art of painting attaches any importance to what we call the subject of a picture—what is represented. To one who feels the language of pictorial form all depends on *how* it is presented, *nothing* on what. Rembrandt expressed his profoundest feelings just as well when he painted a carcass hanging up in a butcher's shop as when he painted the Crucifixion or his mistress. Cézanne, who most of us believed to be the greatest artist of modern times, expressed some of his grandest conceptions in pictures of fruit and crockery on a common kitchen table.

I remember when this fact became clear to me, and the instance may help to show what I mean. In a loan exhibition I came upon a picture by Chardin. It was a signboard painted to hang outside a druggist's shop. It represented a number of glass retorts, a still, and various glass bottles, the furniture of a chemist's laboratory of that time. You will admit that there was not much material for wish-fulfilment (unless the still suggested remote possibilities of alcohol). Well, it gave me a very intense and vivid sensation. Just the shapes of those bottles and their mutual relations gave me the feeling of something immensely grand and impressive and the phrase that came into my mind was "This is just how I felt when I first saw Michel Angelo's frescos in the Sistine Chapel." Those represented the whole history of creation with the tremendous images of Sybils and Prophets, but esthetically it meant something very similar to Chardin's glass bottles. /16/

And here let me allude to a curious phenomenon which I have frequently noticed, namely that even though at the first shock of a great pictorial design the subject appears to have a great deal to do with one's emotional reaction, that part of one's feeling evaporates very quickly; one soon exhausts the feelings connected by associated ideas with the figures, and what remains, what never grows less nor evaporates, are the feelings dependent on the purely formal relations. This indeed may be the explanation of that curious fact that I alluded to, the persistence throughout the ages of works in which formal perfection is attained, and the rapid disappearance and neglect which is the fate of works that make their chief appeal through the associated ideas of the images. . . . /17/

. . . the question occurs, what is the source of the affective quality of certain systems of formal design for those who are sensitive to pure form. Why are we moved deeply by certain sequences of notes which arouse no suggestion of any experience in actual life? Why are we moved deeply by certain dispositions of space in architecture which refer so far as we can tell to no other experience?

One thing I think we may clearly say, namely, that there is a pleasure in the recognition of order, of inevitability in relations, and that the more complex the relations of which we are able to recognize the inevitable interdependence and correspondence, the greater is the pleasure; this of course will come very near to the pleasure derived from the contemplation of intellectual constructions united by logical inevitability. What the source of that satisfaction is would clearly be a problem for psychology.

But in art there is, I think, an affective quality which lies outside that. It is not a mere recognition of order and inter-relation; every part, as well as the whole, becomes suffused with an emotional tone. Now, from our definition of this pure beauty, the emotional tone is not due to any recognizable reminiscence or suggestion of the emotional experiences of life; but I sometimes wonder if it nevertheless does not get its force from arousing some very deep, very vague, and immensely generalized reminiscences. It looks as though art had got access to the substratum of all the emotional colours of life, to something which underlies all the particular and specialized emotions of actual life.

It seems to derive an emotional energy from the very conditions of our existence by its revelation of an emotional significance in time and space. Or it may be that art really calls up, as it were, the /19/ residual traces left on the spirit by the different emotions of life, without however recalling the actual experiences, so that we get an echo of the emotion without the limitation and particular direction which it had in experience. /20/

'PSYCHICAL DISTANCE' AS A FACTOR IN ART AND AN AESTHETIC PRINCIPLE

Edward Bullough

I

1. The conception of 'Distance' suggests, in connexion with Art, certain trains of thought by no means devoid of interest or of speculative importance. Perhaps the most obvious suggestion is that of *actual spatial* distance, i.e. the distance of a work of Art from the spectator, or that of *represented spatial* distance, i.e. the distance represented within the work. Less obvious, more metaphorical, is the /87/ meaning of *temporal* distance. The first was noticed already by Aristotle in his *Poetics;* the second has played a great part in the history of painting in the form of perspective; the distinction between these two kinds of distance assumes special importance theoretically in the differentiation between sculpture in the round, and relief-sculpture. Temporal distance, remoteness from us in point of time, though often a cause of misconceptions, has been declared to be a factor of considerable weight in our appreciation.

It is not, however, in any of these meanings that 'Distance' is put forward here, though it will be clear in the course of this essay that the above mentioned kinds of distance are rather special forms of the conception of Distance as advocated here, and derive whatever *aesthetic* qualities they may possess from Distance in its *general* connotation. This general connotation is 'Psychical Distance.'

A short illustration will explain what is meant by 'Psychical Distance.' Imagine a fog at sea: for most people it is an experience of acute unpleasantness. Apart from the physical annoyance and remoter forms of discomfort such as delays, it is apt to produce feelings of peculiar anxiety, fears of invisible dangers, strains of watching and listening for distant and unlocalised signals. The listless movements of the ship and her warning calls soon tell upon the nerves of the passengers; and that special, expectant, tacit anxiety and nervousness, always associated with this experience, make a fog the dreaded terror of the sea (all the more terrifying because of its very silence and gentleness) for the expert seafarer no less than for the ignorant landsman.

Nevertheless, a fog at sea can be a source of intense relish and enjoyment. Abstract from the experience of the sea fog, for the moment, its danger and practical unpleasantness, just as every one in the enjoyment of a mountain-climb disregards its physical labour and its danger (though, it is not denied, that these may incidentally enter into the enjoyment and enhance it); direct the attention to the features 'objectively' constituting the phenomenon—the veil surrounding you with an opaqueness as of transparent milk, blurring the

From "'Psychical Distance' as a Factor in Art and an Aesthetic Principle," *British Journal of Psychology*, 5 (1912–1913), 87–118.

outline of things and distorting their shapes into weird grotesqueness; observe the carrying-power of the air, producing the impression as if you could touch some far-off siren by merely putting out your hand and letting it lose itself behind that white wall; note the curious creamy smoothness of the water, hypocritically denying as it were any suggestion of danger; and, above all, the strange solitude /88/ and remoteness from the world, as it can be found only on the highest mountain tops: and the experience may acquire, in its uncanny mingling of repose and terror, a flavour of such concentrated poignancy and delight as to contrast sharply with the blind and distempered anxiety of its other aspects. This contrast, often emerging with startling suddenness, is like a momentary switching on of some new current, or the passing ray of a brighter light, illuminating the outlook upon perhaps the most ordinary and familiar objects—an impression which we experience sometimes in instants of direst extremity, when our practical interest snaps like a wire from sheer over-tension, and we watch the consummation of some impending catastrophe with the marvelling unconcern of a mere spectator.

It is a difference of outlook, due—if such a metaphor is permissible—to the insertion of Distance. This Distance appears to lie between our own self and its affections, using the latter term in its broadest sense as anything which affects our being, bodily or spiritually, e.g. as sensation, perception, emotional state or idea. Usually, though not always, it amounts to the same thing to say that the Distance lies between our own self and such objects as are the sources or vehicles of such affections.

Thus, in the fog, the transformation by Distance is produced in the first instance by putting the phenomenon, so to speak, out of gear with our practical, actual self; by allowing it to stand outside the context of our personal needs and ends—in short, by looking at it 'objectively,' as it has often been called, by permitting only such reactions on our part as emphasise the 'objective' features of the experience, and by interpreting even our 'subjective' affections not as modes of *our* being but rather as characteristics of the phenomenon.

The working of Distance is, accordingly, not simple, but highly complex. It has a *negative,* inhibitory aspect—the cutting-out of the practical sides of things and of our practical attitude to them—and a *positive* side—the elaboration of the experience on the new basis created by the inhibitory action of Distance.

2.   Consequently, this distanced view of things is not, and cannot be, our normal outlook. As a rule, experiences constantly turn the same side towards us, namely, that which has the strongest practical force of appeal. We are not ordinarily aware of those aspects of things which do not touch us immediately and practically, nor are we generally conscious of impressions apart from our own self which is impressed. The sudden view of things from their reverse, usually /89/unnoticed, side, comes upon us as a revelation, and such revelations are precisely those of Art. In this most general sense, Distance is a factor in all Art. . . . /90/

II

Distance, as I said before, is obtained by separating the object and its appeal from one's own self, by putting it out of gear with practical needs and ends. Thereby the 'contemplation' of the object becomes alone possible. But it does not mean that the relation between the self and the object is broken to the extent of becoming 'impersonal.' Of the alternatives 'personal' and 'impersonal' the latter surely comes nearer to the truth; but here, as elsewhere, we meet the difficulty of having to express certain facts in terms coined for entirely different uses. To do so usually results in paradoxes, which are nowhere more inevitable than in discussions upon Art. 'Personal' and 'impersonal,' 'subjective' and 'objective' are such terms, devised for purposes other than aesthetic speculation, and becoming loose and ambiguous as soon as applied outside the sphere of their special meanings. In giving preference therefore to the term 'impersonal' to describe the relation between the spectator and a work of Art, it is to be noticed that it is not impersonal in the sense in which we speak of the 'impersonal' character of Science, for instance. In order to obtain 'objectively valid' results, the scientist excludes the 'personal factor,' i.e. his personal wishes as to the validity of his results, his predilection for any particular system to be proved or disproved by his research. It goes without saying that all experiments and investigations are undertaken out of a personal interest in the science, for the ultimate support of a definite assumption, and involve personal hopes of success; but this does not affect the 'dispassionate' attitude of the investigator, under pain of being accused of 'manufacturing his evidence.'

1.   Distance does not imply an impersonal, purely intellectually interested relation of such a kind. On the contrary, it describes a *personal* relation, often highly emotionally coloured, but *of a peculiar character*. Its peculiarity lies in that the personal character of the relation has been, so to speak, filtered. It has been cleared of the practical, concrete nature of its appeal, without, however, thereby losing its original constitution. One of the best-known examples is to be found in our attitude towards the events and characters of the drama: they appeal to us like persons and incidents of normal experience, except that that side of their appeal, which would usually affect us in a directly personal manner, is held in abeyance. This difference, so well known as to be almost trivial, is generally /91/ explained by reference to the knowledge that the characters and situations are 'unreal,' imaginary. In this sense Witasek[1], operating with Meinong's theory of *Annahmen*, has described the emotions involved in witnessing a drama as *Scheingefühle*, a term which has so frequently been misunderstood in discussions of his theories. But, as a matter of fact, the 'assumption' upon which the imaginative emotional reaction is based is not necessarily the condition, but often the consequence, of Distance; that is to say, the converse of the reason usually stated would then be true: viz. that Distance, by changing our relation to the characters, renders them seemingly fictitious, not that the fictitiousness of the characters alters our feelings toward them. It is, of course, to be granted that the actual and admitted unreality of the dramatic action reinforces the effect of Distance. But surely the proverbial unsophisticated yokel whose chivalrous interference in the play on behalf of the hapless heroine can only be prevented by impressing upon him that 'they are only pretending,' is not the ideal type of theatrical audience. The proof of the seeming paradox that it is Distance which primarily gives to dramatic action the appearance of unreality and not *vice versâ*, is the observation that the same filtration of our sentiments and the same seeming 'unreality' of *actual* men and things occur, when at times, by a sudden change of inward perspective, we are overcome by the feeling that "all the world's a stage."

2.   This personal, but 'distanced' relation (as I will venture to call this nameless character of our view) directs attention to a strange fact which appears to be one of the fundamental paradoxes of Art: it is what I propose to call 'the antinomy of Distance.'

It will be readily admitted that a work of Art has the more chance of appealing to us the better it finds us prepared for its particular kind of appeal.

[1] H. Witasek, 'Zur psychologischen Analyse der aesthetischen Einfühlung,' *Ztsch. f. Psychol. u. Physiol. der Sinnesorg.* 1901, xxv. 1 ff.; *Grundzüge der Aesthetik*, Leipzig, 1904. /192/

Indeed, without some degree of predisposition on our part, it must necessarily remain incomprehensible, and to that extent unappreciated. The success and intensity of its appeal would seem, therefore, to stand in direct proportion to the completeness with which it corresponds with our intellectual and emotional peculiarities and the idiosyncracies of our experience. The absence of such a concordance between the characters of a work and of the spectator is, of course, the most general explanation for differences of 'tastes.' /92/

At the same time, such a principle of concordance requires a qualification, which leads at once to the antinomy of Distance.

Suppose a man, who believes that he has cause to be jealous about his wife, witnesses a performance of 'Othello.' He will the more perfectly appreciate the situation, conduct and character of Othello, the more exactly the feelings and experiences of Othello coincide with his own — at least he *ought* to on the above principle of concordance. In point of fact, he will probably do anything but appreciate the play. In reality, the concordance will merely render him acutely conscious of his own jealousy; by a sudden reversal of perspective he will no longer see Othello apparently betrayed by Desdemona, but himself in an analogous situation with his own wife. This reversal of perspective is the consequence of the loss of Distance.

If this be taken as a typical case, it follows that the qualification required is that the coincidence should be as complete as is compatible with maintaining Distance. The jealous spectator of 'Othello' will indeed appreciate and enter into the play the more keenly, the greater the resemblance with his own experience — *provided* that he succeeds in keeping the Distance between the action of the play and his personal feelings: a very difficult performance in the circumstances. It is on account of the same difficulty that the expert and the professional critic make a bad audience, since their expertness and critical professionalism are *practical* activities, involving their concrete personality and constantly endangering their Distance. [It is, by the way, one of the reasons why Criticism is an art, for it requires the constant interchange from the practical to the distanced attitude and *vice versâ,* which is characteristic of artists.]

The same qualification applies to the artist. He will prove artistically most effective in the formulation of an intensely *personal* experience, but he can formulate it artistically only on condition of a detachment from the experience *quâ personal.* Hence the statement of so many artists that artistic formulation was to them a kind of catharsis, a means of ridding themselves of feelings and ideas the acuteness of which they felt almost as a kind of obsession. Hence, on the other hand, the failure of the average man to convey to others at all adequately the impression of an overwhelming joy or sorrow. His personal implication in the event renders it impossible for him to formulate and present it in such a way as to make others, like himself, feel all the meaning and fulness which it possesses for him. /93/

What is therefore, both in appreciation and production, most desirable is the *utmost decrease of Distance without its disappearance.*

3. Closely related, in fact a presupposition to the 'antimony,' is the *variability of Distance.* Herein especially lies the advantage of Distance compared with such terms as 'objectivity' and 'detachment.' Neither of them implies a *personal* relation — indeed both actually preclude it; and the mere inflexibility and exclusiveness of their opposites render their application generally meaningless.

Distance, on the contrary, admits naturally of degrees, and differs not only according to the nature of the *object,* which may impose a greater or smaller degree of Distance, but varies also according to the *individual's capacity* for maintaining a greater or lesser degree. And here one may remark that not only do *persons differ from each other* in their habitual measure of Distance, but that the *same individual differs* in his ability to maintain it in the face of different objects and of different arts.

There exist, therefore, two different sets of conditions affecting the degree of Distance in any given case: those offered by the object and those realised by the subject. In their interplay they afford one of the most extensive explanations for varieties of aesthetic experience, since loss of Distance, whether due to the one or the other, means loss of aesthetic appreciation.

In short, Distance may be said *to be variable both according to the distancing-power of the individual, and according to the character of the object.*

There are two ways of losing Distance: either to 'under-distance' or to 'over-distance.' 'Under-distancing' is the commonest failing of the *subject,* an excess of Distance is a frequent failing of *Art,* especially in the past. Historically it looks almost as if Art had attempted to meet the deficiency of Distance on the part of the subject and had overshot the mark in this endeavour. It will be seen later that this is actually true, for it appears that over-distanced Art is specially designed for a class of appreciation which has difficulty to rise spontaneously to any degree of Distance. The consequence of a loss of Distance through one or other cause is familiar: the verdict in the case of under-distancing is that the work is 'crudely naturalistic,' 'harrowing,' 'repulsive in its realism.' An excess of Distance produces the impression of improbability, artificiality, emptiness or absurdity.

The individual tends, as I just stated, to under-distance rather than to lose Distance by over-distancing. *Theoretically* there is no limit to /94/ the decrease of Distance. In theory, therefore, not only the usual subjects of Art, but even the most personal affections, whether ideas, percepts or emotions, can be sufficiently distanced to be aesthetically appreciable. Especially artists are gifted in this direction to a remarkable extent. The average individual, on the contrary, very rapidly reaches his limit of decreasing Distance, his 'Distance-limit,' i.e. that point at which Distance is lost and appreciation either disappears or changes its character.

In the *practice,* therefore, of the average person, a limit does exist which marks the minimum at which his appreciation can maintain itself in the aesthetic field, and this average minimum lies considerably higher than the Distance-limit of the artist. It is practically impossible to fix this average limit, in the absence of data, and on account of the wide fluctuations from person to person to which this limit is subject. But it is safe to infer that, in art practice, explicit references to organic affections, to the material existence of the body, especially to sexual matters, lie normally below the Distance-limit, and can be touched upon by Art only with special precautions. Allusions to social institutions of any degree of personal importance—in particular, allusions implying any doubt as to their validity—the questioning of some generally recognised ethical sanctions, references to topical subjects occupying public attention at the moment, and such like, are all dangerously near the average limit and may at any time fall below it, arousing, instead of aesthetic appreciation, concrete hostility or mere amusement.

This difference in the Distance-limit between artists and the public has been the source of much misunderstanding and injustice. Many an artist has seen his work condemned, and himself ostracized for the sake of so-called 'immoralities' which to him were *bonâ fide* aesthetic objects. His power of distancing, nay, the necessity of distancing feelings, sensations, situations which for the average person are too intimately bound up with his concrete existence to be regarded in that light, have often quite unjustly earned for him accusations of cynicism, sensualism, morbidness or frivolity. The same misconception has arisen over many 'problem plays' and 'problem novels' in which the public have persisted in seeing nothing but a supposed 'problem' of the moment, whereas the author may have been — and often has demonstrably been — able to distance the subject-matter sufficiently to rise above its practical problematic import and to regard it simply as a dramatically and humanly interesting situation.

The variability of Distance in respect to Art, disregarding for the /95/ moment the subjective complication, appears both as a general feature in Art, and in the differences between the special arts.

It has been an old problem why the 'arts of the eye and of the ear' should have reached the practically exclusive predominance over arts of other senses. Attempts to raise 'culinary art' to the level of a Fine Art have failed in spite of all propaganda, as completely as the creation of scent or liqueur 'symphonies.' There is little doubt that, apart from other excellent reasons[1] of a partly psycho-physical, partly technical nature, the actual, *spatial distance* separating objects of sight and hearing from the subject has contributed strongly to the development of this monopoly. In a similar manner *temporal remoteness* produces Distance, and objects removed from us in point of time are *ipso facto* distanced to an extent which was impossible for their contemporaries. Many pictures, plays and poems had, as a matter of fact, rather an expository or illustrative significance — as for instance much ecclesiastical Art — or the force of a direct practical appeal — as the invectives of many satires or comedies — which seem to us nowadays irreconcilable with their aesthetic claims. Such works have consequently profited greatly by lapse of time and have reached the level of Art only with the help of temporal distance, while others, on the contrary, often for the same reason have suffered a loss of Distance, through *over*-distancing.

Special mention must be made or a group of artistic conceptions which present excessive Distance in their form of appeal rather than in their actual presentation — a point illustrating the necessity of distinguishing between distancing an object and distancing the appeal of which it is the source. I mean here what is often rather loosely termed 'idealistic Art,' that is, Art springing from abstract conceptions, expressing allegorical meanings, or illustrating general truths. Generalisations and abstractions suffer under this disadvantage that they have too much general applicability to invite a personal interest in them, and too little individual concreteness to prevent them applying to us in all their force. They appeal to everybody and therefore to none. An axiom of Euclid belongs to nobody, just because it compels everyone's assent; general conceptions like Patriotism, Friendship, Love, Hope, Life, Death, concern as much Dick, Tom and Harry as myself, and I, therefore, either feel unable to get into any kind of personal relation to them, or, if I do so, they become at once, emphatically and concretely, *my* Patriotism, *my* Friendship, *my* /96/ Love, *my* Hope, *my* Life and Death. By mere force of generalisation, a general truth or a universal ideal is so far distanced from myself that I fail to realise it concretely at all, or, when I do so, I can realise it only as part of my *practical actual being*, i.e., it falls below the Distance-limit altogether. 'Idealistic Art' suffers consequently under the peculiar difficulty that its excess of Distance turns generally into an *under*-distanced appeal — all the more easily, as it is the usual failing of the subject to *under*- rather than to *over*-distance.

The different special arts show at the present time very marked variations

---

[1] J. Volkelt, 'Die Bedeutung der niederen Empfindungen für die aesthetische Einfühlung,' *Ztsch. für Psychol. u. Physiol. der Sinnesorg.* xxxii. 15, 16; *System der Aesthetik*, 1905, 1. 260 ff. /96/

in the degree of Distance which they usually impose or require for their appreciation. Unfortunately here again the absence of data makes itself felt and indicates the necessity of conducting observations, possibly experiments, so as to place these suggestions upon a securer basis. In one single art, viz. the *theatre,* a small amount of information is available, from an unexpected source, namely the proceedings of the censorship committee[1], which on closer examination might be made to yield evidence of interest to the psychologist. In fact, the whole censorship problem, as far as it does not turn upon purely economic questions, may be said to hinge upon Distance; if every member of the public could be trusted to keep it, there would be no sense whatever in the existence of a censor of plays. There is, of course, no doubt that, speaking generally, theatrical performances *eo ipso* run a special risk of a loss of Distance owing to the material presentment[2] of its subject-matter. The physical presence of living human beings as vehicles of dramatic art is a difficulty which no art has to face in the same way. A similar, in many ways even greater, risk confronts *dancing*: though attracting perhaps a less widely spread human interest, its animal spirits are frequently quite unrelieved by any glimmer of spirituality and consequently form a proportionately stronger lure to under-distancing. In the higher forms of dancing technical execution of the most wearing kind makes up a great deal for its intrinsic tendency towards a loss of Distance, and as a popular performance, at least in southern Europe, it has retained much of its ancient artistic glamour, producing a peculiarly subtle balancing of Distance between the pure delight of bodily movement and high technical accomplishment. In passing, it is interesting to observe (as bearing upon the development of Distance), that this art, /97/ once as much a fine art as music and considered by the Greeks as a particularly valuable educational exercise, should — except in sporadic cases — have fallen so low from the pedestal it once occupied. Next to the theatre and dancing stands *sculpture.* Though not using a *living* bodily medium, yet the human form in its full spatial materiality constitutes a similar threat to Distance. Our northern habits of dress and ignorance of the human body have enormously increased the difficulty of distancing Sculpture, in part through the gross misconceptions to which it is exposed, in part owing to a complete lack of standards of bodily perfection, and an inability to realise the distinction between sculptural form and bodily shape, which is the only but fundamental point distinguishing a statue from a cast taken from life. In *painting* it is apparently the form of its presentment and the usual reduction in scale which would explain why this art can venture to approach more closely than sculpture to the normal Distance-limit. As this matter will be discussed later in a special connexion this simple reference may suffice here. *Music* and *architecture* have a curious position. These two most abstract of all arts show a remarkable fluctuation in their Distances. Certain kinds of music, especially 'pure' music, or 'classical' or 'heavy' music, appear for many people over-distanced; light, 'catchy' tunes, on the contrary, easily reach that degree of decreasing Distance below which they cease to be Art and become a pure amusement. In spite of its strange abstractness which to many philosophers has made it comparable to architecture and mathematics, music possesses a sensuous, frequently sensual, character: the undoubted physiological and muscular stimulus of its melodies and harmonies, no less than its rhythmic aspects, would seem to account for the occasional disappearance of Distance. To this might be added its strong tend-

---

[1] Report from the Joint Select Committee of the House of Lords and the House of Commons on the Stage Plays (Censorship), 1909. /97/

[2] I shall use the term 'presentment' to denote the manner of presenting, in distinction to 'presentation' as that which is presented. /97/

ency, especially in unmusical people, to stimulate trains of thought quite disconnected with itself, following channels of subjective inclinations,—day-dreams of a more or less directly personal character. *Architecture* requires almost uniformly a very great Distance; that is to say, the majority of persons derive no aesthetic appreciation from architecture as such, apart from the incidental impression of its decorative features and its associations. The causes are numerous, but prominent among them are the confusion of building with architecture and the predominance of utilitarian purposes, which overshadow the architectural claims upon the attention. /98/

✖ THE DEHUMANIZATION OF ART

José Ortega y Gasset

ARTISTIC ART

If the new art is not accessible to every man this implies that its impulses are not of a generically human kind. It is an art not for men in general but for a special class of men who may not be better but who evidently are different.

One point must be clarified before we go on. What is it the majority of people call aesthetic pleasure? What happens in their minds when they "like" a work of art; for instance, a theatrical performance? The answer is easy. A man likes a play when he has become interested in the human destinies presented to him, when the love and hatred, the joys and sorrows of the personages so move his heart that he participates in it all as though it were happening in real life. And he calls a work "good" if it succeeds in creating the illusion necessary to make the imaginary personages appear like living persons. In poetry he seeks the passion and pain of the man be- /8/ hind the poet. Paintings attract him if he finds on them figures of men or women whom it would be interesting to meet. A landscape is pronounced "pretty" if the country it represents deserves for its loveliness or its grandeur to be visited on a trip.

It thus appears that to the majority of people aesthetic pleasure means a state of mind which is essentially undistinguishable from their ordinary behavior. It differs merely in accidental qualities, being perhaps less utilitarian, more intense, and free from painful consequences. But the object towards which their attention and, consequently, all their other mental activities are directed is the same as in daily life: people and passions. By art they understand a means through which they are brought in contact with interesting human affairs. Artistic forms proper—figments, fantasy—are tolerated only if they do not interfere with the perception of human forms and fates. As soon as purely aesthetic elements predominate and the story of John and Mary grows elusive, most people feel out of their depth and are at a loss what to make of the scene, the book, or the painting. As they have never practiced any other attitude but the practical one in which a man's feelings are aroused and he is emotionally involved, a work that does not invite sentimental intervention leaves them without a cue.

Now, this is a point which has to be made perfectly clear. Not only is grieving and rejoicing at such human destinies as a work of art presents or

From *The Dehumanization of Art, and Notes on the Novel,* tr. Helen Weyl (Princeton, N.J.: Princeton University Press, 1948).

narrates a very different thing from true artistic pleasure, but preoccu- /9/ pation with the human content of the work is in principle incompatible with aesthetic enjoyment proper.

We have here a very simple optical problem. To see a thing we must adjust our visual apparatus in a certain way. If the adjustment is inadequate the thing is seen indistinctly or not at all. Take a garden seen through a window. Looking at the garden we adjust our eyes in such a way that the ray of vision travels through the pane without delay and rests on the shrubs and flowers. Since we are focusing on the garden and our ray of vision is directed toward it, we do not see the window but look clear through it. The purer the glass, the less we see it. But we can also deliberately disregard the garden and, withdrawing the ray of vision, detain it at the window. We then lose sight of the garden; what we still behold of it is a confused mass of color which appears pasted to the pane. Hence to see the garden and to see the windowpane are two incompatible operations which exclude one another because they require different adjustments.

Similarly a work of art vanishes from sight for a beholder who seeks in it nothing but the moving fate of John and Mary or Tristan and Isolde and adjusts his vision to this. Tristan's sorrows are sorrows and can evoke compassion only in so far as they are taken as real. But an object of art is artistic only in so far as it is not real. In order to enjoy Titian's portrait of Charles the Fifth on horse-back we must forget that this is Charles the Fifth in person and see instead a portrait—that is, an image, a fiction. The portrayed person and /10/ his portrait are two entirely different things; we are interested in either one or the other. In the first case we "live" with Charles the Fifth, in the second we look at an object of art.

But not many people are capable of adjusting their perceptive apparatus to the pane and the transparency that is the work of art. Instead they look right through it and revel in the human reality with which the work deals. When they are invited to let go of this prey and to direct their attention to the work of art itself they will say that they cannot see such a thing, which indeed they cannot, because it is all artistic transparency and without substance.

During the nineteenth century artists proceeded in all too impure a fashion. They reduced the strictly aesthetic elements to a minimum and let the work consist almost entirely in a fiction of human realities. In this sense all normal art of the last century must be called realistic. Beethoven and Wagner were realistic, and so was Chateaubriand as well as Zola. Seen from the vantage-point of our day Romanticism and Naturalism draw closer together and reveal their common realistic root.

Works of this kind are only partially works of art, or artistic objects. Their enjoyment does not depend upon our power to focus on transparencies and images, a power characteristic of the artistic sensibility; all they require is human sensibility and willingness to sympathize with our neighbor's joys and worries. No wonder that nineteenth century art has been so popular; it is /11/ made for the masses inasmuch as it is not art but an extract from life. Let us remember that in epochs with two different types of art, one for minorities and one for the majority, the latter has always been realistic.*

I will not now discuss whether pure art is possible. Perhaps it is not; but as the reasons that make me inclined to think so are somewhat long and difficult the subject better be dropped. Besides, it is not of major importance for the matter in hand. Even though pure art may be impossible there doubtless can prevail a

---

* For instance in the Middle Ages. In accordance with the division of society in the two strata of noblemen and commoners, there existed an aristocratic art which was "conventional" and "idealistic," and a popular art which was realistic and satirical. /12/

tendency toward a purification of art. Such a tendency would effect a progressive elimination of the human, all too human, elements predominant in romantic and naturalistic production. And in this process a point can be reached in which the human content has grown so thin that it is negligible. We then have an art which can be comprehended only by people possessed of the peculiar gift of artistic sensibility—an art for artists and not for the masses, for "quality" and not for hoi polloi.

That is why modern art divides the public into two classes, those who understand it and those who do not understand it—that is to say, those who are artists and those who are not. The new art is an artistic art. . . . /12/

A FEW DROPS OF PHENOMENOLOGY

A great man is dying. His wife is by his bedside. A doctor takes the dying man's pulse. In the background two more persons are discovered: a reporter who is present for professional reasons, and a painter whom mere chance has brought here. Wife, doctor, reporter, and painter witness one and the same event. Nonetheless, this identical event—a man's death—impresses each of them in a different way. So different indeed that the several aspects have hardly anything in common. What this scene means to the wife who is all grief has so little to do with what it means to the painter who looks on impassively that it seems doubtful whether the two can be said to be present at the same event. /14/

It thus becomes clear that one and the same reality may split up into many diverse realities when it is beheld from different points of view. And we cannot help asking ourselves: Which of all these realities must then be regarded as the real and authentic one? The answer, no matter how we decide, cannot but be arbitrary. Any preference can be founded on caprice only. All these realities are equivalent, each being authentic for its corresponding point of view. All we can do is to classify the points of view and to determine which among them seems, in a practical way, most normal or most spontaneous. Thus we arrive at a conception of reality that is by no means absolute, but at least practical and normative.

As for the points of view of the four persons present at the deathbed, the clearest means of distinguishing them is by measuring one of their dimensions, namely the emotional distance between each person and the event they all witness. For the wife of the dying man the distance shrinks to almost nothing. What is happening so tortures her soul and absorbs her mind that it becomes one with her person. Or to put it inversely, the wife is drawn into the scene, she is part of it. A thing can be seen, an event can be observed, only when we have separated it from ourselves and it has ceased to form a living part of our being. Thus the wife is not present at the scene, she is in it. She does not behold it, she "lives" it.

The doctor is several degrees removed. To him this is a professional case. He is not drawn into the event with /15/ the frantic and blinding anxiety of the poor woman. However it is his bounden duty as a doctor to take a serious interest, he carries responsibility, perhaps his professional honor is at stake. Hence he too, albeit in a less integral and less intimate way, takes part in the event. He is involved in it not with his heart but with the professional portion of his self. He too "lives" the scene although with an agitation originating not in the emotional center, but in the professional surface, of his existence.

When we now put ourselves in the place of the reporter we realize that we have traveled a long distance away from the tragic event. So far indeed that we have lost all emotional contact with it. The reporter, like the doctor, has been brought here for professional reasons and not out of a spontaneous human interest. But while the doctor's profession requires him to interfere, the reporter's requires him precisely to stay aloof; he has to confine himself to observing. To him the event is a mere scene, a pure spectacle on which he is expected to report in his newspaper column. He takes no feeling part in what is happening here, he is emotionally free, an outsider. He does not "live" the scene, he observes it. Yet he observes it with a view to telling his readers about it. He wants to interest them, to move them, and if possible to make them weep as though they each had been the dying man's best friend. From his schooldays he remembers Horace's recipe: "*Si vis me flere dolendum est primum ipsi tibi*" — if you want me to weep you must first grieve yourself. /16/

Obedient to Horace the reporter is anxious to pretend emotion, hoping that it will benefit his literary performance. If he does not "live" the scene he at least pretends to "live" it.

The painter, in fine, completely unconcerned, does nothing but keep his eyes open. What is happening here is none of his business; he is, as it were, a hundred miles removed from it. His is a purely perceptive attitude; indeed, he fails to perceive the event in its entirety. The tragic inner meaning escapes his attention which is directed exclusively toward the visual part — color values, lights, and shadows. In the painter we find a maximum of distance and a minimum of feeling intervention.

The inevitable dullness of this analysis will, I hope, be excused if it now enables us to speak in a clear and precise way of a scale of emotional distances between ourselves and reality. In this scale, the degree of closeness is equivalent to the degree of feeling participation; the degree of remoteness, on the other hand, marks the degree to which we have freed ourselves from the real event, thus objectifying it and turning it into a theme of pure observation. At one end of the scale the world — persons, things, situations — is given to us in the aspect of "lived" reality; at the other end we see everything in the aspect of "observed" reality.

At this point we must make a remark that is essential in aesthetics and without which neither old art nor new art can be satisfactorily analyzed. Among the diverse aspects of reality we find one from which all the others /17/ derive and which they all presuppose: "lived" reality. If nobody had ever "lived" in pure and frantic abandonment a man's death, the doctor would not bother, the readers would not understand the reporter's pathos, and the canvas on which the painter limned a person on a bed surrounded by mourning figures would be meaningless. The same holds for any object, be it a person, a thing, or a situation. The primal aspect of an apple is that in which I see it when I am about to eat it. All its other possible forms — when it appears, for instance, in a Baroque ornament, or on a still life of Cézanne's, or in the eternal metaphor of a girl's apple cheeks — preserve more or less that original aspect. A painting or a poem without any vestiges of "lived" forms would be unintelligible, i.e., nothing — as a discourse is nothing whose every word is emptied of its customary meaning.

That is to say, in the scale of realities "lived" reality holds a peculiar primacy which compels us to regard it as "the" reality. Instead of "lived" reality we may say "human" reality. The painter who impassively witnesses the death scene appears "inhuman." In other words, the human point of view is that in which we "live" situations, persons, things. And, vice versa, realities — a woman, a countryside, an event — are human when they present the aspect in which they are usually "lived." . . . /18/

FIRST INSTALLMENT ON THE DEHUMANIZATION OF ART

With amazing swiftness modern art has split up into a multitude of divergent directions. Nothing is easier than to stress the differences. But such an emphasis on the distinguishing and specific features would be pointless without a previous account of the common fund that in a varying and sometimes contradictory manner asserts itself throughout modern art. Did not Aristotle already observe that things differ in what they have in common? Because all bodies are colored we notice that they are differently colored. Species are nothing if not modifications of a genus, and we cannot understand them unless we realize that they draw, in their several ways, upon a common patrimony.

I am little interested in special directions of modern /19/ art and, but for a few exceptions, even less in special works. Nor do I, for that matter, expect anybody to be particularly interested in my valuation of the new artistic produce. Writers who have nothing to convey but their praise or dispraise of works of art had better abstain from writing. They are unfit for this arduous task.

The important thing is that there unquestionably exists in the world a new artistic sensibility.* Over against the multiplicity of special directions and individual works, the new sensibility represents the generic fact and the source, as it were, from which the former spring. This sensibility it is worth while to define. And when we seek to ascertain the most general and most characteristic feature of modern artistic production we come upon the tendency to dehumanize art. After what we have said above, this formula now acquires a tolerably precise meaning.

Let us compare a painting in the new style with one of, say, 1860. The simplest procedure will be to begin by setting against one another the objects they represent: a man perhaps, a house, or a mountain. It then appears that the artist of 1860 wanted nothing so much as to give to the objects in his picture the same looks and airs they possess outside it when they occur as parts of the "lived" or "human" reality. Apart from this he may have been animated by other more intricate aesthetic /20/ ambitions, but what interests us is that his first concern was with securing this likeness. Man, house, mountain are at once recognized, they are our good old friends; whereas on a modern painting we are at a loss to recognize them. It might be supposed that the modern painter has failed to achieve resemblance. But then some pictures of the 1860's are "poorly" painted, too, and the objects in them differ considerably from the corresponding objects outside them. And yet, whatever the differences, the very blunders of the traditional artist point toward the "human" object; they are downfalls on the way toward it and somehow equivalent to the orienting words "This is a cock" with which Cervantes lets the painter Orbanejo enlighten his public. In modern paintings the opposite happens. It is not that the painter is bungling and fails to render the natural (natural=human) thing because he deviates from it, but that these deviations point in a direction opposite to that which would lead to reality.

Far from going more or less clumsily toward reality, the artist is seen going against it. He is brazenly set on deforming reality, shattering its human aspect, dehumanizing it. With the things represented on traditional paintings we could have imaginary intercourse. Many a young Englishman has fallen in love with Gioconda. With the objects of modern pictures no intercourse is possible. By divesting them of their aspect of "lived" reality the artist has blown up the

---

* This new sensibility is a gift not only of the artist proper but also of his audience. When I said above that the new art is an art for artists I understood by "artists" not only those who produce this art but also those who are capable of perceiving purely artistic values. /20/

bridges and burned the ships that could have taken us back to our daily world. He leaves us locked up in an abstruse universe, /21/ surrounded by objects with which human dealings are inconceivable, and thus compels us to improvise other forms of intercourse completely distinct from our ordinary ways with things. We must invent unheard-of gestures to fit those singular figures. This new way of life which presupposes the annulment of spontaneous life is precisely what we call understanding and enjoyment of art. Not that this life lacks sentiments and passions, but those sentiments and passions evidently belong to a flora other than that which covers the hills and dales of primary and human life. What those ultra-objects* evoke in our inner artist are secondary passions, specifically aesthetic sentiments.

It may be said that, to achieve this result, it would be simpler to dismiss human forms—man, house, mountain—altogether and to construct entirely original figures. But, in the first place, this is not feasible.† Even in the most abstract ornamental line a stubborn reminiscence lurks of certain "natural" forms. Secondly—and this is the crucial point—the art of which we speak is inhuman not only because it contains no things human, but also because it is an explicit act of dehumanization. In his escape from the human world the young artist cares less for the "*terminus ad quem*," the startling fauna at which he arrives, than for the "*terminus a quo*," the human aspect which he destroys. The question is not to paint something altogether different from /22/ a man, a house, a mountain, but to paint a man who resembles a man as little as possible; a house that preserves of a house exactly what is needed to reveal the metamorphosis; a cone miraculously emerging—as the snake from his slough—from what used to be a mountain. For the modern artist, aesthetic pleasure derives from such a triumph over human matter. That is why he has to drive home the victory by presenting in each case the strangled victim.

It may be thought a simple affair to fight shy of reality, but it is by no means easy. There is no difficulty in painting or saying things which make no sense whatever, which are unintelligible and therefore nothing. One only needs to assemble unconnected words or to draw random lines.* But to construct something that is not a copy of "nature" and yet possesses substance of its own is a feat which presupposes nothing less than genius.

"Reality" constantly waylays the artist to prevent his flight. Much cunning is needed to effect the sublime escape. A reversed Odysseus, he must free himself from his daily Penelope and sail through reefs and rocks to Circe's Faery. When, for a moment, he succeeds in escaping the perpetual ambush, let us not grudge him a gesture of arrogant triumph, a St. George gesture with the dragon prostrate at his feet. /23/

INVITATION TO UNDERSTANDING

The works of art that the nineteenth century favored invariably contain a core of "lived" reality which furnishes the substance, as it were, of the aesthetic body. With this material the aesthetic process works, and its working consists in endowing the human nucleus with glamour and dignity. To the majority of people this is the most natural and the only possible setup of a work of art. Art

* "Ultraism" is one of the most appropriate names that have been coined to denote the new sensibility. /22/
† An attempt has been made in this extreme sense—in certain works by Picasso—but it has failed signally. /22/
* This was done by the dadaistic hoax. It is interesting to note again (see the above footnote) that the very vagaries and abortive experiments of the new art derive with a certain cogency from its organic principle, thereby giving ample proof that modern art is a unified and meaningful movement. /23/

is reflected life, nature seen through a temperament, representation of human destinies, and so on. But the fact is that our young artists, with no less conviction, maintain the opposite. Must the old always have the last word today while tomorrow infallibly the young win out? For one thing, let us not rant and rave. . . . Our firmest convictions are apt to be the most suspect, they mark our limits and our bonds. Life is a petty thing unless it is moved by the indomitable urge to extend its boundaries. Only in proportion as we are desirous of living more do we really live. Obstinately to insist on carrying on within the same familiar horizon betrays weakness and a decline of vital energies. Our horizon is a biological line, a living part of our organism. In times of fullness of life it expands, elastically moving in unison almost with our breathing. When the horizon stiffens it is because it has become fossilized and we are growing old.

It is less obvious than academicians assume that a /24/ work of art must consist of human stuff which the Muses comb and groom. Art cannot be reduced to cosmetics. Perception of "lived" reality and perception of artistic form, as I have said before, are essentially incompatible because they call for a different adjustment of our perceptive apparatus. An art that requires such a double seeing is a squinting art. The nineteenth century was remarkably cross-eyed. That is why its products, far from representing a normal type of art, may be said to mark a maximum aberration in the history of taste. All great periods of art have been careful not to let the work revolve about human contents. The imperative of unmitigated realism that dominated the artistic sensibility of the last century must be put down as a freak in aesthetic evolution. It thus appears that the new inspiration, extravagant though it seems, is merely returning, at least in one point, to the royal road of art. For this road is called "will to style." But to stylize means to deform reality, to derealize; style involves dehumanization. And vice versa, there is no other means of stylizing except by dehumanizing. Whereas realism, exhorting the artist faithfully to follow reality, exhorts him to abandon style. A Zurbarán enthusiast, groping for the suggestive word, will declare that the works of this painter have "character." And character and not style is distinctive of the works of Lucas and Sorolla, of Dickens and Galdós. The eighteenth century, on the other hand, which had so little character was a past master of style. /25/

ESSAY XXIII—OF THE STANDARD OF TASTE

David Hume

The great variety of Taste, as well as of opinion, which prevails in the world, is too obvious not to have fallen under every one's observation. Men of the most confined knowledge are able to remark a difference of taste in the narrow circle of their acquaintance, even where the persons have been educated under the same government, and have early imbibed the same prejudices. But those, who can enlarge their view to contemplate distant nations and remote ages, are still more surprized at the great inconsistence and contrariety. We are apt to call *barbarous* whatever departs widely from our own taste and apprehension: But soon find the epithet of reproach retorted on us. And the highest arrogance and self-conceit is at last startled, on observing an equal assurance on all sides, and

From "Essay XXIII—Of the Standard of Taste," in *Essays Moral, Political, and Literary*, eds. T. H. Green and T. H. Grose (London: Longmans, Green, and Co., 1875), I, 266–284.

scruples, amidst such a contest of sentiment, to pronounce positively in its own favour.

As this variety of taste is obvious to the most careless enquirer; so will it be found, on examination, to be still greater in reality than in appearance. The sentiments of men often differ with regard to beauty and deformity of all kinds, even while their general discourse is the same. There are certain terms in every language, which import blame, and others praise; and all men, who use the same tongue, must agree in their application of them. Every voice is united in applauding elegance, propriety, simplicity, spirit in writing; and in blaming fustian, affectation, coldness, and a false brilliancy: But when critics come to particulars, this seeming unanimity vanishes; and it is found, that they had affixed a very different meaning to their expressions. In all matters of opinion and science, the case is opposite: The difference among men is there oftener found to lie in generals than in particulars; and to be less in reality than in appearance. An explanation of the terms commonly ends the controversy; and the disputants are surprized to find, that they had been quarrelling, while at bottom they agreed in their judgment. . . . /266/

It is natural for us to seek a *Standard of Taste;* a rule, by which the various sentiments of men may be reconciled; at least, a decision, afforded, confirming one sentiment, and condemning another.

There is a species of philosophy, which cuts off all hopes of success in such an attempt, and represents the impossibility of ever attaining any standard of taste. The difference, it is said, is very wide between judgment and sentiment. All sentiment is right; because sentiment has a reference to nothing beyond itself, and is always real, wherever a man is conscious of it. But all determinations of the understanding are not right; because they have a reference to something beyond themselves, to wit, real matter of fact; and are not always conformable to that standard. Among a thousand different opinions which different men may entertain of the same subject, there is one, and but one, that is just and true; and the only difficulty is to fix and ascertain it. On the contrary, a thousand different sentiments, excited by the same object, are all right: Because no sentiment represents what is really in the object. It only marks a certain conformity or relation between the object and the organs or faculties of the mind; and if that conformity did not really exist, the sentiment could never possibly have being. Beauty is no quality in things themselves: It exists merely in the mind which contemplates them; and each mind perceives a different beauty. One person may even perceive deformity, /268/ where another is sensible of beauty; and every individual ought to acquiesce in his own sentiment, without pretending to regulate those of others. To seek the real beauty, or real deformity, is as fruitless an enquiry, as to pretend to ascertain the real sweet or real bitter. According to the disposition of the organs, the same object may be both sweet and bitter; and the proverb has justly determined it to be fruitless to dispute concerning tastes. It is very natural, and even quite necessary, to extend this axiom to mental, as well as bodily taste; and thus common sense, which is so often at variance with philosophy, especially with the sceptical kind, is found, in one instance at least, to agree in pronouncing the same decision.

But though this axiom, by passing into a proverb, seems to have attained the sanction of common sense; there is certainly a species of common sense which opposes it, at least serves to modify and restrain it. Whoever would assert an equality of genius and elegance between OGILBY and MILTON, or BUNYAN and ADDISON, would be thought to defend no less an extravagance, than if he had maintained a mole-hill to be as high as TENERIFFE, or a pond as extensive as the ocean. Though there may be found persons, who give the preference to the former authors; no one pays attention to such a taste; and we pronounce without scruple the sentiment of these pretended critics to be absurd and ridiculous. The principle of the natural equality of tastes is then totally forgot, and while we admit it on some occasions, where the objects seem near an equality, it appears an extravagant paradox, or rather a palpable absurdity, where objects so disproportioned are compared together.

It is evident that none of the rules of composition are fixed by reasonings *a priori,* or can be esteemed abstract conclusions of the understanding, from comparing those habitudes and relations of ideas, which are eternal and immutable. Their foundation is the same with that of all the practical sciences, experience; nor are they any thing but general observations, concerning what has been universally found to please in all countries and in all ages. Many of the beauties of poetry and even of eloquence are founded on falsehood and fiction, on hyperboles, metaphors, and an abuse or perversion of terms from their natural meaning. To check the sallies of the imagination, and to reduce every expression to /269/ geometrical truth and exactness, would be the most contrary to the laws of criticism; because it would produce a work, which, by universal experience, has been found the most insipid and disagreeable. But though poetry can never submit to exact truth, it must be confined by rules of art, discovered to the author either by genius or observation. If some negligent or irregular writers have pleased, they have not pleased by their transgressions of rule or order, but in spite of these transgressions: They have possessed other beauties, which were conformable to just criticism; and the force of these beauties has been able to overpower censure, and give the mind a satisfaction superior to the disgust arising from the blemishes. ARIOSTO pleases; but not by his monstrous and improbable fictions, by his bizarre mixture of the serious and comic styles, by the want of coherence in his stories, or by the continual interruptions of his narration. He charms by the force and clearness of his expression, by the readiness and variety of his inventions, and by his natural pictures of the passions, especially those of the gay and amorous kind: And however his faults may diminish our satisfaction, they are not able entirely to destroy it. Did our pleasure really arise from those parts of his poem, which we denominate faults, this would be no objection to criticism in general: It would only be an objection to those particular rules of criticism, which would establish such circumstances to be faults, and would represent them as universally blameable. If they are found to please, they cannot be faults; let the pleasure, which they produce, be ever so unexpected and unaccountable.

But though all the general rules of art are founded only on experience and on the observation of the common sentiments of human nature, we must not imagine, that, on every occasion, the feelings of men will be conformable to these rules. Those finer emotions of the mind are of a very tender and delicate nature, and require the concurrence of many favourable circumstances to make them play with facility and exactness, according to their general and established principles. The least exterior hindrance to such small springs, or the least internal disorder, disturbs their motion, and confounds the operation of the whole machine. When we would make an experiment of this nature, and would try the force of any beauty or deformity, we must choose with care a /270/ proper time and place, and bring the fancy to a suitable situation and disposition. A perfect serenity of mind, a recollection of thought, a due attention to the object; if any of these circumstances be wanting, our experiment will be fallacious, and we shall be unable to judge of the catholic and universal beauty. The relation, which nature has placed between the form and the sentiment, will at least be more obscure; and it will require greater accuracy to trace and discern it. We shall be able to ascertain its influence not so much from the operation of each particular beauty, as from the durable admiration, which attends those works, that have survived all the caprices of mode and fashion, all the mistakes of ignorance and envy.

The same HOMER, who pleased at ATHENS and ROME two thousand years ago, is still admired at PARIS and at LONDON. All the changes of climate, government, religion, and language, have not been able to obscure his glory. Authority or prejudice may give a temporary vogue to a bad poet or orator; but his reputation will never be durable or general. When his compositions are examined by posterity or by foreigners, the enchantment is dissipated, and his faults appear in their true colours. On the contrary, a real genius, the longer his works endure, and the more wide they are spread, the more sincere is the admiration which he meets with. Envy and jealousy have too much place in a narrow circle; and even familiar acquaintance with his person may diminish the applause due to his performances: But when these obstructions are removed, the beauties, which are naturally fitted to excite agreeable sentiments, immediately display their energy; and while the world endures, they maintain their authority over the minds of men.

It appears then, that, amidst all the variety and caprice of taste, there are certain general principles of approbation or blame, whose influence a careful eye may trace in all operations of the mind. Some particular forms or qualities, from the original structure of the internal fabric, are calculated to please, and others to displease; and if they fail of their effect in any particular instance, it is from some apparent defect or imperfection in the organ. A man in a fever would not insist on his palate as able to decide concerning flavours; nor would one, affected with the jaundice, pretend to give a verdict with regard to colours. In each creature, there is a /271/ sound and a defective state; and the former alone can be supposed to afford us a true standard of taste and sentiment. If, in the sound state of the organ, there be an entire or a considerable uniformity of sentiment among men, we may thence derive an idea of the perfect beauty; in like manner as the appearance of objects in day-light, to the eye of a man in health, is denominated their true and real colour, even while colour is allowed to be merely a phantasm of the senses.

Many and frequent are the defects in the internal organs, which prevent or weaken the influence of those general principles, on which depends our sentiment of beauty or deformity. Though some objects, by the structure of the mind, be naturally calculated to give pleasure, it is not to be expected, that in every individual the pleasure will be equally felt. Particular incidents and situations occur, which either throw a false light on the objects, or hinder the true from conveying to the imagination the proper sentiment and perception.

One obvious cause, why many feel not the proper sentiment of beauty, is the want of that *delicacy* of imagination, which is requisite to convey a sensibility of those finer emotions. This delicacy every one pretends to : Every one talks of it; and would reduce every kind of taste or sentiment to its standard. But as our intention in this essay is to mingle some light of the understanding with the feelings of sentiment, it will be proper to give a more accurate definition of delicacy, than has hitherto been attempted. And not to draw our philosophy from too profound a source, we shall have recourse to a noted story in DON QUIXOTE.

It is with good reason, says SANCHO to the squire with the great nose, that I pretend to have a judgment in wine: This is a quality hereditary in our family. Two of my kinsmen were once called to give their opinion of a hogshead, which was supposed to be excellent, being old and of a good vintage. One of them tastes it; considers it; and after mature reflection pronounces the wine to be good, were it not for a small taste of leather, which he perceived in it. The other, after using the same precautions, gives also his verdict in favour of the wine; but with the reserve of a taste of iron, which he could easily distinguish. You cannot imagine how much they were both ridiculed for their judgment. But who laughed in the end? On emptying the hogshead, there was found at the bottom, an old key with a leathern thong tied to it. /272/

The great resemblance between mental and bodily taste will easily teach us to apply this story. Though it be certain, that beauty and deformity, more than sweet and bitter, are not qualities in objects, but belong entirely to the sentiment, internal or external; it must be allowed, that there are certain qualities in objects, which are fitted by nature to produce those particular feelings. Now as these qualities may be found in a small degree, or may be mixed and confounded with each other, it often happens, that the taste is not affected with such minute qualities, or is not able to distinguish all the particular flavours, amidst the disorder, in which they are presented. Where the organs are so fine, as to allow nothing to escape them; and at the same time so exact as to perceive every ingredient in the composition: This we call delicacy of taste, whether we employ these terms in the literal or metaphorical sense. Here then the general rules of beauty are of use; being drawn from established models, and from the observation of what pleases or displeases, when presented singly and in a high degree: And if the same qualities, in a continued composition and in a smaller degree, affect not the organs with a sensible delight or uneasiness, we exclude the person from all pretensions to this delicacy. To produce these general rules or avowed patterns of composition is like finding the key with the leathern thong; which justified the verdict of SANCHO's kinsmen, and confounded those pretended judges who had condemned them. Though the hogshead had never been emptied, the taste of the one was still equally delicate, and that of the other equally dull and languid: But it would have been more difficult to have proved the superiority of the former, to the conviction of every by-stander. In like manner, though the beauties of writing had never been methodized, or reduced to general principles; though no excellent models had ever been acknowledged; the different degrees of taste would still have subsisted, and the judgment of one man been preferable to that of another, but it would not have been so easy to silence the bad critic, who might always insist upon his particular sentiment, and refuse to submit to his antagonist. But when we show him an avowed principle of art; when we illustrate this principle by examples, whose operation, from his own particular taste, he acknowledges to be conformable to the principle; when we prove, that the same principle may be applied to the pre- /273/ sent case, where he did not perceive or feel its influence: He must conclude, upon the whole, that the fault lies in himself, and that he wants the delicacy, which is requisite to make him sensible of every beauty and every blemish, in any composition or discourse.

It is acknowledged to be the perfection of every sense or faculty, to perceive with exactness its most minute objects, and allow nothing to escape its notice and observation. The smaller the objects are, which become sensible to the eye, the finer is that organ, and the more elaborate its make and composition. A good palate is not tried by strong flavours; but by a mixture of small ingredients, where we are still sensible of each part, notwithstanding its minuteness and its confusion with the rest. In like manner, a quick and acute perception of beauty and deformity must be the perfection of our mental taste; nor can a man be satisfied with himself while he suspects, that any excellence or blemish in a discourse has passed him unobserved. In this case, the perfection of the man, and the perfection of the sense or feeling, are found to be united. A very delicate palate, on many occasions, may be a great inconvenience both to a man himself and to his friends: But a delicate taste of wit or beauty must always be a desirable quality; because it is the source of all the finest and most innocent enjoyments, of which human nature is susceptible. In this decision the sentiments of all mankind are agreed. Wherever you can ascertain a delicacy of taste, it is sure to meet with approbation; and the best way of ascertaining it is to appeal to those models and principles, which have been established by the uniform consent and experience of nations and ages.

But though there be naturally a wide difference in point of delicacy between one person and another, nothing tends further to encrease and improve this talent, than *practice* in a particular art, and the frequent survey or contemplation of a particular species of beauty. When objects of any kind are first presented to the eye or imagination, the sentiment, which attends them, is obscure and confused; and the mind is, in a great measure, incapable of pronouncing concerning their merits or defects. The taste cannot perceive the several excellences of the performance; much less distinguish the particular character of each excellency, and ascertain its quality and degree. If it pronounce the whole in /274/ general to be beautiful or deformed, it is the utmost that can be expected; and even this judgment, a person, so unpractised, will be apt to deliver with great hesitation and reserve. But allow him to acquire experience in those objects, his feeling becomes more exact and nice: He not only perceives the beauties and defects of each part, but marks the distinguishing species of each quality, and assigns it suitable praise or blame. A clear and distinct sentiment attends him through the whole survey of the objects; and he discerns that very degree and kind of approbation or displeasure, which each part is naturally fitted to produce. The mist dissipates, which seemed formerly to hang over the object: The organ acquires greater perfection in its operations; and can pronounce, without danger of mistake, concerning the merits of every performance. In a word, the same address and dexterity, which practice gives to the execution of any work, is also acquired by the same means, in the judging of it.

So advantageous is practice to the discernment of beauty, that, before we can give judgment on any work of importance, it will even be requisite, that that very individual performance be more than once perused by us, and be surveyed in different lights with attention and deliberation. There is a flutter or hurry of thought which attends the first perusal of any piece, and which confounds the genuine sentiment of beauty. The relation of the parts is not discerned: The true characters of style are little distinguished: The several perfections and defects seem wrapped up in a species of confusion, and present themselves indistinctly to the imagination. Not to mention, that there is a species of beauty, which, as it is florid and superficial, pleases at first; but being found incompatible with a just expression either of reason or passion, soon palls upon the taste, and is then rejected with disdain, at least rated at a much lower value.

It is impossible to continue in the practice of contemplating any order of beauty, without being frequently obliged to form *comparisons* between the several species and degrees of excellence, and estimating their proportion to each other. A man, who has had no opportunity of comparing the different kinds of beauty, is indeed totally unqualified to pronounce an opinion with regard to any object presented to him. By comparison alone we fix the epithets of praise or blame, and /275/ learn how to assign the due degree of each. The coarsest daubing contains a certain lustre of colours and exactness of imitation, which are so far beauties, and would affect the mind of a peasant or Indian with the highest admiration. The most vulgar ballads are not entirely destitute of harmony or nature; and none but a person, familiarized to superior beauties, would pronounce their numbers harsh, or narration uninteresting. A great inferiority of beauty gives pain to a person conversant in the highest excellence of the kind, and is for that reason pronounced a deformity: As the most finished object, with which we are acquainted, is naturally supposed to have reached the pinnacle of perfection, and to be entitled to the highest applause. One accustomed to see, and examine, and weigh the several performances, admired in different ages and nations, can only rate the merits of a work exhibited to his view, and assign its proper rank among the productions of genius.

But to enable a critic the more fully to execute this undertaking, he must preserve his mind free from all *prejudice,* and allow nothing to enter into his consideration, but the very object which is submitted to his examination. We may observe, that every work of art, in order to produce its due effect on the mind, must be surveyed in a certain point of view, and cannot be fully relished by persons, whose situation, real or imaginary, is not conformable to that which is required by the performance. An orator addresses himself to a particular audience, and must have a regard to their particular genius, interests, opinions, passions, and prejudices; otherwise he hopes in vain to govern their resolutions, and inflame their affections. Should they even have entertained some prepossessions against him, however unreasonable, he must not overlook this disadvantage; but, before he enters upon the subject, must endeavour to conciliate their affection, and acquire their good graces. A critic of a different age or nation, who should peruse this discourse, must have all these circumstances in his eye, and must place himself in the same situation as the audience, in order to form a true judgment of the oration. In like manner, when any work is addressed to the public, though I should have a friendship or enmity with the author, I must depart from this situation; and considering myself as a man in general, forget, if possible, my individual being and my peculiar circumstances. /276/ A person influenced by prejudice, complies not with this condition; but obstinately maintains his natural position, without placing himself in that point of view, which the performance supposes. If the work be addressed to persons of a different age or nation, he makes no allowance for their peculiar views and prejudices; but, full of the manners of his own age and country, rashly condemns what seemed admirable in the eyes of those for whom alone the discourse was calculated. If the work be executed for the public, he never sufficiently enlarges his comprehension, or forgets his interest as a friend or enemy, as a rival or commentator. By this means, his sentiments are perverted; nor have the same beauties and blemishes the same influence upon him, as if he had imposed a proper violence on his imagination, and had forgotten himself for a moment. So far his taste evidently departs from the true standard; and of consequence loses all credit and authority.

It is well known, that in all questions, submitted to the understanding, prejudice is destructive of sound judgment, and perverts all operations of the intellectual faculties: It is no less contrary to good taste; nor has it less influence to corrupt our sentiment of beauty. It belongs to *good sense* to check its influence in both cases; and in this respect, as well as in many others, reason, if not an essential part of taste, is at least requisite to the operations of this latter faculty. In all the nobler productions of genius, there is a mutual relation and correspondence of parts; nor can either the beauties or blemishes be perceived by him, whose thought is not capacious enough to comprehend all those parts, and compare them with each other, in order to perceive the consistence and uniformity of the whole. Every work of art has also a certain end or purpose, for which it is calculated; and is to be deemed more or less perfect, as it is more or less fitted to attain this end. The object of eloquence is to persuade, of history to instruct, of poetry to please by means of the passions and the imagination. These ends we must carry constantly in our view, when we peruse any performance; and we must be able to judge how far the means employed are adapted to their respective purposes. Besides, every kind of composition, even the most poetical, is nothing but a chain of propositions and reasonings; not always, indeed, the justest and most exact, but still plausible and specious, /277/ however disguised by the colouring of the imagination. The persons introduced in tragedy and epic poetry, must be represented as reasoning, and thinking, and concluding, and acting, suitably to their character and circumstances; and without judgment, as well as taste and invention, a poet can never hope to succeed in so delicate an undertaking. Not to mention, that the same excellence of faculties which contributes to the improvement of reason, the same clearness of conception, the same exactness of distinction, the same vivacity of apprehension, are essential to the operations of true taste, and are its infallible concomitants. It seldom, or never happens, that a man of sense, who has experience in any art, cannot judge of its beauty; and it is no less rare to meet with a man who has a just taste without a sound understanding.

Thus, though the principles of taste be universal, and, nearly, if not entirely the same in all men; yet few are qualified to give judgment on any work of art, or establish their own sentiment as the standard of beauty. The organs of internal sensation are seldom so perfect as to allow the general principles their full play, and produce a feeling correspondent to those principles. They either labour under some defect, or are vitiated by some disorder; and by that means, excite a sentiment, which may be pronounced erroneous. When the critic has no delicacy, he judges without any distinction, and is only affected by the grosser and more palpable qualities of the object: The finer touches pass unnoticed and disregarded. Where he is not aided by practice, his verdict is attended with confusion and hesitation. Where no comparison has been employed, the most frivolous beauties, such as rather merit the name of defects, are the object of his admiration. Where he lies under the influence of prejudice, all his natural sentiments are perverted. Where good sense is wanting, he is not qualified to discern the beauties of design and reasoning, which are the highest and most excellent. Under some or other of these imperfections, the generality of men labour; and hence a true judge in the finer arts is observed, even during the most polished ages, to be so rare a character: Strong sense, united to delicate sentiment, improved by practice, perfected by comparison, and cleared of all prejudice, can alone entitle critics to this valuable character; and the joint /278/ verdict of such, wherever they are to be found, is the true standard of taste and beauty.

But where are such critics to be found? By what marks are they to be known? How distinguish them from pretenders? These questions are embarrassing; and seem to throw us back into the same uncertainty, from which, during the course of this essay, we have endeavoured to extricate ourselves.

But if we consider the matter aright, these are questions of fact, not of sentiment. Whether any particular person be endowed with good sense and a delicate imagination, free from prejudice, may often be the subject of dispute, and be liable to great discussion and enquiry: But that such a character is valuable and estimable will be agreed in by all mankind. Where these doubts occur, men can do no more than in other disputable questions, which are submitted to the understanding: They must produce the best arguments, that their invention suggests to them; they must acknowledge a true and decisive standard to exist somewhere, to wit, real existence and matter of fact; and they must have indulgence to such as differ from them in their appeals to this standard. It is sufficient for our present purpose, if we have proved, that the taste of all individuals is not upon an equal footing, and that some men in general, however difficult to be particularly pitched upon, will be acknowledged by universal sentiment to have a preference above others. . . . /279/

Though men of delicate taste be rare, they are easily to be distinguished in society, by the soundness of their understanding and the superiority of their faculties above the rest of mankind. The ascendant, which they acquire, gives a prevalence to that lively approbation, with which they receive any productions of genius, and renders it generally predominant. Many men, when left to themselves, have but a faint and dubious perception of beauty, who yet are capable of relishing any fine stroke, which is pointed out to them. Every convert to the admiration of the real poet or orator is the cause of some new conversion. And though prejudices may prevail for a time, they never unite in celebrating any rival to the true genius, but yield at last to the force of nature and just sentiment. Thus, though a civilized nation may easily be mistaken in the choice of their admired philosopher, they never have been found long to err, in their affection for a favorite epic or tragic author.

But notwithstanding all our endeavours to fix a standard of taste, and reconcile the discordant apprehensions of men, there still remain two sources of variation, which are not sufficient indeed to confound all the boundaries of beauty and deformity, but will often serve to produce a difference in the degrees of our approbation or blame. The one is the different humours of particular men; the other, the particular manners and opinions of our age and country. The general principles of taste are uniform in human nature: Where men vary in their judgments, some defect or perversion in the faculties may commonly be remarked; proceeding either from prejudice, from want of practice, or want of delicacy; and there is just reason for approving one taste, and condemning another. But where there is such a diversity in the internal frame or external situation as is entirely blameless on both sides, and leaves no room to give one the preference above the other, in that case a certain degree of diversity in judgment is unavoidable, and we seek in vain /280/ for a standard, by which we can reconcile the contrary sentiments.

A young man, whose passions are warm, will be more sensibly touched with amorous and tender images, than a man more advanced in years, who takes pleasure in wise, philosophical reflections concerning the conduct of life and moderation of the passions. At twenty, OVID may be the favourite author; HORACE at forty; and perhaps TACITUS at fifty. Vainly would we, in such cases, endeavour to enter into the sentiments of others, and divest ourselves of those propensities, which are natural to us. We choose our favourite author as we do our friend, from a conformity of humour and disposition. Mirth or passion, sentiment or reflection; whichever of these most predominates in our temper, it gives us a peculiar sympathy with the writer who resembles us.

One person is more pleased with the sublime; another with the tender; a third with raillery. One has a strong sensibility to blemishes, and is extremely studious of correctness: Another has a more lively feeling of beauties, and pardons twenty absurdities and defects for one elevated or pathetic stroke. The ear of this man is entirely turned towards conciseness and energy; that man is delighted with a copious, rich, and harmonious expression. Simplicity is affected by one; ornament by another. Comedy, tragedy, satire, odes, have each its partizans, who prefer that particular species of writing to all others. It is plainly an error in a critic, to confine his approbation to one species or style of writing, and condemn all the rest. But it is almost impossible not to feel a predilection for that which suits our particular turn and disposition. Such preferences are innocent and unavoidable, and can never reasonably be the object of dispute, because there is no standard, by which they can be decided. /281/

⌘ CONFRONTING THE WORK OF ART

Manuel Bilsky

The proverbial confusions of aesthetics apply equally to the philosophical discipline and to the critical activity. "What is aesthetics?" "What is criticism?" Such questions frequently cause despair among those who try to get some clarity about these concepts. And when we try to relate the one to the the other, we add more fuel to what is already a set of burning—if not burned out—issues. I do not intend to get involved in the more abstruse sides of these problems. I want rather to focus on one particular aspect, an eminently practical one, namely, introducing the student to the work of art. What is the most effective way of bringing the student and the work of art together so that what results is a significant experience? Furthermore, I'm presupposing the use of the discussion method, that is, I mean these remarks primarily for the teacher who *discusses* works of art with his class. The lecturer has special problems, important ones, to be sure, but my particular concern is with the learning situation in which the teacher and the student both participate actively.

A psychiatrist, in discussing the doctor-patient relationship, recently said that the first words the patient utters when he enters the office frequently provide an important clue to many aspects of the therapy that follows. Similarly important are the first words that the teacher speaks when he starts the class. The first question he raises will often determine whether the ensuing discussion will be confusion and muddle or fruitful and rewarding. We cannot therefore put too much emphasis on discussing this opening gesture. In such a discussion we don't have to worry very much about theories of meaning or other related philosophical problems. The important issue is the heuristic significance of the opening question, and for the most part we need only bring in common sense considerations. We can leave to others, where they properly belong, such issues as formalism vs. emotionalism, meaning vs. significance, etc., etc. What I shall do, therefore, is suggest in turn a number of questions with which one might begin the discussion of a work of art, trace the possible consequences of asking each question, and then try to evaluate these consequences. If they are undesirable, we have a right, I should think, to reject the question that provokes them. My evaluation will be guided by the goals of clarity and greater practical success in the discussion of works of art. If I were pressed further on this point, I would say that the aim is to make something significant happen

In its present form, this article appears for the first time in this book. It is the original version of an article that appeared in *University College Quarterly*, 6 (Fall, 1960), 5–7.

when the student is in the presence of a work of art, to heighten his enjoyment of it.[1]

The first candidate, the first question with which one might open the discussion of a work of art, is "What do you feel?" The student looks at the picture, say, and the teacher asks him what he feels. Obviously this is an invitation to the student—which unfortunately he too frequently and too readily accepts—to say, "Nothing." And no amount of conjoling will *necessarily* make him say anything else. "But look," the teacher might insist, placing the depiction of a wedding dance beside that of a funeral, "doesn't the one make you feel gay and the other sad?" "I feel lousy," the student might reply, "I awoke with a cold and a headache, and I've felt and still do feel vaguely depressed, and if I were to look at that Brueghel for the next two hours, I'm sure I wouldn't feel any less depressed."

The student, in my opinion, would be quite justified if at that moment, he walked out of the room and never returned. The teacher is confused and is doing very little else but imparting his confusion to the student. He is confusing autobiography with criticism. To insist that the student reveal what he feels is to force him into the posture of confession and is to take him away from the picture. Obviously I can in turn look at a Brueghel oil and a Kollwitz woodcut and say one is gay while the other is sad even though I feel utterly depressed while looking at both of them. Here, then, is the root of this particular confusion: the failure to distinguish between my feeling and the feeling expressed by or in the picture. The same word, namely, "feeling," occurs in both contexts, so the failure to make the distinction is not altogether unnatural.

This confusion is enshrined in a sentence used by the author of a recent book on art appreciation. "There is something gay and relaxing about [its] continuous movement . . . ", he says of a Boucher. "Gay," in this sentence, seems to direct our attention to the picture, but "relaxing" seems rather to designate some kind of psychological effect on or in the spectator—as though all I have to do if I feel nervous and anxious is, instead of reaching for my tranquilizers, to stand before the Boucher for a while and thus save the price of the pills. Perhaps the "ing" form is inadvertent; if the author has used the "ed" form instead—"relaxed" instead of "relaxing"—the import of the sentence would have been quite different, and the confusion somewhat diminished. No less an authority than Hanslick makes the same mistake. He says: "With the technically uninitiated the 'feelings' play a predominant part, while, in the case of the trained musician, they are quite in the background. . . . If every shallow Requiem, every noisy funeral march and every whining Adagio had the power to make us sad, who would care to prolong his existence in such a world?" (*The Beautiful in Music*, pp. 77, 137). The Adagio may certainly be sad, but it doesn't follow that it necessarily makes me actually feel sad. Hanslick fails to distinguish the sadness of the music, which is an expressive property that characterizes the piece, from the sadness I might feel if, say, a close friend were badly injured.

What I am suggesting, then, is that it is important to distinguish two senses

[1] I am taking for granted something which is perhaps arguable, namely, that analysis heightens enjoyment. Many proponents of the "murder-to-dissect" school would undoubtedly deny this, and most vehemently. But to enter into such a controversy would be, for me, pointless. I could grant that no necessary connection exists between analysis and enjoyment, and my investigation would still be relevant, because it's not directed towards proving that any such necessary condition exists. Actually, I could even accept the extreme position, i.e., that enjoyment never follows analysis, and my efforts would still have point. It, the analysis, would result in a heightened awareness of the elements and constituents of the work of art, and this I presuppose as a value. But of course the extreme position is not necessary, so all I need really to assume is that in some cases the one follows from the other, that the analysis results in heightened enjoyment on the part of the spectator. And such an assumption certainly requires no justification.

in which feeling words may be used and then that, except in some special cases, we restrict critical remarks to those which describe what the work expresses and not what the spectator feels. Obviously Brueghel's "Wedding Dance" is a gay picture and Kollwitz's "The Widow" a sad one, and I can say this with good reason without necessarily feeling either gay or sad. I may actually feel the opposite in each case and still recognize the Brueghel as gay and the Kollwitz as sad.

But don't works of art ever make us actually feel anything, someone might ask? How about when I step inside a cathedral? Or see an exciting movie such as the recent French one in which an auto loaded with dynamite went charging around the countryside constantly in danger of exploding? And what about the testimony of a long line of aestheticians, culminating perhaps in Tolstoy, who insist that art is the communication of feeling? Is it not, then, legitimate to ask "What do you feel?" when the primary function of art is, at least according to some eminent authorities, to communicate feelings?

Of course we experience these feelings in the presence of various works of art. As a matter of fact, sometimes what we feel is indistinguishable from what we feel in real life. (These are the special cases I mentioned before. The purpose in discussing them would of course also be special.) For example, the scene in the movie *Gervaise* where two women are fighting and one lacerates the other's ear: the shock and revulsion we feel is extremely intense. Another instance occurs in the opening measures of the introduction to the first movement of Bartok's "Sonata for Two Pianos and Percussion." After a few measures of quiet playing by the pianos of a series of quite ordinary intervals, a sudden very loud, clangorous interruption by what seems to be the whole percussion section plus the two pianos takes place. The effect is, at least the first time you hear it, *actually* frightening. In both these cases, and in many similar ones, I think, where the feeling coincides identically with a similar life feeling, the important distance threshold has been lowered to the extent that one would be justified in saying that the phenomenon in question is no longer a work of art. I am, of course, here following the classic interpretation of Edward Bullough in such cases.

So the answer to the question as to whether works of art ever make us actually feel anything is definitely yes. Again, the relation between what we actually feel in the presence of a work of art and the expressive properties which the work exhibits is an interesting one philosophically. But it has very little if any relevance to or place in the discussion of a work of art. If the discussion of such a relation occurs at all, it will occur only inadvertently or as an indication of a possible shortcoming in the work. The significant questions, the really fruitful ones, will center around the expressive properties in the work and not around the feelings that it elicits in the spectator.

Between the possible questions, then, "What do you see?" and "What do you feel?" the former keeps us within the confines of the work while the latter too often leads us astray. The opening question should not lead the class into a philosophical discussion about whose feelings are involved, or whether the artist is effectively communicating his feelings, and to whom, because then we're getting away from the work of art. The question should rather provoke a discussion of the work being considered, and the one which will do that more effectively and avoid the seductive though irrelevant by-passes of philosophy is "What do you see?"

The second candidate, the second possible opening gesture, is "What do you experience?" or one of its variants such as "Describe your experience of this painting," or "How does your experience of this work differ from your experience of that one?" I find it hard to understand how such an awkward way of wording the opening question could have developed. Perhaps it is an attempt to avoid the difficulties of "feeling, " or perhaps the shade of Dewey is still lurking compellingly in the background. Whatever the cause, the effect is obvious. The question throws us right back into all the problems associated with "feel," only "experience" is even more vague and useless. A judicious application of Occam's razor to questions phrased in this way results in a much healthier and much more fruitful set of questions. "Describe your experience of 'Sunday on the Grande Jatte' "; "What characteristics distinguish your experience of 'The Assumption of the Virgin' " becomes "What characteristics does 'The Assumption of the Virgin' exhibit?"; "How does your experience of Crivelli's 'Crucifixion' differ from your experience of Perugino's 'Crucifixion' "? becomes "How does Crivelli's 'Crucifixion' differ from Perugino's 'Crucifixion' "? Nothing is lost; much is gained in the way of clarity and straightforwardness. And in the new form we also avoid such philosophical pitfalls as the difference between aesthetic experience and ordinary experience, which might otherwise be tempting. The point of all this has already been made, but it needs to be reiterated: when a teacher is discussing a work of art with a group of students, he is or should be discussing art objects and not philosophical problems or autobiographical data.

Perhaps the biggest trap is our next candidate: "What does this work mean?" I am not referring to questions like this which arise from a failure to understand a word in a poem or a grammatical construction. I refer rather to such things as non-objective painting or atonal music where this question also too frequently invites a "Nothing!" reply. Other dangers lurk in the shadows. Before you know it, you're talking about what the artist intended, and this leads directly to the relation between the intention and the accomplishment, which, again, is interesting and important as a philosophical problem, but which takes us far away from our important business, namely, discussing the work that confronts us. Another avenue which beckons when one takes the meaning gambit is the surface meaning depth meaning distinction. On the surface "Guérnica" depicts the horrors of wartorn Spain, but the depth meaning is far more universal in scope: the whole of civilization is really involved. So might the argument run, and from there it's an easy step to the problem of belief, e.g., if I believe with Picasso that the nature of human existence is thus and so, does that enhance the value of the picture? When such a discussion takes place it cannot go very far without the work of art's receding into the background.

Consider, for example, "Dover Beach"; you discuss the obvious things about it with your class: the changing lines reflect the changing character of the sea; the texture of the lines, in places, reflects the tranquility the poem is talking about, the many instances where the sound of the words reflects what the words refer to, "the melancholy, long, withdrawing roar," or "Begin, and cease, and then again begin," for example. Fine! But then you ask, as no less an astute critic than A. C. Bradley recommends, "But doesn't this poem really mean something like 'The world is an unchanging sea of misery?' " Again we're off. Is it really, one could ask. And if it is and I don't think so, will this fact detract from my appreciation of the poem? And if it does, should it? And so on, but the poem is lost; we've left it, and we've become involved in totally irrelevant issues.

My conclusion is obvious, I think, from all I have said so far. I am recommending that the teacher open his discussion with a question that will elicit from the student certain responses directed towards the work itself. The questions will of course vary depending on which art you are discussing. But the important thing in each case is to focus on the work itself and not on irrelevant issues such as philosophical problems. And, in the case of the visual arts, for example, I am suggesting that the most effective means of accomplishing this is through the use of a question like "What do you see?" a question centering around the visual stimulants of the work. This general approach is equally valid for arts other than the visual with, of course, appropriate modifications.

✺ THE ROLE OF THEORY IN AESTHETICS

Morris Weitz

Theory has been central in aesthetics and is still the preoccupation of the philosophy of art. Its main avowed concern remains the determination of the nature of art which can be formulated into a definition of it. It construes definition as the statement of the necessary and sufficient properties of what is being defined, where the statement purports to be a true or false claim about the essence of art, what characterizes and distinguishes it from everything else. Each of the great theories of art—Formalism, Voluntarism, Emotionalism, Intellectualism, Intuitionism, Organicism—converges on the attempt to state the defining properties of art. Each claims that it is the true theory because it has formulated correctly into a real definition the nature of art; and that the others are false because they have left out some necessary or sufficient property. Many theorists contend that their enterprise is no mere intellectual exercise but an absolute necessity for any understanding of art and our proper evaluation of it. Unless we know what art is, they say, what are its necessary and sufficient properties, we cannot begin to respond to it adequately or to say why one work is good or better than another. Aesthetic theory, thus, is important not only in itself but for the foundations of both appreciation and criticism. Philosophers, critics, and even artists who have written on art, agree that what is primary in aesthetics is a theory about the nature of art.

Is aesthetic theory, in the sense of a true definition or set of necessary and sufficient properties of art, possible? If nothing else does, the history of aesthetics itself should give one enormous pause here. For, in spite of the many theories, we seem no nearer our goal today than we were in Plato's time. Each age, each art-movement, each philosophy of art, tries over and over again to establish the stated ideal only to be succeeded by a new or revised theory, rooted, at least in part, in the repudiation of preceding ones. Even today, almost everyone interested in aesthetic matters is still deeply wedded to the hope that the correct theory of art is forthcoming. We need only examine the numerous new books on art in which new definitions are proffered; or, in our own country especially, the basic textbooks and anthologies to recognize how strong the priority of a theory of art is.

In this essay I want to plead for the rejection of this problem. I want to show that theory—in the requisite classical sense—is *never* forthcoming in aesthetics, and that we would do much better as philosophers to supplant the question, "What is the nature of art?," by other questions, the answers to which

"The Role of Theory in Aesthetics," *Journal of Aesthetics and Art Criticism*, 15 (1956), 27–35.

will provide us with all the understanding of the arts there can be. I want to show that the inadequacies of the theories are not primarily occasioned by any legitimate difficulty such e.g., as the vast complexity of art, which might be corrected by further probing and research. Their basic inadequacies reside instead in a fundamental misconception of art. Aesthetic theory—all of it—is wrong in principle /27/ in thinking that a correct theory is possible because it radically misconstrues the logic of the concept of art. Its main contention that "art" is amenable to real or any kind of true definition is false. Its attempt to discover the necessary and sufficient properties of art is logically misbegotten for the very simple reason that such a set and, consequently, such a formula about it, is never forthcoming. Art, as the logic of the concept shows, has no set of necessary and sufficient properties, hence a theory of it is logically impossible and not merely factually difficult. Aesthetic theory tries to define what cannot be defined in its requisite sense. But in recommending the repudiation of aesthetic theory I shall not argue from this, as too many others have done, that its logical confusions render it meaningless or worthless. On the contrary, I wish to reassess its role and its contribution primarily in order to show that it is of the greatest importance to our understanding of the arts.

Let us now survey briefly some of the more famous extant aesthetic theories in order to see if they do incorporate correct and adequate statements about the nature of art. In each of these there is the assumption that it is the true enumeration of the defining properties of art, with the implication that previous theories have stressed wrong definitions. Thus, to begin with, consider a famous version of Formalist theory, that propounded by Bell and Fry. It is true that they speak mostly of painting in their writings but both assert that what they find in that art can be generalized for what is "art" in the others as well. The essence of painting, they maintain, are the plastic elements in relation. Its defining property is significant form, i.e., certain combinations of lines, colors, shapes, volumes—everything on the canvas except the representational elements—which evoke a unique response to such combinations. Painting is definable as plastic organization. The nature of art, what it *really* is, so their theory goes, is a unique combination of certain elements (the specifiable plastic ones) in their relations. Anything which is art is an instance of significant form; and anything which is not art has no such form.

To this the Emotionalist replies that the truly essential property of art has been left out. Tolstoy, Ducasse, or any of the advocates of this theory, find that the requisite defining property is not significant form but rather the expression of emotion in some sensuous public medium. Without projection of emotion into some piece of stone or words or sounds, etc., there can be no art. Art is really such embodiment. It is this that uniquely characterizes art, and any true, real definition of it, contained in some adequate theory of art, must so state it.

The Intuitionist disclaims both emotion and form as defining properties. In Croce's version, for example, art is identified not with some physical, public object but with a specific creative, cognitive and spiritual act. Art is really a first stage of knowledge in which certain human beings (artists) bring their images and intuitions into lyrical clarification or expression. As such, it is an awareness, non-conceptual in character, of the unique individuality of things; and since it exists below the level of conceptualization or action, it is without scientific or moral content. Croce singles out as the defining essence of art this first stage of spiritual life and advances its identification with art as a philosophically true theory or definition. /28/

The Organicist says to all of this that art is really a class of organic wholes consisting of distinguishable, albeit inseparable, elements in their causally efficacious relations which are presented in some sensuous medium. In A. C. Bradley, in piece-meal versions of it in literary criticism, or in my own general-ized adaptation of it in my *Philosophy of the Arts*, what is claimed is that anything which is a work of art is in its nature a unique complex of interrelated parts—in painting, for example, lines, colors, volumes, subjects, etc., all interacting upon one another on a paint surface of some sort. Certainly, at one time at least it seemed to me that this organic theory constituted the one true and real defini-tion of art.

My final example is the most interesting of all, logically speaking. This is the Voluntarist theory of Parker. In his writings on art, Parker persistently calls into question the traditional simple-minded definitions of aesthetics. "The assump-tion underlying every philosophy of art is the existence of some common nature present in all the arts."[1] "All the so popular brief definitions of art—'significant form,' 'expression,' 'intuition,' 'objectified pleasure'—are fallacious, either be-cause, while true of art, they are also true of much that is not art, and hence fail to differentiate art from other things; or else because they neglect some essential aspect of art."[2] But instead of inveighing against the attempt at definition of art itself, Parker insists that what is needed is a complex definition rather than a simple one. "The definition of art must therefore be in terms of a complex of characteristics. Failure to recognize this has been the fault of all the well-known definitions."[3] His own version of Voluntarism is the theory that art is essentially three things: embodiment of wishes and desires imaginatively satisfied, lan-guage, which characterizes the public medium of art, and harmony, which unifies the language with the layers of imaginative projections. Thus, for Parker, it is a true definition to say of art that it is ". . . the provision of satis-faction through the imagination, social significance, and harmony. I am claiming that nothing except works of art possesses all three of these marks."[4]

Now, all of these sample theories are inadequate in many different ways. Each purports to be a complete statement about the defining features of all works of art and yet each of them leaves out something which the others take to be central. Some are circular, e.g., the Bell-Fry theory of art as significant form which is defined in part in terms of our response to significant form. Some of them, in their search for necessary and sufficient properties, emphasize too few properties, like (again) the Bell-Fry definition which leaves out subject-representation in painting, or the Croce theory which omits inclusion of the very important feature of the public, physical character, say, of architecture. Others are too general and cover objects that are not art as well as works of art. Organicism is surely such a view since it can be applied to *any* causal unity in the natural world as well as to art.[5] /29/ Still others rest on dubious principles, e.g., Parker's claim that art embodies imaginative satisfactions, rather than real ones; or Croce's assertion that there is non-conceptual knowledge. Conse-quently, even if art has one set of necessary and sufficient properties, none of the theories we have noted or, for that matter, no aesthetic theory yet pro-posed, has enumerated that set to the satisfaction of all concerned.

Then there is a different sort of difficulty. As real definitions, these theo-ries are supposed to be factual reports on art. If they are, may we not ask, Are they empirical and open to verification or falsification? For example, what

[1]D. Parker, "The Nature of Art," reprinted in E. Vivas and M. Krieger, *The Problems of Aesthetics*, (N.Y., 1953), p. 90. /29/
[2] *Ibid.*, pp. 93–94. /29/
[3] *Ibid.*, p. 94. /29/
[4] *Ibid.*, p. 104. /29/
[5] See M. Macdonald's review of my *Philosophy of the Arts, Mind*, Oct., 1951, pp. 561–564, for a bril-liant discussion of this objection to the Organic theory. /29/

would confirm or disconfirm the theory that art is significant form or embodiment of emotion or creative synthesis of images? There does not even seem to
be a hint of the kind of evidence which might be forthcoming to test these
theories; and indeed one wonders if they are perhaps honorific definitions of
"art," that is, proposed redefinitions in terms of some *chosen* conditions for
applying the concept of art, and not true or false reports on the essential
properties of art at all.

But all these criticisms of traditional aesthetic theories—that they are
circular, incomplete, untestable, pseudo-factual, disguised proposals to change
the meaning of concepts—have been made before. My intention is to go
beyond these to make a much more fundamental criticism, namely, that
aesthetic theory is a logically vain attempt to define what cannot be defined, to
state the necessary and sufficient properties of that which has no necessary and
sufficient properties, to conceive the concept of art as closed when its very use
reveals and demands its openness.

The problem with which we must begin is not "What is art?," but "What
sort of concept is 'art'?" Indeed, the root problem of philosophy itself is to
explain the relation between the employment of certain kinds of concepts and
the conditions under which they can be correctly applied. If I may paraphrase
Wittgenstein, we must not ask, What is the nature of any philosophical x?, or
even, according to the semanticist, What does "x" mean?, a transformation that
leads to the disastrous interpretation of "art" as a name for some specifiable
class of objects; but rather, What is the use or employment of "x"? What does
"x" do in the language? This, I take it, is the initial question, the begin-all if not
the end-all of any philosophical problem and solution. Thus, in aesthetics, our
first problem is the elucidation of the actual employment of the concept of art,
to give a logical description of the actual functioning of the concept including a
description of the conditions under which we correctly use it or its correlates.

My model in this type of logical description or philosophy derives from
Wittgenstein. It is also he who, in his refutation of philosophical theorizing in
the sense of constructing definitions of philosophical entities, has furnished
contemporary aesthetics with a starting point for any future progress. In his
new work *Philosophical Investigations*,[6] Wittgenstein raises as an illustrative
question, What is a game? The traditional philosophical, theoretical answer
would be in terms of some exhaustive set of properties common to all games.
To this Witt- /30/ genstein says, let us consider what we call "games": "I mean
board-games, card-games, ball-games, Olympic games, and so on. What is
common to them all?—Don't say: 'there *must* be something common, or they
would not be called "games"' but *look and see* whether there is anything common
to all.—For if you look at them you will not see something that is common to
all, but similarities, relationships, and a whole series of them at that . . ."

Card games are like board games in some respects but not in others. Not
all games are amusing, nor is there always winning or losing or competition.
Some games resemble others in some respects—that is all. What we find are no
necessary and sufficient properties, only "a complicated network of similarities
overlapping and crisscrossing," such that we can say of games that they form a
family with family resemblances and no common trait. If one asks what a game
is, we pick out sample games, describe these, and add, "This and *similar things*
are called 'games'." This is all we need to say and indeed all any of us knows
about games. Knowing what a game is is not knowing some real definition or

---

[6] L. Wittgenstein, *Philosophical Investigations* (Oxford, 1953), tr. by E. Anscombe; see esp. Part I,
Sections 65–75. All quotations are from these sections. /30/

theory but being able to recognize and explain games and to decide which among imaginary and new examples would or would not be called "games."

The problem of the nature of art is like that of the nature of games, at least in these respects: If we actually look and see what it is that we call "art," we will also find no common properties — only strands of similarities. Knowing what art is is not apprehending some manifest or latent essence but being able to recognize, describe, and explain those things we call "art" in virtue of these similarities.

But the basic resemblance between these concepts is their open texture. In elucidating them, certain (paradigm) cases can be given, about which there can be no question as to their being correctly described as "art" or "game," but no exhaustive set of cases can be given. I can list some cases and some conditions under which I can apply correctly the concept of art but I cannot list all of them, for the all-important reason that unforeseeable or novel conditions are always forthcoming or envisageable.

A concept is open if its conditions of application are emendable and corrigible; i.e., if a situation or case can be imagined or secured which would call for some sort of *decision* on our part to extend the use of the concept to cover this, or to close the concept and invent a new one to deal with the new case and its new property. If necessary and sufficient conditions for the application of a concept can be stated, the concept is a closed one. But this can happen only in logic or mathematics where concepts are constructed and completely defined. It cannot occur with empirically-descriptive and normative concepts unless we arbitrarily close them by stipulating the ranges of their uses.

I can illustrate this open character of "art" best by examples drawn from its sub-concepts. Consider questions like "Is Dos Passos' *U. S. A.* a novel?," "Is V. Woolf's *To the Lighthouse* a novel?," "Is Joyce's *Finnegan's Wake* a novel?" On the traditional view, these are construed as factual problems to be answered yes or no in accordance with the presence or absence of defining properties. But certainly this is not how any of these questions is answered. Once it arises, as it has many times in the development of the novel from Richardson to Joyce (e.g., "Is Gide's *The School for Wives* a novel or a diary?"), what is at stake is no factual /31/ analysis concerning necessary and sufficient properties but a decision as to whether the work under examination is similar in certain respects to other works, already called "novels," and consequently warrants the extension of the concept to cover the new case. The new work is narrative, fictional, contains character delineation and dialogue but (say) it has no regular time-sequence in the plot or is interspersed with actual newspaper reports. It is like recognized novels, A, B, C . . . , in some respects but not like them in others. But then neither were B and C like A in some respects when it was decided to extend the concept applied to A to B and C. Because work N + 1 (the brand new work) is like A, B, C . . . N in certain respects — has strands of similarity to them — the concept is extended and a new phase of the novel engendered. "Is N 1 a novel?," then, is no factual, but rather a decision problem, where the verdict turns on whether or not we enlarge our set of conditions for applying the concept.

What is true of the novel is, I think, true of every sub-concept of art: "tragedy," "comedy," "painting," "opera," etc., of "art" itself. No "Is X a novel, painting, opera, work of art, etc.?" question allows of a definitive answer in the sense of a factual yes or no report. "Is this *collage* a painting or not?" does not rest on any set of necessary and sufficient properties of painting but on whether we decide — as we did! — to extend "painting" to cover this case.

"Art," itself, is an open concept. New conditions (cases) have constantly arisen and will undoubtedly constantly arise; new art forms, new movements will emerge, which will demand decisions on the part of those interested, usually professional critics, as to whether the concept should be extended or not. Aestheticians may lay down similarity conditions but never necessary and sufficient ones for the correct application of the concept. With "art" its conditions of application can never be exhaustively enumerated since new cases can always be envisaged or created by artists, or even nature, which would call for a decision on someone's part to extend or to close the old or to invent a new concept. (E.g., "It's not a sculpture, it's a mobile.")

What I am arguing, then, is that the very expansive, adventurous character of art, its ever-present changes and novel creations, makes it logically impossible to ensure any set of defining properties. We can, of course, choose to close the concept. But to do this with "art" or "tragedy" or "portraiture," etc., is ludicrous since it forecloses on the very conditions of creativity in the arts.

Of course there are legitimate and serviceable closed concepts in art. But these are always those whose boundaries of conditions have been drawn for a *special* purpose. Consider the difference, for example, between "tragedy" and "(extant) Greek tragedy." The first is open and must remain so to allow for the possibility of new conditions, e.g., a play in which the hero is not noble or fallen or in which there is no hero but other elements that are like those of plays we already call "tragedy." The second is closed. The plays it can be applied to, the conditions under which it can be correctly used are all in, once the boundary, "Greek," is drawn. Here the critic can work out a theory or real definition in which he lists the common properties at least of the extant Greek tragedies. Aristotle's definition, false as it is as a theory of all the plays of Aeschylus, Sophocles, and Euripides, since it does not cover some of them,[7] properly called "tragedies," can be /32/ interpreted as a real (albeit incorrect) definition of this closed concept; although it can also be, as it unfortunately has been, conceived as a purported real definition of "tragedy," in which case it suffers from the logical mistake of trying to define what cannot be defined — of trying to squeeze what is an open concept into an honorific formula for a closed concept.

What is supremely important, if the critic is not to become muddled, is to get absolutely clear about the way in which he conceives his concepts; otherwise he goes from the problem of trying to define "tragedy," etc., to an arbitrary closing of the concept in terms of certain preferred conditions or characteristics which he sums up in some linguistic recommendation that he mistakenly thinks is a real definition of the open concept. Thus, many critics and aestheticians ask, "What is tragedy?," choose a class of samples for which they may give a true account of its common properties, and then go on to construe this account of the chosen closed class as a true definition or theory of the whole open class of tragedy. This, I think, is the logical mechanism of most of the so-called theories of the sub-concepts of art: "tragedy," "comedy," "novel," etc. In effect, this whole procedure, subtly deceptive as it is, amounts to a transformation of correct criteria for *recognizing* members of certain legitimately closed classes of works of art into recommended criteria for *evaluating* any putative member of the class.

The primary task of aesthetics is not to seek a theory but to elucidate the concept of art. Specifically, it is to describe the conditions under which we employ the concept correctly. Definition, reconstruction, patterns of analysis

---

[7] See H. D. F. Kitto, *Greek Tragedy* (London, 1939), on this point. /32/

are out of place here since they distort and add nothing to our understanding of art. What, then, is the logic of "X is a work of art"?

As we actually use the concept, "Art" is both descriptive (like "chair") and evaluative (like "good"); i.e., we sometimes say, "This is a work of art," to describe something and we sometimes say it to evaluate something. Neither use surprises anyone.

What, first, is the logic of "X is a work of art," when it is a descriptive utterance? What are the conditions under which we would be making such an utterance correctly? There are no necessary and sufficient conditions but there are the strands of similarity conditions, i.e., bundles of properties, none of which need be present but most of which are, when we describe things as works of art. I shall call these the "criteria of recognition" of works of art. All of these have served as the defining criteria of the individual traditional theories of art; so we are already familiar with them. Thus, mostly, when we describe something as a work of art, we do so under the conditions of there being present some sort of artifact, made by human skill, ingenuity, and imagination, which embodies in its sensuous, public medium—stone, wood, sounds, words, etc.—certain distinguishable elements and relations. Special theorists would add conditions like satisfaction of wishes, objectification or expression of emotion, some act of empathy, and so on; but these latter conditions seem to be quite adventitious, present to some but not to other spectators when things are described as works of art. "X is a work of art and contains *no* emotion, expression, act of empathy, satisfaction, etc.," is perfectly good sense and may frequently be true. "X is a work of art and . . . was made by no one," or . . . "exists only in the mind and /33/ not in any publicly observable thing," or . . . "was made by accident when he spilled the paint on the canvas," in each case of which a normal condition is denied, are also sensible and capable of being true in certain circumstances. None of the criteria of recognition is a defining one, either necessary or sufficient, because we can sometimes assert of something that it is a work of art and go on to deny any one of these conditions, even the one which has traditionally been taken to be basic, namely, that of being an artifact: Consider, "This piece of driftwood is a lovely piece of sculpture." Thus, to say of anything that it is a work of art is to commit oneself to the presence of *some* of these conditions. One would scarcely describe X as a work of art if X were not an artifact, or a collection of elements sensuously presented in a medium, or a product of human skill, and so on. If none of the conditions were present, if there were no criteria present for recognizing something as a work of art, we would not describe it as one. But, even so, no one of these or any collection of them is either necessary or sufficient.

The elucidation of the descriptive use of "Art" creates little difficulty. But the elucidation of the evaluative use does. For many, especially theorists, "This is a work of art" does more than describe; it also praises. Its conditions of utterance, therefore, include certain preferred properties or characteristics of art. I shall call these "criteria of evaluation." Consider a typical example of this evaluative use, the view according to which to say of something that it is a work of art is to imply that it is a *successful* harmonization of elements. Many of the honorific definitions of art and its sub-concepts are of this form. What is at stake here is that "Art" is construed as an evaluative term which is either identified with its criterion or justified in terms of it. "Art" is defined in terms of its evaluative property, e.g., successful harmonization. On such a view, to say "X is a work of art" is (1) to say something which is taken *to mean* "X is a successful harmonization" (e.g., "Art *is* significant form") or (2) to say something praiseworthy *on the basis* of its successful harmonization. Theorists are never clear whether it is (1) or (2) which is being put forward. Most of them, concerned as they are with this evaluative use, formulate (2), i.e., that feature of art that *makes* it art in the praise-sense, and then go on to state (1), i.e., the definition of "Art" in terms of its art-making feature. And this is clearly to confuse the conditions under which we say something evaluatively with the meaning of what we say. "This is a work of art," said evaluatively, cannot mean "This is a successful harmonization of elements"—except by stipulation—but at most is said in virtue of the art-making property, which is taken as a (the) criterion of "Art," when "Art" is employed to assess. "This is a work of art," used evaluatively, serves to praise and not to affirm the reason why it is said.

The evaluative use of "Art," although distinct from the conditions of its use, relates in a very intimate way to these conditions. For, in every instance of "This is a work of art" (used to praise), what happens is that the criterion of evaluation (e.g., successful harmonization) for the employment of the concept of art is converted into a criterion of recognition. This is why, on its evaluative use, "This is a work of art" implies "This has P," where "P" is some chosen art-making property. Thus, if one chooses to employ "Art" evaluatively, as many do, /34/ so that "This is a work of art and not (aesthetically) good" makes no sense, he uses "Art" in such a way that he refuses to *call* anything a work of art unless it embodies his criterion of excellence.

There is nothing wrong with the evaluative use; in fact, there is good reason for using "Art" to praise. But what cannot be maintained is that theories of the evaluative use of "Art" are true and real definitions of the necessary and sufficient properties of art. Instead they are honorific definitions, pure and simple, in which "Art" has been redefined in terms of chosen criteria.

But what makes them—these honorific definitions—so supremely valuable is not their disguised linguistic recommendations; rather it is the *debates* over the reasons for changing the criteria of the concept of art which are built into the definitions. In each of the great theories of art, whether correctly understood as honorific definitions or incorrectly accepted as real definitions, what is of the utmost importance are the reasons proffered in the argument for the respective theory, that is, the reasons given for the chosen or preferred criterion of excellence and evaluation. It is this perennial debate over these criteria of evaluation which makes the history of aesthetic theory the important study it is. The value of each of the theories resides in its attempt to state and to justify certain criteria which are either neglected or distorted by previous theories. Look at the Bell-Fry theory again. Of course, "Art is significant form" cannot be accepted as a true, real definition of art; and most certainly it actually functions in their aesthetics as a redefinition of art in terms of the chosen condition of significant form. But what gives it its aesthetic importance is what lies behind the formula: In an age in which literary and representational elements have become paramount in painting, *return* to the plastic ones since these are indigenous to painting. Thus, the role of the theory is not to define anything but to use the definitional form, almost epigrammatically, to pin-point a crucial recommendation to turn our attention once again to the plastic elements in painting.

Once we, as philosophers, understand this distinction between the formula and what lies behind it, it behooves us to deal generously with the traditional theories of art; because incorporated in every one of them is a debate over and argument for emphasizing or centering upon some particular feature of art which has been neglected or perverted. If we take the aesthetic theories literally, as we have seen, they all fail; but if we reconstrue them, in terms of their function and point, as serious and argued-for recommendations to concentrate on certain criteria of excellence in art, we shall see that aesthetic theory is far from worthless. Indeed, it becomes as central as anything in aesthetics, in our understanding of art, for it teaches us what to look for and how to look at it in art. What is central and must be articulated in all the theories are their debates over the reasons for excellence in art—debates over emotional depth, profound truths, natural beauty, exactitude, freshness of treatment, and so on, as criteria of evaluation—the whole of which converges on the perennial problem of what makes a work of art good. To understand the role of aesthetic theory is not to conceive it as definition, logically doomed to failure, but to read it as summaries of seriously made recommendations to attend in certain ways to certain features of art. /35/

Appendices

Edgar Allan Poe's THE CASK OF AMONTILLADO

The thousand injuries of Fortunato I had borne as I best could, but when he ventured upon insult I vowed revenge. You, who so well know the nature of my soul, will not suppose, however, that I gave utterance to a threat. *At length* I would be avenged; this was a point definitely settled—but the very definitiveness with which it was resolved precluded the idea of risk. I must not only punish but punish with impunity. A wrong is unredressed when retribution overtakes its redresser. It is equally unredressed when the avenger fails to make himself felt as such to him who has done the wrong.

It must be understood that neither by word nor deed had I given Fortunato cause to doubt my good will. I continued, as was my wont, to smile in his face, and he did not perceive that my smile *now* was at the thought of his immolation.

He had a weak point—this Fortunato—although in other regards he was a man to be respected and even feared. He prided himself on his connoisseurship in wine. Few Italians have the true virtuoso spirit. For the most part their enthusiasm is adopted to suit the time and opportunity, to practise imposture upon the British and Austrian *millionaires*. In painting and gemmary, Fortunato, like his countrymen, was a quack, but in the matter of old wines he was sincere. In this /167/ respect I did not differ from him materially;—I was skilful in the Italian vintages myself, and bought largely whenever I could.

It was about dusk, one evening during the supreme madness of the carnival season, that I encountered my friend. He accosted me with excessive warmth, for he had been drinking much. The man wore motley. He had on a tight-fitting parti-striped dress, and his head was surmounted by the conical cap and bells. I was so pleased to see him that I thought I should never have done wringing his hand.

I said to him—"My dear Fortunato, you are luckily met. How remarkably well you are looking to-day. But I have received a pipe of what passes for Amontillado, and I have my doubts."

"How?" said he. "Amontillado? A pipe? Impossible! And in the middle of the carnival!"

"I have my doubts," I replied; "and I was silly enough to pay the full Amontillado price without consulting you in the matter. You were not to be found, and I was fearful of losing a bargain."

"Amontillado!"

"The Cask of Amontillado," *The Complete Works of Edgar Allan Poe,* ed. James A. Harrison (New York: Thomas Y. Crowell, 1902), VI, 167–175.

"I have my doubts."

"Amontillado!"

"And I must satisfy them."

"Amontillado!"

"As you are engaged, I am on my way to Luchresi. If any one has a critical turn it is he. He will tell me —"

"Luchresi cannot tell Amontillado from Sherry."

"And yet some fools will have it that his taste is a match for your own."

"Come, let us go."

"Whither?" /168/

"To your vaults."

"My friend, no; I will not impose upon your good nature. I perceive you have an engagement. Luchresi —"

"I have no engagement; — come."

"My friend, no. It is not the engagement, but the severe cold with which I perceive you are afflicted. The vaults are insufferably damp. They are encrusted with nitre."

"Let us go, nevertheless. The cold is merely nothing. Amontillado! You have been imposed upon. And as for Luchresi, he cannot distinguish Sherry from Amontillado."

Thus speaking, Fortunato possessed himself of my arm; and putting on a mask of black silk and drawing a *roquelaire* closely about my person, I suffered him to hurry me to my palazzo.

There were no attendants at home; they had absconded to make merry in honour of the time. I had told them that I should not return until the morning, and had given them explicit orders not to stir from the house. These orders were sufficient, I well knew, to insure their immediate disappearance, one and all, as soon as my back was turned.

I took from their sconces two flambeaux, and giving one to Fortunato, bowed him through several suites of rooms to the archway that led into the vaults. I passed down a long and winding staircase, requesting him to be cautious as he followed. We came at length to the foot of the descent, and stood together upon the damp ground of the catacombs of the Montresors.

The gait of my friend was unsteady, and the bells upon his cap jingled as he strode.

"The pipe," he said. /169/

"It is farther on," said I; "but observe the white web-work which gleams from these cavern walls."

He turned towards me, and looked into my eyes with two filmy orbs that distilled the rheum of intoxication.

"Nitre?" he asked, at length.

"Nitre," I replied. "How long have you had that cough?"

"Ugh! ugh! ugh! — ugh! ugh! ugh! — ugh! ugh! ugh! — ugh! ugh! ugh! — ugh! ugh! ugh!"

My poor friend found it impossible to reply for many minutes.

"It is nothing," he said, at last.

"Come," I said, with decision, "we will go back; your health is precious. You are rich, respected, admired, beloved; you are happy, as once I was. You are a man to be missed. For me it is no matter. We will go back; you will be ill, and I cannot be responsible. Besides, there is Luchresi —"

"Enough," he said; "the cough is a mere nothing; it will not kill me. I shall not die of a cough."

"True — true," I replied; "and, indeed, I had no intention of alarming you unnecessarily—but you should use all proper caution. A draught of this Medoc will defend us from the damps."

Here I knocked off the neck of a bottle which I drew from a long row of its fellows that lay upon the mould.

"Drink," I said, presenting him the wine.

He raised it to his lips with a leer. He paused and nodded to me familiarly, while his bells jingled.

"I drink," he said, "to the buried that repose around us." /170/

"And I to your long life."

He again took my arm, and we proceeded.

"These vaults," he said, "are extensive."

"The Montresors," I replied, "were a great and numerous family."

"I forget your arms."

"A huge human foot d'or, in a field azure; the foot crushes a serpent rampant whose fangs are imbedded in the heel."

"And the motto?"

"*Nemo me impune lacessit.*"

"Good!" he said.

The wine sparkled in his eyes and the bells jingled. My own fancy grew warm with the Medoc. We had passed through long walls of piled skeletons, with casks and puncheons intermingling, into the inmost recesses of the catacombs. I paused again, and this time I made bold to seize Fortunato by an arm above the elbow.

"The nitre!" I said; "see, it increases. It hangs like moss upon the vaults. We are below the river's bed. The drops of moisture trickle among the bones. Come, we will go back ere it is too late. Your cough——"

"It is nothing," he said; "let us go on. But first, another draught of the Medoc."

I broke and reached him a flagon of De Grâve. He emptied it at a breath. His eyes flashed with a fierce light. He laughed and threw the bottle upwards with a gesticulation I did not understand.

I looked at him in surprise. He repeated the movement—a grotesque one.

"You do not comprehend?" he said.

"Not I," I replied. /171/

"Then you are not of the brotherhood."

"How?"

"You are not of the masons."

"Yes, yes," I said; "yes, yes."

"You? Impossible! A mason?"

"A mason," I replied.

"A sign," he said, "a sign."

"It is this," I answered, producing from beneath the folds of my *roquelaire* a trowel.

"You jest," he exclaimed, recoiling a few paces. "But let us proceed to the Amontillado."

"Be it so," I said, replacing the tool beneath the cloak and again offering him my arm. He leaned upon it heavily. We continued our route in search of the Amontillado. We passed through a range of low arches, descended, passed on, and descending again, arrived at a deep crypt, in which the foulness of the air caused our flambeaux rather to glow than flame.

At the most remote end of the crypt there appeared another less spacious. Its walls had been lined with human remains, piled to the vault overhead, in the fashion of the great catacombs of Paris. Three sides of this interior crypt were still ornamented in this manner. From the fourth side the bones had been thrown down, and lay promiscuously upon the earth, forming at one point a mound of some size. Within the wall thus exposed by the displacing of the bones, we perceived a still interior crypt or recess, in depth about four feet, in width three, in height six or seven. It seemed to have been constructed for no especial use within itself, but formed merely the interval between two of the colossal supports of the roof of the catacombs, and was backed by one of their circumscribing walls of solid granite. /172/

It was in vain that Fortunato, uplifting his dull torch, endeavoured to pry into the depth of the recess. Its termination the feeble light did not enable us to see.

"Proceed," I said; "herein is the Amontillado. As for Luchresi—"

"He is an ignoramus," interrupted my friend, as he stepped unsteadily forward, while I followed immediately at his heels. In an instant he had reached the extremity of the niche, and finding his progress arrested by the rock, stood stupidly bewildered. A moment more and I had fettered him to the granite. In its surface were two iron staples, distant from each other about two feet, horizontally. From one of these depended a short chain, from the other a padlock. Throwing the links about his waist, it was but the work of a few seconds to secure it. He was too much astounded to resist. Withdrawing the key I stepped back from the recess.

"Pass your hand," I said, "over the wall; you cannot help feeling the nitre. Indeed, it is *very* damp. Once more let me *implore* you to return. No? Then I must positively leave you. But I must first render you all the little attentions in my power."

"The Amontillado!" ejaculated my friend, not yet recovered from his astonishment.

"True," I replied; "the Amontillado."

As I said these words I busied myself among the pile of bones of which I have before spoken. Throwing them aside, I soon uncovered a quantity of building stone and mortar. With these materials and with the aid of my trowel, I began vigorously to wall up the entrance of the niche.

I had scarcely laid the first tier of the masonry /173/ when I discovered that the intoxication of Fortunato had in a great measure worn off. The earliest indication I had of this was a low moaning cry from the depth of the recess. It was *not* the cry of a drunken man. There was then a long and obstinate silence. I laid the second tier, and the third, and the fourth; and then I heard the furious vibrations of the chain. The noise lasted for several minutes, during which, that I might hearken to it with the more satisfaction, I ceased my labours and sat down upon the bones. When at last the clanking subsided, I resumed the trowel, and finished without interruption the fifth, the sixth, and the seventh tier. The wall was now nearly upon a level with my breast. I again paused, and holding the flambeaux over the mason-work, threw a few feeble rays upon the figure within.

A succession of loud and shrill screams, bursting suddenly from the throat of the chained form, seemed to thrust me violently back. For a brief moment I hesitated, I trembled. Unsheathing my rapier, I began to grope with it about the recess; but the thought of an instant reassured me. I placed my hand upon the solid fabric of the catacombs, and felt satisfied. I reapproached the wall; I replied to the yells of him who clamoured. I re-echoed, I aided, I surpassed them in volume and in strength. I did this, and the clamourer grew still.

It was now midnight, and my task was drawing to a close. I had completed the eighth, the ninth and the tenth tier. I had finished a portion of the last and the eleventh; there remained but a single stone to be fitted and plastered in. I struggled with its weight; I placed it partially in its destined position. But now there came from out the niche a low laugh that erected /174/ the hairs upon my head. It was succeeded by a sad voice, which I had difficulty in recognizing as that of the noble Fortunato. The voice said —

"Ha! ha! ha! — he! he! he! — a very good joke, indeed — an excellent jest. We will have many a rich laugh about it at the palazzo — he! he! he! — over our wine — he! he! he!"

"The Amontillado!" I said.

"He! he! he! — he! he! he! — yes, the Amontillado. But is it not getting late? Will not they be awaiting us at the palazzo, the Lady Fortunato and the rest? Let us be gone."

"Yes," I said, "let us be gone."

"For the love of God, Montresor!"

"Yes," I said, "for the love of God!"

But to these words I hearkened in vain for a reply. I grew impatient. I called aloud —

"Fortunato!"

No answer. I called again —

"Fortunato!"

No answer still. I thrust a torch through the remaining aperture and let it fall within. There came forth in return only a jingling of the bells. My heart grew sick; it was the dampness of the catacombs that made it so. I hastened to make an end of my labour. I forced the last stone into its position; I plastered it up. Against the new masonry I re-erected the old rampart of bones. For the half of a century no mortal has disturbed them. *In pace requiescat!* /175/

※

STUDY QUESTIONS

Part I: PRELIMINARIES

Abrams:

1. What is "the total situation of a work of art"?
2. What might a critic ask and say about a work of art if, for example, his theory of art were orientated towards the audience?

Aristotle:

1. In his definition of tragedy, which element in the total situation of a work of art does Aristotle emphasize?
2. What are his standards of excellence for tragedy?
3. How would he distinguish tragedy from comedy and lyric poetry?
4. With which element in tragedy is he most concerned? Why?

Sidney:

1. With which element in the total situation of a work of art is Sidney most concerned?
2. How would Sidney determine the value of a poem?
3. How does he distinguish "true" poetry from other kinds of poetry?
4. Does Sidney place as much emphasis on the formal elements of poetry as Aristotle does? Why or why not?
5. How might Sidney and Aristotle define art? Would their standards of excellence be the same? Why or why not?

Véron:

1. According to Véron, what is the source of art?
2. Which element in the total situation of a work of art does Véron emphasize?
3. How does he measure the merit of a work of art?
4. For what reasons does Véron reject the imitation theory of art?
5. What do people admire in a work of art?
6. What constitutes beauty in a work of art?
7. What does Véron say about the value of the content and the form of a work of art?
8. Can a picture be about something ugly and still be a work of art? Explain.
9. What is aesthetics?
10. What are the two distinct kinds of art? How are they different?
11. How is modern art doubly expressive?
12. Other things being equal, do the kinds of emotions and thoughts expressed in a work of art determine its value? Explain your answer.
13. Does originality of thought and feeling contribute to the value of a work of art? Explain.
14. What is style?
15. Must the artist be sincere? Why? How can his audience determine his sincerity? What would result if the audience could not determine the sincerity of the artist?
16. How is the artist different from the scientist and the realist?
17. Would Véron call a photographer an artist and a photograph a work of art? Explain.

Brooks:

1. According to Brooks, what does the formalist critic want to do?
2. What "two popular tests for literary value" does the formalist critic reject? Why does he reject them?
3. According to Brooks, what is the critic's job?

General:

1. Which writers in this section employ one or the other of the "two popular tests for literary value"?
2. Other than Brooks, which writer in this section is also a formalist critic? Support your answer with reasons.
3. According to Aristotle, Sidney, and Véron, of what does the activity of the artist consist?
4. Do any of the writers in this section believe that a work of art acquires its value from something outside itself? Explain your answer.
5. What standards do the writers in this section use to determine the value of a work of art?
6. Do any of these writers believe that the "significance and value [of a work of art] are determined without any reference beyond itself"? Explain.

Part II: *LEO TOLSTOY*

What Is Art?

Chapter 4:
1. ". . . all aesthetic definitions of beauty lead to two fundamental conceptions." What are they?
2. Tolstoy refers to metaphysical definitions of beauty. What are they? Why does he reject them?
3. Why does "no objective definition of beauty" exist?
4. Explain the art-food analogy. Why does Tolstoy use it?

Chapter 5:
1. What is the inaccuracy of all the definitions that Tolstoy discusses?
2. What is the first step in correctly defining art?
3. How are art and speech similar; how are they different?
4. On what is the activity of art based?
5. When does a communication become a work of art?
6. Tolstoy seems to have two senses of art, limited and unlimited. Explain.
7. What feelings can an artist communicate?
8. What, by definition, does Tolstoy exclude from the realm of art?

Chapter 10:
1. Why does Tolstoy reject the idea that art can be good when the majority of men cannot understand it?
2. Why is certain art unintelligible to "great masses"?

Chapter 12:
1. Why is an art critic unnecessary?
2. What do critics do that is detrimental to art?

Chapter 15:
1. What distinguishes real art from its counterfeit? Explain.
2. What does a real work of art destroy?
3. Apart from subject matter, what is Tolstoy's standard of excellence in art?
4. On what does the degree of infectiousness of a work of art depend? Explain.
5. Which condition of infectiousness is most important? Explain.
6. Must a work of art have individuality, clearness, and sincerity in equal portions? Explain.

Chapter 16:
1. What is the purpose of art?
2. "How in art are we to decide what is good and what is bad in subject-matter?"
3. What is "religious perception"?
4. If the religious perception varies with the epoch, does art vary in any way? Explain.
5. How is Tolstoy's standard of excellence for subject matter both universal and particular?
6. What is the religious perception of our time? How does Tolstoy use it to determine what is good and bad art?
7. What was the chief mistake made by people of the upper classes during the Renaissance?

8. What is the great misfortune of the people of the upper classes of our time?
9. What are the two kinds of feelings that unite all men? What are their relationships to the art of our time?
10. Explain: "The art of our time should be appraised differently from former art. . . ."
11. What is the primary medium of religious art? Explain.
12. What are the media of universal art? Explain.
13. What spoils the universality of modern literature and music?
14. Which art medium most satisfies the demands of universal Christian art? Explain.
15. Concerning decorative art, is Tolstoy's view similar or dissimilar to Véron's? How? What is decorative art?
16. Does Tolstoy believe that Beethoven's *Ninth Symphony* is not art at all, or just not good art? Explain.

God Sees the Truth, But Waits

1. What is the plot of the story? Does it contain any unexpected incidents? If so, are they plausible? Where does the climax occur?
2. Describe the character of Aksënov. Compare it to that of Semënich. Which of the two would you regard as a "Tolstoyan" character? Why?
3. The theme of a story can be either the dominant mood of the story or the message or lesson that the story suggests. In which sense does this story contain a theme? What is it?
4. Although the story ends with Aksënov's death, the conclusion is clearly a triumph for him. How would you explain this?
5. To what extent do Aksënov's religious convictions shape the action of the story? To what extent do they determine the value of the story?
6. What kind of rating would Tolstoy put on the story? For what reasons? Would you agree with him?
7. What is the significance of the title?

A Prisoner in the Caucasus

1. Near the beginning of the story, Zhílin fights the Tartars. On the basis of what happens in the fight, describe Zhílin's character.
2. Are there other incidents in the story which substantiate your judgment about Zhílin's character? Compare the character of Kostílin to that of Zhílin.
3. Can you say anything in general about the character of the Tartars? How does it compare with that of Zhílin? Describe the setting in the Tartar village. What role does the setting have in relation to character?
4. Why, in Section V, does Zhílin refuse to leave Kostílin? Is he justified? Later in the story, he does leave him. Is this a breakdown in consistency of character portrayal?
5. What evidence of religious feeling do you find in the story? Does it function as an integral part of the story? Explain your answer.
6. What is the theme of the story? For what reasons would Tolstoy approve of this story?

Part III: THE CRITICS

Tolstoy's Theory

Lee:

1. According to Lee, how is Tolstoy's position on art related to his position on other practices, institutions, and ideas?
2. How does Tolstoy's condemnation of science "help us to a rapid understanding of one half of his condemnation of art—its condemnation as morally useless"?
3. Why does Lee say Tolstoy is wrong in trying to judge "the question of art by the whole practice of literature"? What is "the question of art"?
4. Does Lee suggest a definition of art in terms of pleasure and beauty?
5. How does Lee use science to show that art "has a right to live and a duty to fulfill, quite apart from any help it may contribute to the enforcement of a moralist's teachings"? What sciences does she use?
6. What differentiates art from the "mere practical or aimless exercise"?
7. What is Tolstoy's second plea against art? What is his first plea against it?
8. How does Lee answer Tolstoy's criticism of impressionistic painters? Does her answer to this criticism suggest her answer to Tolstoy's second plea against art? What is her answer to this plea?
9. Concerning art and its audience, how is Tolstoy's historical sense deficient? What error, according to Lee, does this deficiency cause him to commit?
10. "As regards the continuity of artistic development," what are the "two notable causes of disturbance"?
11. What has resulted from these disturbances?
12. Does Lee use the results of these disturbances to enforce her criticism of Tolstoy's second plea against art?
13. What has scientific and industrial progress contributed to the "difference which separates the aesthetic conditions of our century from those of every other one"?
14. With which of Tolstoy's ideas does Lee agree? Why?
15. With which of his ideas does she disagree? Why?

Macy:

1. According to Macy, what are the "general biases and limitations which . . . affect Tolstoi's work"?
2. What biases and limitations affect Macy's work?
3. What does Macy like about Tolstoy's work?
4. On what grounds does Macy reject Tolstoy's conclusion that beauty is no standard of art?
5. How, according to Macy, is beauty related to pleasure?
6. What relationship does Macy establish among beauty, pleasure, and art?
7. How is Tolstoy's approach to questions of art related to Plato's?
8. What great value of art, according to Macy, does Tolstoy fail to see?
9. Where in Part IV of his essay does Macy display his own narrowness in matters of art?
10. Does Macy believe that "unto the pure all things are pure"? Explain.
11. How does Tolstoy's theory of art resemble Ruskin's? How are the two theories different?
12. Does Macy believe in "art for art's sake"? Explain.
13. What is the "play of art"?

14. According to Macy, who is a qualified critic of art? Why does he reject Tolstoy's peasant as a critic?
15. What does Macy mean when he asks whether a peasant can tell "Homer's 'Iliad' from a book of fairy-tales"? Would the *Iliad* be any different if the peasant knew it was not a fairy tale?
16. What is the "highest criterion of artistic values"?

Knowlson:
1. What is Tolstoy's "religious perception"?
2. What are the "palpable weaknesses in the chain of argument" used by Tolstoy in his "threefold indictment" of modern art?
3. Which of Tolstoy's arguments does Knowlson reject? Why?
4. What is Knowlson's conception of the critic's job? What is Lourié's conception of it?
5. Why does Knowlson reject Tolstoy's main thesis?
6. What does Knowlson mean when he says, "Let the multitude wait"?
7. What is Knowlson's opinion of the peasant as an art critic? Whom does he use to support his opinion?

Symons:
1. What is Symons demonstrating with the many references to artists and works of art on pages 84–85?
2. What is Tolstoy's "quite unjustifiable assumption"? Why is it unjustifiable?
3. How does Tolstoy confuse art with progress?
4. To what "precipices are we led at every moment by the theory which makes feeling the test of art"?
5. What does Symons suggest about the qualifications and methods of the competent art critic when he says that "neither the uneducated judgement nor the instincts of the uneducated can ever come to have more than the slightest value in the determination of what is true or false in art"?
6. Does Tolstoy claim that the peasant can judge what is true or false in art, or does he claim that the peasant can determine what is good and bad art?

Flaccus:
1. Did Tolstoy develop his attitude about art suddenly?
2. When is Tolstoy's judgement about art most true?
3. Why is Tolstoy's theory of art "entitled to a hearing"?
4. What tests "give the key to Tolstoy's theory of art"?
5. What is Flaccus' opinion about Tolstoy's first three tests for art? How does he support his opinion?
6. Concerning Tolstoy's fourth test for art, what "two questions immediately shake themselves free"?
7. According to Flaccus, what does Tolstoy mean when he says that the artist must have "a correct, that is, moral relation . . . to his subject"?
8. What idea is Flaccus trying to establish on pages 89–91?
9. Why must Tolstoy's "criticisms on modern art . . . be viewed in the light of his attitude toward modern culture"?
10. Why is Tolstoy "not to be ranked as an enemy of art . . . but a critic"?
11. Where does Tolstoy get "his test of true art"?
12. Where lies the "deeper" fault of Tolstoy's theory of art? Where is Tolstoy "weakest"?
13. How is Tolstoy's theory "not disappointing as a problem"?
14. Does Flaccus believe that art should be confined to mere moral problems?

Hearn:
1. Are the two objections to Tolstoy's theory those of Hearn?
2. What is "a superior nervous system"?
3. What evidence does Hearn supply to prove that the peasant is a qualified critic of beauty?
4. Does Tolstoy claim that the peasant is a qualified critic of beauty or of art?
5. What is one of Tolstoy's "little mistakes"? Why does he make it?
6. Why can Hearn not strictly observe Tolstoy's principles?
7. In general, does Hearn agree or disagree with Tolstoy's principles of art, especially those concerning the peasant? Explain.

Knox (Tolstoy's Esthetic Definition . . .):
1. What are the two distinct elements of Tolstoy's philosophy of art?
2. What are the three concepts involved in Tolstoy's aesthetic definition of art?
3. What is the solution to the controversy as to whether art is expression or communication?
4. How does Tolstoy's theory differ from Véron's?
5. On what grounds does Knox support Tolstoy's theory against those of Véron, Ducasse, and Croce?
6. How does Knox use the ideas of Grosse and Hirn?
7. Why does Knox reject Tolstoy's concept of art as the infectious communication of emotion?

Knox (Notes on the Moralistic Theory . . .):
1. How does Tolstoy fit into Knox's discussion of Plato and Aristotle?
2. How are the theories of Plato and Tolstoy similar?
3. In what ways do "the final concrete conclusions of the two masters differ a little"?
4. Does Knox himself expound a moral theory of art? Explain.
5. Why, according to Knox, is Plato's and Tolstoy's view of art "really a negation of the moral function of art"?

Tolstoy's Ideas

Finklestein:
1. According to Finklestein, to understand art we must know two things. What are they and why are they important?
2. What is the aesthetic emotion? For what reasons is Finklestein opposed to theories which rely on it?
3. What are the constituents of a work of art? How does Finklestein account for the power of a work of art?
4. What is the difference between art and ordinary communication?
5. What is a form? Explain how the development of the modern conception of the artist took place.
6. Finally, how does Finklestein define the work of art?

Khrushchev Hits "Donkey" Art:
1. The concept of realistic art appears several times in the article. What does it mean? How is it opposed to formalistic art? What is "donkey" art?
2. What, according to *Pravda*, is the function of art? How can certain trends be "incorrect"? What, according to Khrushchev, is good art? How would you criticize his description?

Abercrombie:

1. This article presupposes a knowledge of Croce, but is such knowledge necessary for an understanding of Abercrombie's positive contribution?
2. Describe the ways language resembles art.
3. Explain Dante's remark: "It is more human to be heard than to hear." How is this remark related to expression and communication?
4. What is the essential nature of communicated expression? How is the effectiveness of art related to its power to communicate? Do you agree with Abercrombie on this point?
5. How does Abercrombie distinguish aesthetics from theory of art? What is the point of the distinction? How does he distinguish art from nature? How does he distinguish the artist from the non-artist?
6. Abercrombie considers two objections to his views. What are these objections and how does he answer them?

Hospers:

1. Explain the expressionist theory, as Hospers describes it.
2. For what are the words *transmit, deposit, convey* possible substitutions? For what reasons does Hospers reject the substitution of these words? What is the point of Hospers' argument here?
3. Hospers lists four possible objections to any formulation of the expressionist theory. What are they? Which do you regard as the most forceful? Why?
4. Under what conditions does Hospers regard the fourth objection as fatal to the expressionist theory?
5. What are Hospers' objections to amending the theory to read ". . . what the artist intended the audience to feel"?

Montague:

1. What important point characterizes both Kant and Santayana?
2. Explain moralism, realism, and unrealism. On what grounds does Montague criticize them? With which is he most sympathetic? What reservations does he have?
3. Explain: "Unrealist artists . . . revel in a collectivistic narcissism." Why is the exclusiveness of the formalists inevitable?
4. What is aesthetic pluralism? What does the title of the article mean, i.e., "Beauty Is Not All"?

Ducasse:

1. What is ugly art? In which sense does Ducasse use this expression to support his assertion that there is no necessary connection between art and beauty? Explain how his conclusion follows.
2. To what extent does Ducasse use Tolstoy and Véron in his analysis of art? How does his account differ from Tolstoy's?
3. What is Ducasse's definition of art? How does his definition rule out shouts of joy? Explain how his characterization of art does not involve beauty.
4. How does Ducasse distinguish the aesthetic, the inquisitive, and the practical attitudes? Trace the reasoning by which this distinction results in the characterization of beauty as independent of art.
5. Finally, how does Ducasse answer the question in the title of his article?

Poe:

1. What is the "heresy of *The Didactic*"? Why does Poe object to it?
2. Might Poe agree with the concept of "art for art's sake"? Explain.

3. What are the "three most obvious distinctions of the mind"? Which "informs us of the Beautiful"?
4. Why is "mere repetition . . . not poetry"? What is poetry?
5. What do poetry and music do to and for their audience?
6. What is the "Poetic Sentiment"? Is it restricted to poetry? Why?
7. What value does Poe place on meter, rhythm, and rhyme? Is his opinion of them different from Sidney's? Explain.
8. Through which art medium does the soul "most nearly attain the great end for which . . . it struggles"? For what great end does the soul struggle?
9. How might Poe distinguish poetry from a collage?
10. The "incitements of Passion or the precepts of Duty, or even the lessons of Truth" serve what function in a poem?

Wilde:
1. What does the artist do?
2. What does the critic do?
3. Does Wilde believe that beauty lies in the beholder?
4. What does art have to do with morality?
5. How does Wilde's theory resemble Poe's?
6. What is the value of art?
7. What does Wilde suggest about reading ideas and impressions into a work of art?
8. Which of Tolstoy's ideas does Wilde oppose?
9. Is Wilde a formalist critic in any sense? Explain.

Fry:
1. What is impure art? In what sense are advertisements and clothes impure art? When are pictures impure art? Are photographs always impure?
2. What is the aesthetic emotion? Why is it rarely aroused by "The Star Spangled Banner"? What is the connection between the aesthetic emotion and form? Why is the aesthetic emotion so rare?
3. For the formalist, what is the role of the subject in a painting?
4. What is the source of the pleasure the formalist gets from the aesthetic emotion?

Bullough:
1. How does the insertion of Distance transform the appearance of the fog at sea?
2. How does Distance "filter" our relation to the characters in a drama?
3. Explain the antimony of Distance. Can you tell a jealous husband witnessing a performance of *Othello* to "maintain distance"? How effective will his attempt be? In appreciation and production, what Distance relation is most desirable?
4. Explain the variables in the Distance relationship. How do the arts differ in the Distance required?

Ortega:
1. Distinguish human sensibility from aesthetic sensibility. What is "true artistic pleasure"? What is "aesthetic enjoyment proper"?
2. What is the point of the dying-man example?
3. Compare how Ortega and Bullough use the term "Distance."
4. What is dehumanization? Why does Ortega oppose complete abstraction in art?

Hume:

1. What is a standard of taste? How does Hume distinguish between a judgment and a sentiment? Which is beauty?
2. Hume describes two views as to the possible reconciliation of opposed evaluations. What are they? Which one does he prefer? For what reasons does he prefer it?
3. Where do rules of art come from? How widespread is the sentiment of beauty?
4. Explain the Sancho Panza example. What is Hume's reason for using it?
5. Hume's discussion of the characteristics of a good critic centers around the following points: delicacy, practice, comparison, prejudice, and good sense. Explain each of these. What results from a deficiency in any one of them? If a critic has all these characteristics to a high degree, what follows about the validity of his judgments?
6. What circumstances inevitably produce differences in value judgments? How, finally, would Hume compare a value judgment to a judgment of fact?

Bilsky:

1. In general, what method does Bilsky suggest to test the value of questions one might ask about works of art?
2. What are the objections to asking "What do you feel?" about a work of art? What are the two senses in which "feeling" words may be used? Why does Bilsky prefer the question "What do you see?" to "What do you feel?"?
3. What are his objections to the questions "What do you experience?" and "What does this work mean?"?
4. Compare the validity of Bilsky's remarks when they are applied to the different art forms.

Weitz:

1. What is a "theory of art"? How is it different from a theory in science? Why does Weitz think that people cannot formulate a theory of art?
2. Distinguish closed concepts from open concepts.
3. What, for Weitz, is the real problem in aesthetics? How can one solve it?
4. What is the role of decision?
5. How does Weitz criticize Aristotle's theory of tragedy?
6. What is the logic of "X is a work of art"?
7. What, finally, is the role of theory in aesthetics?

TOPICS FOR ESSAYS

These topics vary in complexity; some of them require research outside this book.

1. Tolstoy extends Véron's definition of art. Show how and why he does so.
2. Summarize Tolstoy's definition of art, then criticize it the way Weitz would.

3. Compare and contrast the theories of Tolstoy and Sidney.
4. Summarize any objection to Tolstoy's principles, then explain why you support the objection.
5. Using the essays of Lee, Hearn, Macy, and Hume, discuss the peasant as a qualified art critic.
6. Demonstrate that Bilsky's essay is an application of the formalist critic's position on art criticism.
7. Is a bullfight a work of art? Support your answer by appealing to various authors that discuss such a possibility either directly or indirectly. What are your views?
8. What is a critical standard? Give the views of at least three authors (other than Tolstoy) as to what the correct critical standards are. In each case, explain how Tolstoy would criticize them.
9. Various authors distinguish what Aristotle called the theoretical, the practical, and the productive (e.g., Ducasse talks about the inquisitive, the practical, and the aesthetic). Explain the distinction, the grounds on which various authors make it, and its significance insofar as works of art are concerned. What would Tolstoy say about the distinction and its relation to works of art?
10. Both Bullough and Ortega use the concept of Distance. Do they use it in the same way? How is the concept of Distance related to the notion of abstraction in art?
11. What is the formalist view in aesthetics? Which of the authors in this book would subscribe to such a view? Document your answer and explain why you think the authors belong in this category. For what reasons do Marxists reject the formalist view?
12. Ortega's article contains two seemingly contradictory assertions. In one place he says that no such thing as a complete abstraction exists; in another place he says that the artist should not abstract completely. Try to figure out a sense in which these two assertions are not contradictory.
13. Finklestein and Bilsky meet in an art museum. They stand together before Whistler's "Mother" or Picasso's "Guernica." Suggest their conversation, letting each man present his theory as clearly as possible. They should focus on their points of disagreement, if any. With which (if either) do you agree?
14. On page 174 of *What Is Art?* Tolstoy gives the procedure for testing a work claiming to be art. Test "The Cask of Amontillado" as Tolstoy would.
15. Show how Tolstoy and Bilsky (or Brooks) would differ in their critical approach to, for example, "God Sees the Truth, But Waits." What would be the first question each critic would ask?
16. Using the theories of as many critics as you can, test the validity of Abrams' idea that critical theories are orientated towards one of the four elements in the total situation of a work of art.
17. Compare and contrast the aesthetic principles of Aristotle and Sidney.
18. Use the theories of Tolstoy and Abercrombie in a discussion of the question "Is everybody an artist?"
19. Summarize the objections to Tolstoy and the grounds for them that appear in the first group of articles in Part Three.
20. Relate to Tolstoy's ideas the ideas in Finklestein and in "Khrushchev Hits 'Donkey' Art."
21. Summarize and criticize the objections to Tolstoy made by Phythian, Spielmann, Yarros, and Doumic.
22. Beauty has long been associated with art. What arguments have been made for and against beauty as a criterion for art?

23. Read Tolstoy's other essays on art and relate the ideas in them to those in *What Is Art?*

24. What is an aesthetic theory? Does Tolstoy have one theory or several theories? If he has several of them, are they consistent or inconsistent? In what way are they consistent or inconsistent?

25. Art has always had its censors, and censors have always had their conceptions about art. What ideas about art are either implicitly or explicitly stated by the people who advocate censorship of *Lady Chatterley's Lover,* for example? What ideas about art are expressed by those people who oppose censorship of the book?

26. Trace in Maude, Simmons, and Rolland the evolution of Tolstoy's ideas about art that appear in *What Is Art?*

27. On what grounds do Poe and Wilde oppose Tolstoy? Do they oppose each other in any way?

28. Read one of Tolstoy's other words (for example, *Resurrection, Anna Karenina,* or *The Kreutzer Sonata*) and apply his test for a work of art to it.

29. Show how Fry and Montague oppose Tolstoy, if they do, and then analyze the differences, if any, between Fry and Montague.

30. Alymer Maude consistently supports Tolstoy's aesthetic principles. Summarize his support and the reasons he rejects the opposition of other critics to Tolstoy's ideas.

31. On what basis could Tolstoy (or anyone) say that such popular arts as jazz and rock 'n' roll are immoral?

32. Both Plato and Aristotle agree in general with Tolstoy that art has a moral function; they also agree that music can perform such a function. Explain as specifically as you can how music can function in this way. See, for example, Aristotle's *Politics* and Plato's *Republic.*

33. Explore the possible answers to the following question: "Is Poe's 'The Cask of Amontillado' a work of art?"

34. When Hitler came into power, he eliminated from the German scene all non-representational sculpture because he believed it was decadent art. What would Tolstoy say to such an action?

35. When Boris Pasternak won the Nobel Prize for literature, the Russian government would not let him claim his prize. The government held that Pasternak's book told lies about the Russian society. Explain why Tolstoy would approve or disapprove of the government's action.

36. Read all of *What Is Art?* and decide whether the selection in this book is a fair representation of Tolstoy's ideas. If it is a fair representation, explain why it is. If it is not a fair representation or in any way distorts Tolstoy's ideas, explain the additional ideas that would make the selection a fair and undistorted one and why they should be added.

37. Compare and contrast Weitz's ideas about art that appear in his *Philosophy of the Arts* and "The Role of Theory in Aesthetics."

38. You have read Brooks' "The Formalist Critics." Now read his *The Well Wrought Urn* and analyze the critical approach he uses in it. You might ask, for example, whether he is consistent in his theory and practice of criticism.

39. Clive Bell is well known for his conception of art as "significant form." Read his *Art* and compare and contrast his ideas to those of Tolstoy.

40. Hospers and Weitz state objections to Tolstoy's theory of art. Are their objections the same? Explain. With what are both Hospers and Weitz much concerned?

41. Using the ideas of as many authors as you can, analyze the meaning of the concept of art as expression.

42. Summarize Bullough's ideas about Distance, then state Longman's criticism of them.
43. Read Wordsworth's "Preface" to the 1800 edition of *Lyrical Ballads*, then compare his ideas about poetry (e.g., his concept of the language of poetry) to Tolstoy's ideas about art.
44. Read Wimsatt and Beardsley's "The Intentional Fallacy" and "The Affective Fallacy." Which of Tolstoy's ideas do they reject? Why do they reject them? With which authors in this book are they similar? How are they similar to them?

✳

SELECTED BIBLIOGRAPHY

Articles

Abercrombie, Lascelles, "Communication Versus Expression in Art," *British Journal of Psychology*, 14 (1923), 68–78.

Aiken, Henry, "Criteria for an Adequate Aesthetics," *Journal of Aesthetics and Art Criticism*, 7 (1948), 141–158.

Arnheim, Rudolph, "The Priority of Expression," *Journal of Aesthetics and Art Criticism*, 8 (1949), 106–109.

Belgion, Montgomery, "Expression of Emotion," *Southern Review*, 3 (1938), 783–789.

Bilsky, Manuel, "Confronting the Work of Art," *University College Quarterly*, 6:1 (1960), 5–7.

Brooks, Cleanth, "The Formalist Critics," *Kenyon Review*, 13 (1951), 72–81.

Bullough, Edward, "Psychical Distance as a Factor in Art and an Aesthetic Principle," *British Journal of Psychology*, 5 (1912–1913), 87–118.

Coomaraswamy, Ananda K. "Intention," *American Bookman*, 1 (1944), 41–48.

Doumic, René, "Count Tolstoi's Ideas on Art," *Living Age*, 218 (1898), 607–614.

Ducasse, Curt J., "What has Beauty to do with Art?" *Journal of Philosophy*, 25 (1928), 181–185.

Gotshalk, D. W., "Aesthetic Expression," *Journal of Aesthetics and Art Criticism*, 13 (1954), 80–85.

———, "Art and Beauty," *Monist*, 41 (1931), 624–632.

Hornblow, Arthur, "Tolstoi's Denunciation of Contemporary Art," *Bookman*, 12 (1900), 383–387.

Huneker, James, "Dostoievsky and Tolstoy," *The Forum*, 54 (August, 1915), 201–216.

Hyde, George M., "Tolstoy's Gospel of Art," *Bookman*, 8 (1898), 148–150.

"Khrushchev Hits 'Donkey' Art," *The Ann Arbor News*, December 3, 1962, p. 6.

Knox, Israel, "Tolstoi's Esthetic Definition of Art," *Journal of Philosophy*, 27 (1930), 65–70.

———, "Notes on the Moralistic Theory of Art: Plato and Tolstoy," *International Journal of Ethics*, 41 (July, 1930), 507–510.

[Lee, Vernon], "Tolstoi's Views of Art," *Quarterly Review,* 191 (April, 1900), 359–372. Reprinted in Vernon Lee's *Gospels of Anarchy.*

Longman, Lester, "The Concept of Psychical Distance," *Journal of Aesthetics and Art Criticism,* 6 (1947), 31–36.

Lourié, Ossip, "Tolstoi et l'Art," *Revue Philosophe,* 47 (1899), 76–86.

Lovett, Robert Morss, "Tolstoy: The Lesson of the Artist," *New Republic,* 56 (Sept. 5, 1928), 63–66.

Macy, John Albert, "Tolstoi's Moral Theory of Art," *Century Magazine,* 62 (1901), 298–307.

Margolis, Joseph, "Mr. Weitz and the Definition of Art," *Philosophical Studies,* 9 (1958), 88–94.

Maude, Alymer, "Tolstoy's Theory of Art," *The Contemporary Review,* 78 (1900), 241–254. Reprinted in Maude's *Tolstoy and His Problems.*

Mayo, Bernard, "Poetry, Language and Communication," *Philosophy,* 29 (1954), 131–145.

More, Paul E., "The Ancient Feud between Philosophy and Art," *The Atlantic Monthly,* 86 (1900), 337–347.

Murry, John Middleton, "The Essence of Art," *The Forum,* 74 (1925), 562–573. This is the first version of "The Romantic Fallacy."

————, "The Romantic Fallacy," *Criterion,* 4 (1926), 521–537.

Phythian, Ernest J., "Tolstoy's *What Is Art?*" *Manchester Quarterly,* 20 (1901), 184–203.

Rahv, Phillip, "Concerning Tolstoy," *Partisan Review,* 13 (Sept.–Oct., 1946), 420–432.

Spielmann, M. H., *What Is Art?* (A review), *Literature,* 3 (1898), 77–79.

"Tolstoy on Art," *The Nation,* 67 (1898), 275–276, 308–309.

"Tolstoy and His Theories," *The Critic,* 33 (1898), 184–189.

Weitz, Morris, "The Role of Theory in Aesthetics," *Journal of Aesthetics and Art Criticism,* 15 (1956), 27–35.

Wimsatt, William K., Jr., and Monroe C. Beardsley, "The Affective Fallacy," *Sewanee Review,* 57 (1949), 31–55.

————, "The Intentional Fallacy," *Sewanee Review,* 54 (1946), 468–488.

Yarros, Victor, "Tolstoi on Art and Beauty," *The Dial,* 24 (1898), 249–251.

Zink, Sidney, "The Moral Effect of Art," *Ethics,* 60 (1950), 261–274.

Books

Abrams, M. H., *The Mirror and the Lamp* (New York: Oxford University Press, 1953).

Allen, Gay Wilson, and Harry Hayden Clark, eds., *Literary Criticism: Pope to Croce* (Detroit: Wayne State University Press, 1962). Anthology.

Aristotle, *The Poetics of Aristotle,* tr., S. H. Butcher, 4th ed. (London: Macmillan and Co., Ltd., 1907).

Beardsley, Monroe C., *Aesthetics: Problems in the Philosophy of Criticism* (New York: Harcourt, Brace, and Co., 1958).

Bell, Clive, *Art* (London: Chatto and Windus, 1914).

Brooks, Cleanth, *The Well Wrought Urn* (New York: Harcourt, Brace, and Co., 1947).

Carritt, E. F., *The Theory of Beauty* (London: Methuen and Co., Inc., 1914).

————, ed., *Philosophies of Beauty* (London: Oxford University Press, 1931). Anthology.

Chesterton, G. K., *Varied Types* (New York: Dodd, Mead, and Co., 1921).

Collingwood, R. G., *Principles of Art* (New York: Oxford University Press, 1938).

Ducasse, Curt J., *The Philosophy of Art* (London: Allen and Unwin, 1929).

Farrell, James, *Literature and Morality* (New York: Vanguard Press, Inc., 1947).

Finklestein, Sidney, *Art and Society* (New York: International Publishers Co., Inc., 1947).

Flaccus, L. Wm., *Artists and Thinkers* (New York: Longmans, Green, and Co., Inc., 1916).

Fry, Roger, *Vision and Design* (London: Wm. Clowes and Son, 1920).

_____, *The Artist and Psycho-Analysis* (London: L. and V. Woolf, 1924).

Garrod, H. W., *Tolstoi's Theory of Art* (Oxford: The Clarendon Press, 1935).

Gilbert, Allan H., ed., *Literary Criticism: Plato to Dryden* (Detroit: Wayne State University Press, 1962). Anthology.

Goldberg, Gerald, and Nancy Goldberg, eds., *The Modern Critical Spectrum* (Englewood Cliffs, New Jersey: Prentice-Hall, Inc., 1962). Anthology.

Gotshalk, D. W., *Art and Social Order* (Chicago: University of Chicago Press, 1947).

Hearn, Lafcadio, *Life and Literature* (New York: Dodd, Mead, and Co., 1929).

Hospers, John, "The Concept of Artistic Expression," *Proceedings of the Aristotelian Society*, 55 (1954–1955), 313–344 (London: Harrison and Sons, Ltd., 1955).

Hugo, Howard, ed., *Aspects of Fiction: A Handbook* (Boston: Little, Brown, and Co., 1962). Anthology.

Hume, David, *Essays Moral, Political, and Literary*, eds. T. H. Greene and T. H. Grose, 2 vols. (London: Longmans, Green, and Co., 1875).

Knowlson, T. S., *Leo Tolstoy: A Biographical and Critical Study* (New York: Fredrick Warne and Co., 1904).

Lee, Vernon (pseud. for Viola Paget), *Gospels of Anarchy* (London: T. Fisher Unwin, 1908).

Levich, Marvin, ed., *Aesthetics and the Philosophy of Criticism* (New York: Random House, 1963). Anthology.

Listowel, Earl of, *A Critical History of Modern Aesthetics* (London: G. Allen and Unwin, Ltd., 1933).

Lucas, F. L., *Literature and Psychology* (Ann Arbor, Michigan: University of Michigan Press, 1957).

Macy, John Albert, *The Critical Game* (New York: Boni and Liveright, 1922).

Maude, Alymer, *Tolstoy and His Problems* (New York: Funk and Wagnalls Co., 1904).

_____, *Life of Tolstoy*, 2 vols. (New York: Dodd, Mead, and Co., 1911).

_____, *Tolstoy on Art and Its Critics* (London: H. Milford, 1925).

Mead, Hunter, *An Introduction to Aesthetics* (New York: The Ronald Press, 1952).

Montague, Wm. P., *The Ways of Things* (New York: Prentice-Hall, Inc., 1940).

More, P. E., *Shelburne Essays*, First Series (New York: G. P. Putnam's Sons, 1904).

Morris, William, *Selected Writings and Designs*, ed. Asa Briggs (Baltimore, Maryland: Penguin Books, 1962).

Nahm, Milton C., *Aesthetic Experience and Its Presuppositions* (New York: Harper and Brothers, 1946).

Ortega y Gasset, José, *The Dehumanization of Art, and Notes on the Novel*, tr. Helen Weyl (Princeton: Princeton University Press, 1948).

Osborne, Harold, *Aesthetics and Criticism* (London: Routledge and Kegan Paul, Ltd., 1955).

Pepper, Stephen C., *The Basis of Criticism in the Arts* (Cambridge, Massachusetts: Harvard University Press, 1945).

_____, *Principles of Art Appreciation* (New York: Harcourt, Brace, and Co., 1949).

Peters, Robert L., ed., *Victorians on Literature and Art* (New York: Appleton-Century-Crofts, Inc., 1961). Anthology.

Poe, Edgar Allan, *The Complete Works of Edgar Allan Poe*, ed. James A. Harrison (New York: T. Y. Crowell, 1902), Vols. 6, 14.

Prall, D., *Aesthetic Judgement* (New York: T. Y. Crowell Co., 1929).

Rader, Melvin, ed., *A Modern Book of Esthetics*, 3rd ed. (New York: Henry Holt and Co., 1960). Anthology.

Read, Herbert, *The Meaning of Art* (Baltimore, Maryland: Penguin Books, 1963).

Reid, Louis A., *A Study in Aesthetics* (New York: Macmillan Co., 1931).

Richards, I. A., *Principles of Literary Criticism* (New York: Harcourt, Brace, and Co., 1925).

Rolland, Romain, *Tolstoy*, tr. Bernard Miall (New York: E. P. Dutton and Co., 1911).

Ruskin, John, *Selections and Essays*, ed. Frederick W. Roe (New York: Charles Scribner's Sons, 1946).

Shipley, Joseph, ed., *Dictionary of World Literature* (New York: The Philosophical Library, 1943).

Sidney, Sir Philip, *The Defense of Poesy*, ed. Albert S. Cook (Boston: Ginn and Co., 1890).

Simmons, Ernest J., *Leo Tolstoy* (Boston: Little, Brown, and Co., 1946).

Steiner, George, *Tolstoy or Dostoevsky: An Essay in the Old Criticism* (New York: Knopf, 1959).

Symons, Arthur, *The Symbolist Movement in Literature* (London: Constable, 1911).

————, *Studies in Prose and Verse* (New York: E. P. Dutton and Co., 1904).

Tolstoi, Leo, *What Is Art?* tr. Charles Johnson (Philadelphia: Henry Altemus, 1898).

Tolstoy, Leo, *What Is Art?* tr. Alymer Maude (London: Walter Scott, Ltd., 1899).

————, *Twenty-Three Tales*, trs. Louise and Alymer Maude (London: Oxford University Press, 1906).

————, *The Complete Works of Count Tolstoy*, tr. and ed. Leo Wiener, 24 vols. (Boston: D. Estes and Co., 1904–1905).

————, *The Complete Works of Leo Tolstoy*, tr. Alymer Maude, 21 vols. (London: Oxford University Press, 1928).

————, *The Works of Lyof N. Tolstoi*, 16 vols. (New York: Charles Scribner's Sons, 1929).

Véron, Eugene, *Aesthetics*, tr. W. H. Armstrong (London: Chapman and Hall, 1879).

Vivas, Eliseo, and Murray Krieger, eds., *The Problems of Aesthetics* (New York: Rinehart and Co., 1958). Anthology.

Wellek, René, and Austin Warren, *Theory of Literature* (New York: Harcourt, Brace, and World, Inc., 1956).

Widmer, Kingsley and Eleanor, eds., *Literary Censorship* (San Francisco: Wadsworth Publishing Co., Inc., 1961).

Wilde, Oscar, *The Picture of Dorian Gray* (New York: Ward and Lock, 1895).

Wimsatt, Wm. K., Jr. and Cleanth Brooks, eds., *Literary Criticism: A Short History* (New York: Alfred A. Knopf, 1957).

Yassukovitch, Antonina, ed., *Tolstoi In English, 1878–1929: A List of Works By and About Tolstoi in the New York Public Library* (New York: New York Public Library, 1929).

Zabel, Morton Dauwen, ed., *Literary Opinion in America*, 2 vols. (New York: Harper and Row, 1962). Anthology.